Recovering from the Anabaptist Vision

T&T CLARK STUDIES IN ANABAPTIST THEOLOGY AND ETHICS

Series editors:

Malinda Berry
Paul Martens

Recovering from the Anabaptist Vision

New Essays in Anabaptist Identity and Theological Method

Edited by
Laura Schmidt Roberts, Paul Martens, and Myron A. Penner

t&tclark

T&T CLARK

Bloomsbury Publishing Plc

50 Bedford Square, London, WC1B 3DP, UK

1385 Broadway, New York, NY 10018, USA

BLOOMSBURY, T&T CLARK and the T&T Clark logo are trademarks of Bloomsbury Publishing Plc

First published in Great Britain, 2020

Copyright © Laura Schmidt Roberts, Paul Martens, Myron A. Penner and contributors, 2020

Laura Schmidt Roberts, Paul Martens and Myron A. Penner have asserted their right under the Copyright, Designs and Patents Act, 1988, to be identified as Editors of this work.

Cover image © enviromantic/Getty

All rights reserved. No part of this publication may be reproduced or transmitted in any form or by any means, electronic or mechanical, including photocopying, recording, or any information storage or retrieval system, without prior permission in writing from the publishers.

Bloomsbury Publishing Plc does not have any control over, or responsibility for, any third-party websites referred to or in this book. All internet addresses given in this book were correct at the time of going to press. The author and publisher regret any inconvenience caused if addresses have changed or sites have ceased to exist, but can accept no responsibility for any such changes.

A catalogue record for this book is available from the British Library.

A catalog record for this book is available from the Library of Congress.

ISBN: HB: 978-0-5676-9274-0
PB: 978-0-5676-9273-3
ePDF: 978-0-5676-9276-4
eBook: 978-0-5676-9275-7

Typeset by Deanta Global Publishing Services, Chennai, India

To find out more about our authors and books visit www.bloomsbury.com and sign up for our newsletters.

CONTENTS

Series Preface Malinda Berry and Paul Martens vii
Preface Myron A. Penner viii

1 Challenge and Opportunity: The Quest for Anabaptist Theology Today *Paul Martens* 1

2 Contours and Possibilities for an Anabaptist Theology *Karl Koop* 17

3 Refiguration, Configuration: Tradition, Text, and Narrative Identity *Laura Schmidt Roberts* 33

4 Mennonite Women Doing Theology: A Methodological Reflection on Twenty-Five Years of Conferences *Carol Penner* 53

5 Queering Anabaptist Theology: An Endeavor in Breaking Binaries as Hermeneutical Community *Stephanie Chandler Burns* 77

6 On the Need for Critical-Contextual and Trauma-Informed Methods in Mennonite Theology *Melanie Kampen* 93

7 The Ecumenical Vocation of Anabaptist Theology *Jeremy M. Bergen* 103

8   Dialogue as Theological Method: Mennonite Missionaries, West African Churches, and Twenty-First-Century Anabaptist Identity
    R. Bruce Yoder   127

9   Restlessness as Theological Method
    Paul Doerksen   151

Notes on Contributors   169
Bibliography   170
Index   186

SERIES PREFACE

T&T Clark Studies in Anabaptist Theology and Ethics is dedicated to displaying the vibrant global resurgence of theological reflection and praxis in and adjacent to the Anabaptist tradition. In a world that is fraught with overt and covert forms of violence, this series provides a platform for new ways of seeing, understanding, and living what it means to love one's enemy and one's neighbor with the peace of God that surpasses much of the wisdom of the day.

With debts to the New Testament, the early church, and late-medieval reformers, Anabaptism emerged as a loosely organized Christian movement in sixteenth-century Europe. Today the heirs of this continually evolving and sometimes highly contested tradition—whether called Mennonite, Brethren, Hutterite, Amish, or any number of other designations—are scattered around the world and especially the Global South. Therefore, while recognizing that the preponderance of academic theology in the peace church tradition still occurs in North America and Europe, this series is committed to publishing voices that represent the theological imaginations, concerns, heartbreaks, and convictions of the entire global Anabaptist family. To that end, volumes draw from established and emerging voices and take a variety of forms, including but not limited to monographs, case studies, and edited collections.

T&T Clark Studies in Anabaptist Theology and Ethics is published under the editorial direction of the Institute of Mennonite Studies, the research and publication agency of Anabaptist Mennonite Biblical Seminary in Elkhart, Indiana. The Institute of Mennonite Studies was founded in 1958 to promote and create opportunities for research, conversation, and publication on topics and issues vital to the Anabaptist faith tradition. For more information or to submit a proposal to the series, please visit www.ambs.edu/ims.

Malinda Berry, Anabaptist Mennonite Biblical Seminary
Paul Martens, Baylor University

PREFACE

The chapters in this book were solicited and organized as part of the Anabaptist Theology Project initiated by the Humanitas Anabaptist-Mennonite Centre at Trinity Western University. The Humanitas Centre exists to help articulate and develop an Anabaptist perspective, integrating established and emerging voices with learning across academic disciplines, in order to engage both the academy and a wider public. The first phase of this foray into Anabaptist theological method began as a workshop at Trinity Western that I organized in 2016 involving Jeremy Bergen, Karl Koop, Laura Schmidt Roberts, and Paul Martens. The focus of the workshop was to attempt to answer the question: Is there an Anabaptist theological method? Each presented papers on aspects of Anabaptist theological method, versions of which appear in this volume.

Several themes and related questions emerged during those initial meetings. First was the issue of continuity and discontinuity between our contemporary theological context and the early Anabaptists in sixteenth-century Europe. Workshop participants were uneasy with the attempt to distill Anabaptism into "core essentials," while recognizing that the particular historical trajectory of Anabaptist movements from the sixteenth century to today do share important family resemblances. A second issue concerned the need for engaging global Anabaptism in any real attempt to flesh out Anabaptist theological method. Workshop participants were all white North Americans and certainly not representative of the diverse tapestry of global Anabaptism. While the conference that emerged as the second phase of this initiative broadened the conversation partners somewhat, the participants in the initial workshop and contributors to this volume are primarily from a North American context. A third issue concerned the way in which Anabaptism has existed historically and does and should exist today in relation to other Christian traditions and other faith traditions. And, finally, woven through these themes and others in those initial conversations was the legacy of John Howard Yoder, most notably the way in which the damage caused by his decades of sexual abuse requires a reorienting of contemporary Anabaptist theology. Each of these initial themes was also identified by later participants in the project as well as by contributors to this volume.

The second phase of the Anabaptist Theology Project was a conference organized by Humanitas at Trinity Western in June 2017 on the theme Anabaptist Theology: Methods and Practices. Papers were solicited that addressed theological method in general and Anabaptist theological method in particular. Earlier versions of the chapters in this volume were presented at the Humanitas conference.

The third phase of the project is the present book. In diverse ways and drawing on different resources, the nine chapters that compose this book both articulate and model ways in which Anabaptist theology can be done. In Chapter 1, Paul Martens notes that as the Mennonite community continues to come to terms with John Howard Yoder's public reckoning, Anabaptist theologians are poised to return to areas of inquiry historically important to Anabaptist and Mennonite theology, including the relationships of Mennonites to Anabaptism, church to state, the personal to the political, and church to world. In Chapter 2, Karl Koop suggests that Anabaptist theologians look to their tradition with a view to refigure that tradition according to a trinitarian and christological framework and in ways that reflect the lived experience of those within it. Laura Schmidt Roberts, in Chapter 3, extends the theme of refiguring theology with a thorough application of Paul Ricoeur's hermeneutical approach to Anabaptist traditions and the ongoing question of theological identity.

In Chapter 4, Carol Penner observes that the eight Women Doing Theology conferences between 1992 and 2016 employed a theological approach that is both feminist and Anabaptist. Stephanie Chandler Burns then brings queer theology into constructive conversation with Anabaptist theology in Chapter 5. In Chapter 6, Melanie Kampen recommends a de-colonizing method for Anabaptist theology that seeks out and attempts to alleviate the suffering of those harmed by violence, power, domination, and trauma.

Jeremy Bergen, in Chapter 7, locates Anabaptist theology within the context of the church catholic, arguing that Anabaptist theology exists properly only as a reform movement within, and for the sake of, the wider church. In Chapter 8, R. Bruce Yoder argues that the dialogical approach to theology emerging out of the experience of Mennonite Missionaries and African Independent Churches is a useful model for twenty-first-century global Anabaptist theology. Finally, in Chapter 9, Paul Doerksen draws on both theological and literary resources in recommending that theology reject the aim of rational certainty and instead adopt a methodological stance of humility, reverence, finitude, and mobility.

It is with deep gratitude that I acknowledge and thank the many people who helped bring this volume to fruition. The initial workshop participants mentioned above—Jeremy Bergen, Karl Koop, Laura Schmidt Roberts, and Paul Martens—served as the core planning team for this project. Each brought a valued set of skills, experiences, and contacts, all wrapped in a genuine collegiality that has made this project a joy to pursue. Laura Schmidt Roberts has steered the editorial process with both grace and wisdom. Dorothy M. Peters took the lead in conference planning and logistics, and the success of the 2017 Humanitas conference was due in large measure to her excellent work. Thanks as well to Malinda Berry and Paul Martens for including this volume in their series, to David Cramer of the Institute for Mennonite Studies for his editorial oversight of the manuscript, and to Anna Turton at T&T Clark for shepherding the manuscript to publication. Last, but certainly not least, this book could not have come about without the generous donors to the Humanitas Anabaptist-Mennonite Centre who support the vision of developing and articulating an academically informed and culturally engaged Anabaptism. I hope that this volume is a contribution to the ongoing work of shaping that perspective.

Myron A. Penner
Director, Humanitas Anabaptist-Mennonite Centre
Trinity Western University

1

Challenge and Opportunity

The Quest for Anabaptist Theology Today

Paul Martens

In recent decades, Anabaptism has gained a level of fame—and not mere infamy—far beyond what it enjoyed in the last five hundred years. Yet increased scrutiny has accompanied this newfound attention; the contestation of "Anabaptist" has increased relative to its rise in popularity. In this chapter, I engage just one adjectival application of Anabaptist—Anabaptist theology—to question and volatilize what I take to be the dominant North American understanding of the term.

Among the past generation or two of theologians and ethicists in North America (and especially for non-Mennonite theologians during this time), John Howard Yoder was the dominant and almost de facto voice of Anabaptist thought. With the recent unmasking of his sexual violence, however, his role as the authoritative arbiter of Anabaptist theology has been destroyed. The ascription of the term "Today" in the subtitle of this chapter is, therefore, conditioned by both the constructive role Yoder played in creating the context of contemporary understandings of Anabaptism and the virtual vacuum left within the discourse after Yoder's public reckoning.

This chapter aims to (a) illuminate why Yoder's theological vision was so tempting and (b) call into question the legitimacy of the contextual demands that gave his vision so much explanatory power with the goal of (c) illuminating how Yoder's theological vision is unable to address some of the most critical questions up for debate in contemporary Anabaptist theology. Before justifying this damning conclusion, however, it is necessary to reexamine the basic category assumed thus far: "Anabaptism."

Anabaptism Is Not Anabaptism—or Is It?

To unpack the power of Yoder's theological vision, it is helpful to look briefly at the historiography of Anabaptism. In other words, it is always helpful to remember that the way the term "Anabaptism" is used today is a theological reconstruction employed to address the current context and thus reflects a select appropriation of history for a normative end. This is not necessarily a critique, but it is an acknowledgment that a methodological choice has been made. It is also highly unlikely that any of the sixteenth-century Anabaptists counted under this umbrella understood the term to mean what it meant in most contemporary appropriations.

In the beginning of the story—in the sixteenth century—the theological world was not formless and void on the eve of the Protestant Reformation, despite the popular image that the first Anabaptists appeared as "meteors against the night."[1] In previous centuries, reform movements like the Waldensians, Jan Hus, John Wycliffe, and the Brethren of the Common Life within Roman Catholicism served as forerunners of the Protestant Reformation and had much in common with early Anabaptism. All of the first-generation Anabaptists, whether vocational theologians or not, learned doctrines and practices that were not self-consciously Anabaptist per se in their Christian formation. Their eventual Anabaptist theological identity—the term tied to their voluntary adult rebaptism—was therefore adopted through difference in

---

[1] William R. Estep, *The Anabaptist Story: An Introduction to Sixteenth-Century Anabaptism*, 3rd ed. (Grand Rapids: Eerdmans, 1996), 29.

relation to Catholic, Lutheran, and eventually Calvinist theological positions.

Unsurprisingly, the term Anabaptist is merely one of the many denigrating designations used by their sixteenth-century enemies. They were also referred to as Donatists, heretics, Schwärmerei (enthusiasts), Cathars, and restitutionists—the list, often also tied to historical precursors, goes on. Since the sixteenth century, the debate has continued, with the basic question being: Is the group of reformers that emerged after Luther and Zwingli sufficiently unified to fall under one umbrella and, if so, what should it be called: radical reformers, the second front, or the left (or even communist) wing of the Reformation? Leonard Verduin's *The Reformers and Their Stepchildren* is but one example of how this question was asked and answered by historians half a century ago.[2] Another more sympathetic form of this debate within Mennonite historiography came to the conclusion that polygenesis—and not monogenesis—is the best way to understand the emergence of sixteenth-century Anabaptism.[3]

My point in raising this historical question is fairly simple and absolutely pedantic to Mennonite historians: we must recognize that whatever is referred to as Anabaptist theology today is a reconstruction that is, at best, either loosely or selectively tied to the sixteenth century. Each reconstruction entails two elements that can be queried. The first element concerns designation: Why this particular term and not others, especially when rebaptism ceases to be a significant marker in later centuries? Harold Bender himself acknowledged that "the Anabaptists themselves used no common name," and perhaps the closest thing to a unified self-designation would be the use of "Brethren."[4] The second element concerns description: What are the criteria by which one stands within the boundaries of Anabaptism? Certainly, generally recognizable communities within the radical reformation emerged;

---

[2]Leonard Verduin, *The Reformers and Their Stepchildren* (Grand Rapids: Eerdmans, 1964).
[3]James T. Stayer, Werner O. Packull, and Klaus Depperman, "From Monogenesis to Polygenesis: The Historical Discussion of Anabaptist Origins," *Mennonite Quarterly Review* 49 (1975): 83–121.
[4]Harold S. Bender, Robert Friedmann, and Walter Klaassen, "Anabaptism," *Global Anabaptist Mennonite Encyclopedia Online* (1990 [1955]), http://gameo.org/index.php?title=Anabaptism&oldid=143474.

the Schleitheim group, the Marpeck circle, the Mennonites, and the Hutterites are but a few examples. The theology that guided and emerged from these communities was also unique and contingently tied to the identity and practices of these communities. For example, it is difficult to read the *Schleitheim Confession*'s condemnation of popish and re-popish works and its demand for separation from the world as a theological position apart from the kind of exilic community it represents.[5] Likewise, it is difficult to read *The Mirror of the Martyrs* and its defense of believer's baptism (and those that suffered because of it) as anything but a defense of and exhortation to a specific community that understood itself as the faithful remnant, literally the ana-baptists, the "Christminded," the "Apostle-minded," or the "Gospel-minded," to use the language of the text itself.[6] But looking outside the various communities that have remained relatively stable because of their communal separateness from the world (e.g., the Holdeman Mennonites, the Hutterites, and the Amish), appeals to a kind of pan-Anabaptism always take on a description that is novel and shaped at least as much by twenty- and twenty-first-century contexts as the sixteenth.

How Harold Bender Anchored Anabaptism

As I see it, nearly the entire contemporary debate around Anabaptist methodological questions is indebted to the work of Harold Bender. His *Anabaptist Vision* provided a positive and constructive response to the deepest yearnings of the Mennonites of his day and, in the process, launched North American Anabaptist theology on a trajectory that we are just beginning to recognize and recover from. In the words of John Roth, Bender's *Anabaptist Vision*

> served as a symbolic theological anchor within the Mennonite Church. In the tumultuous era following Second World War, as

---

[5]See *The Schleitheim Confession*, ed. and trans. John Howard Yoder (Scottdale, PA: Herald, 1977).
[6]Thieleman J. van Braght, *The Bloody Theater or Martyrs Mirror*, translated by Joseph F. Sohn (Scottdale, PA: Herald, 1950), 16.

Mennonites became increasingly acculturated into the mainstream culture of North America, Bender's summary of Anabaptism's essential features became a lodestar for leaders throughout the church, a source of identity and renewal amidst the buffeting forces of change.[7]

Beginning in the late nineteenth century and increasingly in the early twentieth century, the world that Mennonites encountered—particularly in North America—had become quite different. In short, the Industrial Revolution, colonialism and global trade, the rise of technology and all its social entailments—including and perhaps especially social mobility—and the temptation of the American dream gradually but radically altered the communities and the world in which Anabaptists found themselves. This assimilation of Anabaptist communities into a rapidly changing world quickly generated significant sociological attention,[8] but it also required theological attention. J. C. Wenger's prefatory comments in his *Introduction to Theology* gesture in this direction:

> During the last century, when Mennonites in North America made the transition from German to English, they suddenly found themselves cut off from the writings of Menno Simons, Dirck Philips, T. J. van Braght . . . as well as their confessions of faith, catechisms, and devotional literature. This brought about a certain disorientation, a cutting loose from the historical moorings. Although the brotherhood was saved by the introduction of the Sunday school, and was greatly revived by the ensuing interest in Bible study and missions, there arose a generation of leaders who were but superficially acquainted with the fundamental doctrines and insights of their Anabaptist forefathers. These new

---

[7] John D. Roth, "Living Between the Times: 'Anabaptist Vision and Mennonite Reality' Revisited," in *Refocusing a Vision*, ed. John D. Roth (Goshen: Mennonite Historical Society, 1995), 51.
[8] See, for example, Rodney J. Sawatsky, "Domesticating Sectarianism: Mennonites in the U.S. and Canada in Comparative Perspective," *The Canadian Journal of Sociology* 3, no. 2 (1978), 233–44; and Leo Driedger and J. Harold Kauffman, "Urbanization of Mennonites: Canadian and American Comparisons," *Mennonite Quarterly Review* 56 (1982), 269–90.

leaders attempted to formulate singlehandedly the outlines of a theology which would give our people a renewed sense of mission and thus prevent the further exodus of the ablest young people, and subsequent disintegration of the group. These formulations tended to cluster about nonresistance, nonconformity, and the ordinances: but nonresistance was thought of too exclusively in terms of a rejection of military service in time of war and little effort was made to develop a broad social ethic in terms of New Testament Christianity.[9]

From this moment onward, Mennonite theology could not help but become deeply invested—both intentionally and unintentionally—in the maintenance or reconstruction of an Anabaptist identity. A decade earlier, in the uncertain days of the Second World War, Harold Bender also appealed to history—to a specific strand of the sixteenth century—to describe a synthetic Anabaptist identity that served the purposes of being both summarily descriptive of the sixteenth century and normative for the twentieth:

> Although the definitive history of Anabaptism has not yet been written, we know enough today to draw a clear line of demarcation between original evangelical and constructive Anabaptism on the one hand, which was born in the bosom of Zwinglianism in Zurich, Switzerland, in 1525, and established in the Low Countries in 1533, and the various mystical, spiritualistic, revolutionary, or even antinomian related and unrelated groups on the other hand, which came and went like the flowers of the field in those days of the great renovation. The former, Anabaptism proper, maintained an unbroken course in Switzerland, South Germany, Austria, and Holland throughout the sixteenth century, and has continued until the present day in the Mennonite movement, now almost 500,000 baptized members strong in Europe and America. There is no longer any

---

[9] J. C. Wenger, *Introduction to Theology: A Brief Introduction to the Doctrinal Content of Scripture Written in the Anabaptist-Mennonite Tradition* (Scottdale, PA: Herald, 1966), vii.

excuse for permitting our understanding of the distinct character of this genuine Anabaptism to be obscured.[10]

Bender's tone is not nearly as pessimistic as Wenger's; his range of vision is also not nearly as broad. In essence, Bender selected Anabaptism as the appropriate nomenclature for the purpose of selecting one preferred historical strand that would then be distilled into three easily accessible themes by Bender: discipleship, voluntary church membership, and nonviolence. On this foundation, he then set about inducting young Mennonites into this new Anabaptist world, introducing them to the true understanding of the sixteenth century, and sending them out beyond the Mennonite world to get world-class educations. On this foundation, he energetically committed himself to reinforcing and building Mennonite institutions. And while not strictly speaking a theologian himself, he believed that the basic tenets of the early Anabaptists could be understood in English as well as in the original languages. The classic example of this can be found in the opening lines of his *Vision*. Citing Rufus Jones, he enjoins that the Anabaptist movement

> must be pronounced one of the most momentous and significant undertakings in man's eventful religious struggle after the truth. It gathered up the gains of earlier movements, it is the spiritual soil out of which all nonconformist sects have sprung, and it is the first plain announcement in modern history of a programme for a new type of Christian society which the modern world, especially in America and England, has been slowly realizing—an absolutely free and independent religious society, and a State in which every man counts as a man, and has his share in shaping both Church and State.[11]

And so, against the threat of acculturation and loss of theological identity, Bender provided a synthesized Anabaptism that anchored

---

[10]Harold S. Bender, *The Anabaptist Vision* (Goshen, IN: Mennonite Historical Society, 1944), 8. For a fuller assessment of how Bender's distillation of Anabaptism is carried forward and developed by Yoder and J. Denny Weaver, see Paul Martens, "How Mennonite Theology became Superfluous in Three Easy Steps: Bender, Yoder, Weaver," *Journal of Mennonite Studies* 33 (2015), 149–66.
[11]Bender, *Anabaptist Vision*, 3.

the Mennonite church by appropriating what he took to be the best of the sixteenth century to affirm the best of the modern (i.e., American and English) world.

Yoder and the Sinking of the Mennonite Ship

One of the young Mennonites who Bender inducted into his version of the Anabaptist world and then sent globetrotting for the purposes of gaining greater experience and a world-class education was John Howard Yoder. Yoder fulfilled the promise pursued by both Wenger and Bender—namely, "the development of a broad social ethic" (Wenger) for "a new type of Christian society" that the modern world is slowly realizing (Bender).

Since the Reformation, radical reformers were generally biblicists. They had a generally high and somewhat literal understanding of the Bible; searching the scriptures for truth was as important to Conrad Grebel and Balthasar Hubmaier as it was to Menno Simons and Thieleman van Braght. Yoder's genius, methodologically speaking, was that he was able to create a theology that integrated a version of Bender's understanding of sixteenth-century Anabaptism with late-twentieth-century critical biblical scholarship—thereby bypassing the persistent systematic theology versus biblical theology debates in Anabaptist circles[12]—in a manner that crystallized a social identity beyond the particularities of any specific Anabaptist community. In this way, Yoder's theology demonstrated that one could hold tight to both sixteenth-century history and biblical scholarship and still be faithfully relevant in the modern world. He seemed to be able to deliver the best of both worlds. And, as such, Yoder's theology perfectly met the needs of an increasingly assimilated Mennonite world in need of identity affirmation in a way that was seemingly consonant with the sixteenth century, intellectually satisfying, and self-consciously nonsectarian.

---

[12]This debate was still alive and well until the 1990s, as is evident by the publication of Ben C. Ollenburger, ed., *So Wide a Sea: Essays on Biblical and Systematic Theology* (Elkhart: Institute for Mennonite Studies, 1991).

Although sales and anecdotal comments suggest that *The Politics of Jesus* is Yoder's definitive text (and it is the text that works the hardest to perform the previously stated methodology), I believe that the theological vision sketched in a sermon originally preached in 1968 and later published under the title "The Original Revolution" is the sharpest and clearest account of what is fundamental to Yoder's thought and what has given it its lasting power.

By defining gospel as "revolution" and collapsing the personal and the political, Yoder was able to construct an understanding of Anabaptism in which the gospel was "the original revolution: the creation of a distinct community with its own set of deviant values and its coherent way of incarnating them."[13] The community that gathered around Jesus, again bridging description and normativity, was a sociological reality that was voluntary, was mixed in composition, and lived with a new pattern of relating to the world in a distinctly and idiosyncratically New Testament fashion. This new pattern of relating to the world was not tied to the specifics of lived Mennonite, Hutterite, or Amish experience. Instead, it was a movement that was temptingly relevant: political, demythologized, and distilled in a manner that transcended awkward Mennonite historic particularities. Yoder's new vision or hermeneutic divided the world into a new typology: those who live according to the practices of the new eon (the *agape* of the kingdom of God) and those who live according to the practices of the old eon that is doomed and passing away (especially the use of force and self-defense). The faithful church is the first fruits of the new eon, and "the ultimate meaning of history"—the victory of the Lamb—"is to be found in the work of the church."[14]

Yoder's "church" here is something of an abstraction, and he was very cautious of using the designation Anabaptist for his new political description. He is certainly not referring to the Mennonite church, which he resisted vigorously from his early days to his last and which in his estimation had become a *Corpusculum Christianum*, a miniature version of medieval Christianity.[15] His theological

---

[13]John Howard Yoder, *The Original Revolution: Essays on Christian Pacifism* (Scottdale, PA: Herald, 2003), 28.
[14]Yoder, *Original Revolution*, 61.
[15]John Howard Yoder, "Anabaptist Vision and Mennonite Reality," in *Consultation on Anabaptist-Mennonite Theology*, edited by A. J. Klassen (Fresno: Council of Mennonite Seminaries, 1970), 6–7.

vision, which he claimed reflected the grain of the universe, echoed the confidence of Bender's claim that the basic insights of the Anabaptists are being realized in all that is great in the modern civil societies of the English world. It answered the need for a socially relevant Anabaptist identity that remained nonviolent and nonconformist without plain dress, barns, or bishops. Politics—specifically the politics of Jesus—became the defining difference between the church (the distinct society with its deviant values) and the watching world.

Once non-Mennonites like Stanley Hauerwas got hold of this idea, a movement was started. Dissertations were written, books were published, conferences were held, and neo-Anabaptism was born. Yes, there were other Mennonite theologians in the latter half of the twentieth century (Gordon Kaufman, A. James Reimer, J. Lawrence Burkholder, and Gayle Gerber Koontz are but of few of the more influential). However, it is clear that Yoder was, for over a generation of non-Mennonites and most Mennonites, the overarching arbiter of Anabaptist—and not particularly Mennonite—theology. Because of his reading of Anabaptism, it became increasingly possible to see how its politics could be easily adopted and grafted into theological traditions not historically associated with the radical reformation, hence the emergence of naked or hyphenated Anabaptism (e.g., Anglican Anabaptist) in many quarters. And once this point is reached, Anabaptist theology becomes something different and separate from Mennonite theology. Even the frequent appearance of the term "Anabaptist-Mennonite" today dialectically infers the existence of a category of Mennonite that does not qualify as truly Anabaptist.

Perhaps one of the best illustrations of the sinking of the Mennonite ship that occurs through and following Yoder is provided by Keith Graber Miller: "It is quite possible that as Anabaptist themes are embraced by broader Christian thinkers and communities such as Stanley Hauerwas, Sojourners, and the 'emergent church' movement, these people, publications, and bodies of believers will carry forward important Anabaptist convictions as much or more so than do many of the ethnic institutional Anabaptist churches."[16] After Yoder, a powerful form of Bender's Anabaptist

---

[16]Keith Graber Miller, "Anabaptist Ethics," in *The Dictionary of Scripture and Ethics*, edited by Joel Green (Grand Rapids: Baker Academic, 2011), 65.

anchor remains, waiting to be embraced by any and all who are willing to practice the politics of the new revolution.

Then along came a group of persistent Mennonite women, led chiefly by Ruth Krall, who were committed to revealing precisely how deviant Yoder's revolutionary politics were. They were, in effect, the first to fight for the reality and persistence of a lived community behind the political abstractions of Yoder's Anabaptism.

Releasing John Howard Yoder

By Yoder's own admission, he and an unspecified number of women engaged in superficial touch as a natural greeting, discussion of possible deeper meaning of touch, more "meaningful touch," these same expressions with a layer of expectation (e.g., behind a closed door, accompanied by lap-sitting, with a less fleeting kiss), token partial disrobing, total disrobing, specific touching of penis or pubis, and exploration of partial or interrupted arousal and intermission.[17] Two mental health professionals working closely with Yoder as part of his eventual disciplinary process believe that he sexually violated more than 100 women.[18] His advances also included making suggestive comments, sending sexually explicit correspondence, and surprising women with physical coercion; his activities ranged across a spectrum from sexual harassment in public places to, more rarely, sexual intercourse. Some women found his sexual aggressions to be relatively inconsequential; other women's experiences across several continents were devastating, with trauma exacting a steep toll on marriages and careers.[19]

For good reason, some women in the Mennonite world had been resistant to elevating Yoder's thought for years. After years of partial information, whispers, dismissals, and denials within the Mennonite world, the lid was finally blown off Yoder's sexual experimentation for good in January 2015 with the publication of Rachel Waltner Goossen's historical summary of Mennonite responses to Yoder's sexual abuse in the *Mennonite Quarterly Review*. The immediate,

---

[17]Rachel Waltner Goossen, "'Defanging the Beast': Mennonite Responses to John Howard Yoder's Sexual Abuse," *Mennonite Quarterly Review* 89 (2015): 7.
[18]Goossen, "Defanging the Beast," 10.
[19]Ibid., 11.

haunting question for many that emerged was something like, *How in the world could Yoder do this?*

There is no doubt that qualified psychological assessments might be helpful here. That said, the theological answer is startlingly simple and problematic: in a world where church and world are defined sociologically and reified in opposition to one another, the deviant, revolutionary practices of true Christianity's "grand, noble experiment" could always be justified as a pilot project that would necessarily violate societal norms and therefore be challenged by the majority.[20] As Yoder claimed in *The Priestly Kingdom*, "We educate ourselves in the reasonable expectation that when we see things differently from others, we will often be seeing them more truly."[21] And he always had the "Get out of jail free" card: attempts to force him to stop would be met with the charge of Constantinianism against the Mennonite *Corpusculum Christianum*.

In light of Yoder's actions, it is important to recognize that a generation or two (and perhaps more) of those engaged in the enterprise of Anabaptist theology in North America (and beyond) have been traumatized and betrayed by the actions and authority of a serial sexual abuser. Even though many individuals in or in proximity to Mennonite theological study and institutions may have come through these years apparently unscathed, the tone, composition of interlocutors, content, and methodology of Anabaptist theology today is shaped and scarred in already recognizable and as yet unknown ways.

Like Bender's *Vision*, Yoder's theology had a kind of universal elegance and heuristic simplicity that made it incredibly tempting. With the final public revelations of his sexual abuse, however, the Mennonite world became aware that it may have rested on a problematic foundation: Its assumed historical, theological, and communal foundation—the very community in which he was educated, that sent him to Europe to work and study, and received him back as a theological and institutional leader—was essentially evacuated and depersonalized in the service of particular politics,

---

[20] This is the terminology Yoder used in approaching Carolyn Heggen ("Tina"), quoted in Tom Price, "Yoder's Actions Framed in Writings," *Elkhart Truth*, July 15, 1992.
[21] John Howard Yoder, *The Priestly Kingdom: Social Ethics as Gospel* (Notre Dame, IN: University of Notre Dame Press, 1984), 95.

a particular posture vis-à-vis the watching world. I suspect it is precisely this abstract foundation that made the vision so powerful in the first place.

The Need for New Light

In these years after Yoder's public reckoning, questions in Anabaptist theology presumed closed are suddenly thrown wide open. Increasingly, it is clear that they were closed because Yoder's form of Anabaptist theology either provided a convincing answer or prescinded from treating them seriously as questions. Allow me to illustrate with reference to four issues in Anabaptist theology that demand reconsideration.

Mennonites and Anabaptism

Yoder's theology had a far too simple understanding of the relationship between the sixteenth and the twenty-first centuries. Simplified understandings of the world have an explanatory power that entices many even though its simplicity misinforms and betrays reality. To my mind, the categories that Bender proposed and Yoder then modified for the purpose of transcending the particularities of Mennonite experience have turned out to be abstractions that distort and can pervert what it means to live as a Christian. They are abstractions because they are, literally, drawn apart from the lived communities in which they are allegedly rooted. So what are we then to make of those particularities that were superseded? The questions that remain open in the wake of the emergence of a kind of pan-Anabaptist theology are many: In what way is Anabaptism today linked to (a) sixteenth-century texts and ideas, (b) faith communities that have roots in the sixteenth century, (c) people who have ethnic ties to the communities that emerged in the sixteenth century (whether or not they claim the religious convictions of those communities), and (d) practices or themes that have become popularized under the name of Anabaptism in the last century? Or, in short, what criteria mark someone as an Anabaptist (assuming rebaptism is no longer intimately tied to the contemporary designation)? Bender and Yoder both answer this question unsatisfactorily, yet it remains relevant to both Mennonites and self-proclaimed Anabaptists in North America, Europe, Africa, South America, and the rest of the world.

This initial question presumes that there is, at least at this point, something called Anabaptist theology. How one answers these questions, however, will determine whether such a thing as Anabaptist theology is possible, necessary, or desirable moving forward. It is conceivable that one might even conclude that pursuing this question at all is but an extension of the Bender trajectory in a new way. Yet if one decides that Anabaptist theology is a possibility, and if it stands in some sort of continuity with what has been referred to as Anabaptism to this point in history, then the following questions become relevant as well.

Church and State

Yoder's distillation of the church to a sociological expression of deviance and revolution operated on the background assumption that the violence in question was an expression of the state or governing authority (and this applies even to his extended attempt to refine Constantinianism into neo-neo-neo-neo-Constantinianism).[22] Under the shadow of Vietnam and the Cold War, this binary of faithfulness versus Constantinian violence was incredibly attractive to many, yet it was also relatively blind to the ways violence can be perpetuated structurally in racial, gendered, and ethnic ways. It did not have categories for moral reflection on violence toward animals or the even more indirect slow violence committed against the environment, those beyond our borders, and the unborn. The question, raised in response to Yoder's particular description, is twofold. First, how does one address violence expressed in the aforementioned ways (and certainly others) that cannot neatly be lumped under the umbrella of Constantinianism? Or is a new understanding of the church's relation to the state or governing body needed to address the nearly infinite performances of violence that occur in our everyday practices? Second, has an overly realized eschatological understanding of Anabaptism's new aeon blinded us

---

[22]See Yoder, *Priestly Kingdom*, 135–46.

to the many ways that violence occurs within the church (to which Yoder's own resistance to his church seems to be Exhibit A)?

Personal and Political

Yoder's theology collapsed the personal and the political. As a means of challenging the superficial and therapeutic notions of self-discovery prevalent within much of American individualism in popular culture, this insight was seen as a purposive breath of fresh air. Yet it also discounts much of the history of Christian spirituality and the importance of the yearning of the heart, the mystery of God, and the role of desire. Further, his theology virtually throws away some of the psychological and spiritual tools that could have clarified his sexual politics as addiction or violence. The question that remains open after Bender, Yoder, and their heirs (including Hauerwas) is whether matters of the heart are always resolved by joining in the practices of the revolutionary community or whether a different understanding of Anabaptism needs to be either rehabilitated or imagined. At stake in this question is Yoder's identification of sociological trends as capturing the meaning of the gospel in its fullness, an identification that again abstracts the gospel from the integrity or wholeness of the person.

Church and World

Finally, Yoder's theology depended on the practices of the church to give meaning to history. Against the claims to divinity often intimated by modern nations, this was seen as a necessary proclamation, but the rest of creation then essentially became a meaningless backdrop to the political unfolding of history. Later in his life, Yoder admitted that he wasn't much good to his children, which isn't surprising given that categories like "spouse" and "children" had no significant theological importance in his revolutionary community (to say nothing of non-human animals and their progeny, other living things, or the earth as an expression of God's creative goodness). In light of this profoundly deficient understanding of the politics of the church, how do Anabaptists begin to understand the role of the church in relation to the natural world?

Conclusion

Anabaptist theology today, like much of the Mennonite world, is reeling from Yoder's public reckoning. In my mind, the task is to make sense not merely of his downfall but also of his rise to power and the convictions that made his theology so attractive in the first place. As people interested in the future of Anabaptist theology, we are inevitably seeking ways to address the challenges of our age without making the mistakes of those who came before us. It is now abundantly clear that Yoder is not the saint who can save us. His vision is impotent to address the challenges that we face. As we turn our gaze from Yoder, may we find other theological visions within and beyond the Mennonite world that challenge and encourage us anew.

Today, there is no single voice that speaks for Anabaptist theology. It is a contested conversation with a history, a present, and a future—as it always has been. Today, North American Mennonites are just beginning to recover from the *Anabaptist Vision*. Our particular present stands in the shadow of our recent past, and we have no desire to repeat that past. We are once again on a journey toward a new future with the hope and expectation that there are new dreams and visions yet to be poured out among us.

2

Contours and Possibilities for an Anabaptist Theology

Karl Koop

In the final two decades of the twentieth century, scholars were engaged in issues around the nature of Mennonite theology. A key question that surfaced at the time was whether Mennonite theology should have an ecumenical orientation or whether it should reflect a more particularistic mindset.[1] A. James Reimer was perhaps the most persistent in appealing to the wider Christian tradition even while maintaining Anabaptist-Mennonite convictions. Reimer looked to classical orthodoxy for his theological imagination and emphasized the Triune God and particularly the universal work of the Spirit as the basis for understanding the church catholic.[2]

I find myself generally in agreement with Reimer's line of reasoning. Contemporary Anabaptist communities ought to reject sectarian or partisan approaches that fail to adequately take into account the contributions of the wider Christian world. Theology must be ecumenical and dialogical in nature and recognize the various gifts of the church catholic that extends across time and

---

[1] A summary of some of these publications can be found in David C. Cramer, "Mennonite Systematic Theology in Retrospect and Prospect," *Conrad Grebel Review* 31, no. 3 (Fall 2013): 256, n. 4.
[2] See A. James Reimer, *Mennonites and Classical Theology: Dogmatic Foundations for Christian Ethics* (Kitchener, ON: Pandora, 2001).

space. I am convinced, however, that Anabaptists doing theology should be attentive to the particularities of their tradition even as they work within wider ecumenical frameworks.[3] We are, after all, always located within specific traditions—denominational or nondenominational, religious or nonreligious—and we always "bring tradition-shaped perspectives to our interpretation of human existence."[4] Ecumenism works best when interlocutors are honest about who they are and when they are able to demonstrate a capacity to bring something of themselves and the richness of their particular faith heritage to the table. Just as individuals have received spiritual charisms for the benefit of the local church, so also do theological traditions have gifts for the benefit of the church universal (1 Cor 12).[5] So, theologians who count themselves as being a part of the Anabaptist family—Baptists, Brethren in Christ, Church of the Brethren, Mennonites, and others—should not be apologetic about proceeding in an Anabaptist key.

In what follows I add my voice to the discussion about what it might mean to proceed theologically in this way.[6] I begin by addressing some of the problems that we encounter when we appeal to the Anabaptist tradition. I argue that while it is challenging to articulate what such a tradition might look like, it is nevertheless possible to identify family semblances that characterize the tradition, which may serve to orient Anabaptist theologizing. Yet responsible theology is not about the repristination of a previous faith culture. Contemporary Anabaptist theologians should not blindly appropriate their tradition without taking seriously a hermeneutics

---

[3] Here I am in agreement with David C. Cramer, who argues that Mennonites should be more radically particularistic at the same time that ecumenical and interreligious work is already underway. See Cramer, "Mennonite Systematic Theology," 257.
[4] Laura Schmidt Roberts, "(Re)Figuring Tradition," *Conrad Grebel Review* 21, no. 2 (Spring 2003), 74.
[5] A. James Reimer discusses the richness that denominations bring to the church universal. See his "Mennonites and the Church Universal," in *Without Spot or Wrinkle: Reflecting Theologically on the Nature of the Church*, edited by Karl Koop and Mary Schertz (Elkhart, IN: Institute of Mennonite Studies, 2000), 106–10. This essay was later published as "Mennonites and the Church Universal: Ecumenical Gifts of the Spirit," in A. James Reimer, *Mennonites and Classical Theology*, 537–52.
[6] I am using the term "Anabaptist" rather than "Mennonite" or "Anabaptist-Mennonite" because I am seeking to articulate a theology for an audience that is broader than my own stream within Anabaptism, which is Mennonite.

of tradition that also assumes some "(re)figuring" of tradition.⁷ In the latter part of this chapter I suggest a theological framework as a way of proceeding in an Anabaptist key that takes seriously the Anabaptist tradition but also leaves open the possibility of refiguring it. Here I suggest a trinitarian and christological framework that holds together the importance of Scripture, tradition, and the lived experience of the Christian community.

Problems in Appealing to the Anabaptist Tradition

Appealing to the Anabaptist tradition has its challenges. I have vivid memories of being a part of a theological colloquium at Humboldt University in Berlin in the mid-1990s. My Lutheran and Reformed friends would often ask me about what the Anabaptist tradition had to say about this or that topic, and I remember having difficulty articulating anything coherent, given Anabaptism's diverse beginnings. At the time, Reformation historians were highlighting the polygenetic origins of Anabaptism as a necessary corrective to a previous historiographical tradition that had failed to take seriously the plurality of sixteenth-century Anabaptist beginnings. In this intellectual environment, as both a historian and a theologian, my challenge was to give a coherent answer without adding endless qualifications. So, given that my sixteenth-century tradition was not that unified, my approach going forward was to draw from the confessional tradition that seemed to have some level of consistency and coherence over the long term. In the many confessions of faith that Anabaptists and Mennonites wrote and adopted over an almost-500-year period, I was convinced that one could recognize a *coherent*, even systematic theology that addressed all of the "common places" of Christian belief. Such attention to the confessional heritage, I believed, could help orient the contemporary church in its life and mission in the world.⁸

---

⁷This is terminology that I am borrowing from Laura Schmidt Roberts in her article "(Re)figuring Tradition," 71–81.
⁸This is a part of the argument in my work *Anabaptist-Mennonite Confessions of Faith: The Development of a Tradition* (Kitchener, ON: Pandora, 2004). For

Confessions of faith, however, are only one part of the Anabaptist story and do not adequately capture the full religious expression of a given community, and confessional statements do not tell us how people actually lived. By the end of the sixteenth century and on into the seventeenth century, we encounter Anabaptist traditions that are not only concerned about doctrine but also focused on mystical and "spiritual" experience; here and there we meet not only separatists but also ecumenically engaged actors who fraternized easily with Catholics and trans-denominational Collegiants alike. As the seventeenth century progresses, we meet an evolving Anabaptism of even wider contrasting religiosities from the devoutly pietistic and inwardly focused to the highly rationalistic and worldly oriented. In the mid-eighteenth century we find, here and there, pietistic impulses, and then a few decades later we discover in some quarters not an insignificant number of proponents of the French Revolution embodied among young Swiss enthusiasts and Dutch Patriots. As we enter the nineteenth century in Germany, we see the rise of hyper-nationalism that adumbrates the fervent militarism exemplified among not an insignificant number of Mennonites during the twentieth-century world wars. Among these various periods of contrasting expressions of lived experience, we find instances of the "quiet in the land," occurrences of a people devoted to simplicity, to the practice of mutual aid and nonresistance—instances that contemporary Mennonites and other Anabaptist groups have typically associated with their own heritage. Yet, given more careful attention to what was really going in these centuries of the modern era, we are forced to admit that such descriptions are truncated and incomplete, and they are often projections of our contemporary ideals.[9]

---

an overview of these Anabaptist confessions of faith, see Karl Koop, *Confessions of Faith in the Anabaptist Tradition 1527–1660* (Kitchener, ON: Pandora, 2006); Howard John Loewen, *One Lord, One Church, One Hope, and One God: Mennonite Confessions of Faith* (Elkhart, IN: Institute of Mennonite Studies, 1985).
[9] A comprehensive bibliographical summary of works that describe this plurality cannot be included here. The following writings are only a sampling: Andrew C. Fix, *Prophecy and Reason: The Dutch Collegiants in the Early Enlightenment* (Princeton, NJ: Princeton University Press, 1991); August den Hollander, Alex Noord, Mirjam van Veen, and Anna Voolstra, eds., *Religious Minorities and Cultural Diversity in the Dutch Republic: Studies Presented to Piet Visser on the Occasion of his 65th Birthday* (Leiden: Brill, 2014); Mark Janzen, *Mennonite German Soldiers: Nation, Religion,*

The burden of history, then, is that we are up against a tradition that seems to be a complex of varying lived experiences that from the very beginning to the very end have been shaped by a wide range of social and religious factors. This has created a diversity that points to the multiplicity of faith expressions that we find among members of the Anabaptist family in its developing, evolving, and dynamic renditions up to the present day. In taking seriously the Anabaptist faith tradition, whether it is the sixteenth century or the centuries following or whether it is taking into account the rapidly expanding manifestations of a movement that we see today in the charismatic Global South, what we are likely to encounter is something that is much more difficult to pinpoint than what we may have first imagined. This can make it exceedingly difficult to invoke with integrity the tradition for our own purposes. In their mission statements, for example, some Mennonite institutions will identify with the Anabaptist tradition in some way. But what does such an identification mean when the tradition itself is untethered and unfixed?

The challenge of defining the tradition may seem unsettling, but perhaps we can imagine seeing the varied landscape positively as an example of theological adaptability and contextuality. Of course, not all past expressions of our faith traditions are life-giving and faithful, so a discerning process of the past is important. But the plurality of expression over a 500-year period may hint at a richness that mirrors the multicolored tapestry that characterizes the Christian tradition as a whole—a mosaic that will always elude our interest to neatly define or possess, which itself may be seen as a virtue. Such thinking clearly calls into question "essentialist"

---

and Family in the Prussian East, 1772–1880 (Notre Dame, IN: University of Notre Dame, 2010); Karl Koop, "A Complication for the Mennonite Peace Tradition: Wilhelm Mannhardt's Defense of Military Service," *Conrad Grebel Review* 34, no. 1 (Winter 2016): 28–48; John D. Roth and James M. Stayer, eds., *A Companion to Anabaptism and Spiritualism, 1521–1700*, edited by John D. Roth and James M. Stayer (Leiden: Brill, 2007); John D. Roth, "Pietism and the Anabaptist Soul," in *The Dilemma of Anabaptist Piety*, edited by Stephen L. Longnecker (Bridgewater: Forum for Religious Studies, 1997), 17–33; Mirjam van Veen, Piet Visser, and Gary Waite, *Sisters: Myth and Reality of Anabaptist, Mennonite and Doopsgezind Women, ca 1525–1900*; Piet Visser, *Broeders in de geest: De doopsgezinde bijdragen van Dierick en Jan Philipsz. Schabaelje tot de Nederlandse stichtelijke literatuur*, 2 vols. (Deventer: Sub Rosa, 1988).

understandings of what the Anabaptist tradition looks like. It does not presume clearly defined definitions, boundaries, or "distinctives" but rather assumes expressions of hybridity—that is, the intermixing of ideas and behaviors between and across religious traditions. In taking the long view, however, it may also be possible to identify a certain trajectory, a mix of ingredients that can provide a measure of *ressourcement* or "retrieval" for doing theology in an Anabaptist key.[10]

Persistent Patterns and Family Semblances

One of the ways it might be possible to think about the shape of the Anabaptist tradition for resourcing the present is to ask whether there are repeated or persistent patterns of belief and action over the 500-year story that have stubbornly resurfaced again and again and have thus stood the test of time. In taking the long view—in examining the broad sweep of religious expression among the conservative, the old order, the new order, and the progressives; in looking at reoccurring patterns among contemporary Anabaptist communities in the South as well as the North; in becoming acquainted with the Anabaptists who were mystics, pietists, evangelicals, and charismatics; in encountering the creativity of the artist, poet, entrepreneur, agriculturalist, baker, gardener, home manager; in encountering the laity as well as the resident theologians—can we observe recognizable shapes and threads, a tapestry of rituals and habits that have tenaciously held their ground over time and place? In examining the various faith expressions that have come down through the centuries—catechisms, confessions of faith, concordances, hymns, prayer books, stories of martyrdom, diaries, poetry, writings of fiction, and so on—can we

---

[10]Here I am in sympathy with W. David Buschart and Kent D. Eilers who have aligned themselves with a number of movements of retrieval that have emerged in recent decades, for example, the *nouvelle theologie*, postliberalism, ancient-future movements, and paleo-orthodoxy. See W. David Buschart and Kent D. Eilers, *Theology as Retrieval: Receiving the Past, Renewing the Church* (Downers Grove, IL: IVP Academic, 2015).

find noticeable common components of a faith culture or ethos that may be identified as "Anabaptist"?

Within this mode of inquiry, I suspect, we will find neither fixed nor thick boundaries distinguishing Anabaptism from its surrounding religious environs. After all, the boundary lines between Anabaptist communities and the wider Christian world have always been porous, allowing for stimuli to flow freely in both directions leading to various forms of religious hybridity. Nevertheless, if we are patient and look for patterns, it may be possible for us to recognize certain identifiable family semblances that tell us something about the shape of the Anabaptist communion across time and space. For instance, while noticing many exceptions in the Anabaptist story, we may nevertheless see a persistent commitment in most groups to a Triune God and an ongoing emphasis on the centrality of Jesus Christ as savior and supreme example. We may notice enduring practices of communal readings of Scripture and common liturgical and song traditions that in their various harmonies sound out a certain Anabaptist ring or tone. We may find a certain sensibility concerning the rites of believers' baptism and communion focused on memory, fellowship, and accountability, or we may notice a specific emphasis on orthopraxis (not simply orthodoxy). We may sense a strong loyalty to the concept of discipleship—to a lived, participatory faith affected inwardly and at the same time devoted outwardly to simplicity and to the practices of mutual aid, nonresistance, peace building, and service. We may also encounter a certain reservation about, or suspicion toward, the ways of the "world." Of course, not all Anabaptist groups reflect these patterns, and none of these characteristics can really be truly considered Anabaptist distinctives per se—these features are readily found, after all, in other Christian traditions. What makes the aforementioned description Anabaptist is that many of these characteristics are persistent or repetitive from one region to another and from one era to the next. And it may be in the combination of the features that we recognize a definable tradition.

Still, any appeal to tradition will assume some level of discussion and debate without reaching a final or totalizing definition. We may together witness recognizable family semblances, but we will not necessarily always agree on how the details should be nuanced. Thus, we can assume that there will be some sifting and sorting going on; there will be a hermeneutics of tradition at play. Finding a usable past will invariably include some level of judgment and adjudication, especially as contexts change or as new experiences and encounters call for new interpretive frameworks. The act of traditioning will always involve some (re)figuring of tradition.

Responsible traditioning, then, presumes that one views the past not "regulatively" but "orientationally." As Nathanael Inglis has noted, on one hand, traditions can function regulatively "when serving as norms that justify the status quo, legitimate the authority of community leaders, or secure hierarchical boundaries. In an exclusive sphere of influence, traditions can be elevated as authoritative, indisputable guides for the present and future."[11] On the other hand, traditions can function orientationally "by providing symbolic material that people draw upon to understand who they are and how they relate to one another. In this way, traditions are the building blocks of individual and collective identities."[12]

This latter understanding, in my view, ought to characterize the process of traditioning that is determined not only, as Harry Huebner puts it, "in reference to what has made sense in the past (although it does that)" but also "in relation to experiences and ways of thinking in the lives of people today."[13] This involves the risk of humbly re-presenting the Christian faith, involving both old and new concepts and actions. It is less about an intellectual puzzle to be solved and more about pursuing mystery, a pilgrimage characterized by faith seeking understanding.

What might such a theological pilgrimage look like? And what approach might help along the way in discerning whether a tradition is still tenable? Communities seeking a faithful way forward will need to begin somewhere and will need to proceed with some beginning commitments. In the following, I suggest one

---

[11]Nathanael Inglis, "The Importance of Gordon Kaufman's Constructive Theological Method for Contemporary Anabaptist-Mennonite Theology," *Conrad Grebel Review* 34, no. 2 (Spring 2016): 145. For his ideas Inglis is adapting John Thompson's schema, which includes *normative, legitimating, hermeneutic,* and *identity* aspects of tradition. See Paul Heelas, Scott Lash, and Paul Morris, eds., *Detraditionalization: Critical Reflections on Authority and Identity* (Cambridge, MA: Blackwell, 1996), 92–93.
[12]Inglis, "Constructive Theological Method," 145.
[13]Harry Huebner, "Imagination/Tradition: Disjunction or Conjunction?" in *Mennonite Theology in Face of Modernity: Essays in Honor of Gordon D. Kaufman,* edited by Alain Epp Weaver (North Newton, KS: Bethel College, 1996), 76.

way of moving forward in an Anabaptist key. It is a cursory outline with an invitation to further reflection and discussion.

A Trinitarian and Christological Framework to Which Scripture Bears Witness

The starting point of Anabaptist theology, in my view, should include attentiveness to the Triune God. This is a confession of faith that has its basis in the scriptural witness and the experience of the church. In the various theological treatises, prayer books, songbooks, and other liturgical expressions over a 500-year period, Anabaptists have confessed their belief in the one God of Israel, even as they have declared Jesus Christ as Lord and have recognized the ongoing work of the Spirit in the life of the believer and the Christian community.

Within this threefold understanding, the second person of the Trinity has played a unique role in the tradition. In seeking to understand most fully the nature of God, Anabaptist expressions of belief have emphasized that, while God can be revealed in nature and in history, the fullness of revelation comes decisively in the person of Jesus Christ, the Word made flesh (John 1:14). For Anabaptists, this Word made flesh has persistently been understood as the decisive basis, criterion, and norm for what it means to live as a disciple in the world. As Menno Simons repeatedly reminded his readers in all of his writings, "For no one can lay any foundation other than the one that has been laid; that foundation is Jesus Christ" (1 Cor 3:13).[14] Thus, any refiguring of tradition will need to take into account this foundational norm.

In Anabaptism, this christological basis has sometimes been expressed through propositional or narrative renderings of Scripture.[15] But also noticeable in the tradition are the persistent

---

[14]This is the motto that introduces virtually every writing in Menno Simons's complete works. See *The Complete Writings of Menno Simons c. 1496–1561*, edited by J. C. Wenger; translated by Leonard Verduin (Scottdale, PA: Herald, 1984 [1956]).
[15]For instance, the propositional approach was taken up in the early decades of the twentieth century by Daniel Kauffman. See his *Doctrines of the Bible: A Brief*

strands that describe the way discipleship is ontologically grounded in the person of Jesus Christ, the one in whom the Christian community finds its identity and through whom the church is empowered to live in faithfulness. In this rendering, the emphasis is on being united in Christ, participating in the divine nature of Christ, and living in the Spirit of Christ.[16] More than simply focusing on the historical actions of Jesus of Nazareth, whom believers are called to literally imitate, this Anabaptist perspective views Jesus of the Gospels as the head of "a living and active body into which believers are united by faith and baptism."[17] The relationship is imitative but also ontological in a way that has an impact on one's very being.

Important to note in this discussion is that Scripture is not understood as the supreme norm for Christian belief and practice; the person of Jesus Christ holds this place. Contemporary theologians like Daniel Migliore have noted that Scripture understood in this way is the Word of God "in a derivative sense."[18] Or, as Karl Barth insisted, Scripture is a *witness* to the living Word. "A real witness,"

Discussion of the Teachings of God's Word (Scottdale, PA: Mennonite Publishing House, 1928). A notable proponent of the narrative approach is J. Denny Weaver, "A Believers' Church Christology," *Mennonite Quarterly Review* 58, no. 2 (April 1983): 112–31.

[16]William Keeney was perhaps one of the first scholars to notice the theme of divinization or deification in early Anabaptism, but he tended to view these themes in moral terms, not as ontological or substantial. Brian Hamilton, who is critical of the way Harold S. Bender and J. Denny Weaver reduce Christ to the historical and ethical realm, argues persuasively the inextricable connection between the ontological and the historical in the thought of Michael Sattler. See his essay "The Ground of Perfection: Michael Sattler on 'The Body of Christ,'" in *New Perspectives in Believers Church Ecclesiology*, edited by Abe Dueck, Helmut Harder, and Karl Koop (Winnipeg: CMU Press, 2010), 143–60. In my own interpretation of Menno Simons's peace theology, I have argued that identification with Christ must be understood as a particular ontology in which recipients of the new birth do not simply follow a code of ethics or law; "they have a new identity, having been united in the very being of Christ that compels them to live in a radically different way." So Karl Koop, "A Complication for the Mennonite Peace Tradition," 37. For a list of biblical passages that highlight the connection between the ontological and the historical, see John Howard Yoder, *The Politics of Jesus: Vicit Agnus Noster*, 2nd ed. (Grand Rapids: Eerdmans, 1994), 112–33.

[17]Hamilton, "The Ground of Perfection," 151.

[18]Daniel Migliore, *Faith Seeking Understanding: An Introduction to Christian Theology*, 3rd ed. (Grand Rapids: Eerdmans, 2014), 53.

Barth maintained, "is not identical with that to which it witnesses, but it sets it before us."¹⁹ In this case Barth was following the reformers who typically understood Scripture to be "authoritative not in itself" but as it set forth Christ because it functioned "in the community of faith by the power of the Spirit to create a liberating and renewing relationship with God through Christ."²⁰ Many sixteenth- and seventeenth-century Anabaptists made a similar distinction in that they differentiated between the written and the living Word. The Waterlander Mennonites, for example, were quite insistent in saying that the written Word by itself could not induce a life of holiness within the believer. Only the living Word, the eternal Word, Jesus Christ, they maintained, had the power to bring salvation.²¹

Within the twofold Word of God, the words of Scripture bear witness and are thus provisional or penultimate in position, pointing beyond to the divine presence of God.²² To say that the written Word is provisional or penultimate does not take away from its authority; nevertheless, its provisional nature qualifies its position in relation to the one who is considered to be the supreme norm. Positively worded, Scripture is the primary "testimony of the eye witnesses."²³ For this reason, the church of the ages and the various strands of Anabaptism have confessed that precisely through this

---

[19] Karl Barth, *Church Dogmatics*, 1/2 (Edinburgh: T&T Clark, 1956/1963), 463, quoted in Migliore, *Faith Seeking Understanding*, 52.
[20] Migliore, *Faith Seeking Understanding*, 53.
[21] "Thirteen Articles" in Koop, *Confessions of Faith in the Anabaptist Tradition*, 159–63. This line of thinking was followed by early Anabaptist thinkers such as Hans Denck and Ulrich Stadler. See Walter Klaassen, *Anabaptism in Outline* (Scottdale, PA: Herald, 1981), 142–47. The more recent *Confession of Faith in a Mennonite Perspective* also prioritizes the living Word when it states: "God has spoken above all in the living Word who became flesh and revealed the truth of God faithfully . . . . We believe that God continues to speak through the living and written Word. Because Jesus Christ is the Word become flesh, Scripture as a whole has its center and fulfillment in him." *Confession of Faith in a Mennonite Perspective* (Scottdale, PA: Herald, 1995), art. IV, 21.
[22] For further discussion on the penultimate nature of the sources of theology, see Douglas John Hall, *Thinking the Faith: Christian Theology in a North American Context* (Minneapolis: Fortress, 1991), 432–43.
[23] Karl Barth, *Church Dogmatics*, 1/1 (Edinburgh: T & T Clark, 1956/1963), 98–124, quoted in Hall, *Confessing the Faith*, 441.

medium the divine voice can be heard.[24] But how exactly is this voice heard and understood?

Tradition and the Lived Experience of the Community

In Orthodox and Catholic traditions, it is typically assumed that the divine voice can properly be heard only in the context of the Christian church, specifically through the church's hierarchy. Within contemporary Protestantism, especially evangelicalism, there is a tendency to read Scripture individualistically with the assumption that it can or indeed should be read in an unmediated way. In practice, however, it is not possible to read the Bible in the absence of some tradition. There is no reading *sola scriptura* via scripture alone. Like all interpretive activity, the reading of Scripture cannot take place from some neutral standpoint; it is always historically, culturally, and personally grounded somewhere. The sixteenth-century reformers recognized their dependency on tradition by emphasizing the orthodox traditions of the church and respecting the newly formed hierarchies of the Protestant state churches. For the Anabaptists, the accent on ecclesiology meant, above all, the discerning that took place within the local gathered community of believers in worship and in service. It is this entity that was seen—uniquely so during the Protestant Reformation—as the primary location for discernment. With reference to the Anabaptist tradition, as Fernando Enns has noted, "the gathered congregation in worship and in service to others is considered as the primary reality of the church of Jesus Christ."[25]

---

[24]One of the strongest declarations of the Spirit speaking through Scripture comes through in the Westminster Confession of 1646, article X: "The Supreme Judge, by which all controversies of religion are to be determined, and all decrees of councils, opinions of ancient writers, doctrines of men, and private spirits, are to be examined, and in whose sentence we are to rest, can be no other but the Holy Spirit speaking in the Scripture." See John H. Leith, *Creeds of the Churches: A Reader in Christian Doctrine from the Bible to the Present*, 3rd ed. (Atlanta: John Knox, 1982), 196.
[25]Fernando Enns, "Introduction," in *Mennonites in Dialogue: Official Reports from International and National Ecumenical Encounters, 1975–2012*, edited by Fernando Enns and Jonathan Seiling (Eugene, OR: Wipf & Stock, 2015), 1.

It is in this context that Scripture is read, interpreted, and applied to daily life.

In describing this approach in sixteenth-century Anabaptism, John Howard Yoder used the terminology of "the Rule of Paul," based on 1 Cor 14, where discernment was carried out among ordinary Christians in the context of the congregation. Yoder argued that this paradigm was followed by the Anabaptists, who relied on the gathered body, the written Word, and the Spirit for their process of discernment.[26] In my view Yoder exaggerates the role of the laity and does not take seriously enough the role of Anabaptist leaders in the community's discerning process or the extent to which Anabaptist leaders from different regions typically consulted with one another.[27] But he is right in pointing out that for early Anabaptists it was expected that the Spirit spoke only when Christians were "gathered in readiness to hear it speak to their current needs and concerns."[28] Other scholars have made similar observations, noting that the Anabaptists correlated faithful understanding of Scripture with obedience. Cornelius J. Dyck referred to this as an "epistemology of obedience," where the truths of faith were discovered in the context of "actual faithfulness in discipleship."[29]

What this epistemology of obedience points to is the significance of "lived experience," a way of knowing that is inherently participatory.[30] "Participation in Christ," "partaking of the divine nature," or "living in the Spirit" does not stop with biblical exegesis.

---

[26]John Howard Yoder, "The Hermeneutics of the Anabaptists," in *Essays on Biblical Interpretation: Anabaptist-Mennonite Perspectives*, edited by Willard M. Swartley (Elkhart, IN: Institute of Mennonite Studies, 1984), 11–28.

[27]See my discussion on this topic in "Worldly Preachers and True Shepherds: Anabaptist Anticlericalism in the Lower Rhine," in *The Heart of the Matter: Pastoral Ministry in Anabaptist Perspective*, edited by Erik Sawatzky (Scottdale, PA: Herald, 2004), 24–38; previously published as "Worldly Preachers and True Shepherds: Anticlericalism and Pastoral Identity among Anabaptists in the Lower Rhine," *Mennonite Quarterly Review* 76, no. 4 (October 2002): 399–411.

[28]Yoder, "Hermeneutics of the Anabaptists," 21.

[29]Cornelius J. Dyck, "Hermeneutics and Discipleship," in *Essays on Biblical Interpretation*, 30. See also Ben Ollenburger, "The Hermeneutics of Obedience," in the same volume, 45–61.

[30]Harry Huebner, "Participation, Peace, and Forgiveness: Milbank and Yoder in Dialogue," in *The Gift of Difference: Radical Orthodoxy, Radical Reformation*, edited by Chris K. Huebner and Tripp York (Winnipeg: CMU Press, 2010), 195.

Decisions about slavery, head covering, same-sex marriage, or "medical assistance in dying" are not addressed simply via a community's focus on the biblical text or biblical scholarship. Discernment must be carried out in the context of prayer, worship, and the lived experience of community as it is engaged in the world. As the Eastern Orthodox Church would have it, *lex orandi* precedes *lex credendi*—liturgy and prayer must precede our theologizing. Our problem, as Harry Huebner has put it, is that we "attempt to go directly from the Bible to the community of faith. We have spent much time learning the traditions of the Bible, that is, cultivating the skills of biblical interpretation, but very little time in the important part of the interpretive process which entails embodying that understanding in the life of the community of faith."[31] As Huebner reminds his readers, "The Mennonite theologian Hans Denck knew this long ago, when he said that 'We cannot know Christ unless we follow him daily in life.'"[32]

There is always the danger that such an epistemology will become vulnerable to the whims and wants of our subjectivities or will succumb to the influences of contemporary cultural norms. Yet, at its best, lived experience within the Christian community is anchored to the "mind of Christ" and guided by the Spirit of God. By faith Christians patiently trust that the Spirit will lead toward what is good and true. In this respect, the lived experience of faith is more about a pilgrimage or sojourn that travels in familiar terrain but sometimes ventures into uncharted territory.

Such travel should never take place in isolation. Churches that become self-contained and independent are always in danger of manufacturing their own heresies. One of the ways Anabaptist communities can resist isolation is to continually remind themselves that they are a part of the church catholic, the Christian community that exists through time and space. While it is true that the Anabaptist ecclesiological accent is typically the local gathered community of believers, this community needs to be always open to broadening the circle of discourse with the recognition that no tradition by itself can have the final say. Embracing the church

---

[31]Harry Huebner, "Imagination/Tradition: Conjunction or Disjunction?" in *Mennonite Theology in Face of Modernity: Essays in Honor of Gordon D. Kaufman* (North Newton, KS: Bethel College, 1996), 76.
[32]Huebner, "Imagination/Tradition," 76.

universal means listening to local voices but then also the voices of the whole church. Anabaptist communities have much to learn from their brothers and sisters in Christ—their Orthodox, Roman Catholic, and Protestant neighbors, those that fall within liberal as well as conservative streams, and those who live in the South as well as the North. Moreover, conversations of discernment should not be limited to the Christian world but should also extend to other religions and to those with no religious affiliation, for surely the Spirit of God is at work in all places and times.

Conclusion

In this chapter I have suggested that Anabaptists doing theology should be attentive to their particular tradition, recognizing the complexities but also holding out the possibility of identifying persistent patterns and family semblances within the tradition. I have also suggested that the act of traditioning will always involve some (re)figuring of tradition—that traditions ought to function orientationally rather than regulatively. And finally, I have suggested a trinitarian and christological framework that seeks to hold together the importance of Scripture, tradition, and the lived experience of the Christian community.

Often sources in Christian theology are viewed in hierarchical and discrete fashion. For example, within the structure of the Wesleyan Quadrilateral, Scripture is often considered first, followed by tradition, reason, and experience. For Protestants, Scripture usually takes precedence and is seen as theology's "norming norm,"[33] whereas in Orthodoxy and Catholicism the role of tradition is highlighted alongside of Scripture. While I am not disputing the primacy of Scripture—Scripture is the primary "testimony of the eye witnesses"—I am suggesting a triadic model that suggests holding together Scripture, tradition, and the lived experience of the Christian community, a model that is perichoretic, embracing interdependence.

---

[33]See Stanely J. Grenz and John R. Franke, *Beyond Foundationalism: Shaping Theology in a Postmodern Context* (Louisville, KY: Westminster John Knox, 2001), 57–92.

The Anabaptist vision described in this chapter views the Christian way more like a pilgrimage than a system of doctrinal and ethical tenets. "Far from producing a closed or complacent attitude," such faith hopes to awaken humility, "wonder, inquiry, and exploration."[34] It is less about a book and more about trust and a relationship with a personal creator God who has been made known above all in Jesus and who continues to be present in the world through the Spirit. Any sojourn of this kind will surely be fraught with missteps along the way, which is to be expected of a community characterized by failures of many kinds. But by the grace of God, may this way of sojourning constantly seek renewal and be filled with courageous faith, hope, and love.

---

[34]Migliore, *Faith Seeking Understanding*, 4.

3

Refiguration, Configuration

Tradition, Text, and Narrative Identity

Laura Schmidt Roberts

Introduction

Anabaptist theologizing finds itself beset by a challenge both old and new: a construal of its tradition that adequately accounts for its pluriformity (historical and contemporary) and its recognizable identity. For scholars in Canada and the United States, the question takes a particular cast in light of twentieth-century ecclesial, historiographical, and sociocultural shifts that profoundly reshape communal identity. The development and functional normativity of Harold S. Bender's Swiss-Brethren-based "Anabaptist Vision"[1] as a norm for communal identity was important as Canadian and American Mennonites moved out of rural enclaves and the sociocultural boundary markers native to those settings were lost.[2]

---

[1] Harold S. Bender, *The Anabaptist Vision* (Scottdale, PA: Herald, 1944).
[2] Paul Toews, *Mennonites in American Society, 1930–1970* (Scottdale, PA: Herald, 1996), 36–39, 84–106.

The subsequent demise of this "normative" vision came from multiple factors—theological critiques, polygenesis historiography, historiographic shifts away from idealist approaches toward sociopolitical history—and returned questions of communal identity to the fore.[3] The ongoing negotiation of Anabaptist theological identity in this period after the normative vision is marked by attempts to make theological sense of the realities of historical and contemporary pluralism within the tradition. As theologians turn to more explicit—even systematic—theology to address these concerns, the definition and function of tradition in theologizing emerge as significant issues. Indeed, the definition of the parameters and uniqueness of the tradition are one way to read much of the theological work (and arguments!) that develop among North American scholars beginning in the 1980s. These questions are made more complex for theologians in denominations born of historic Anabaptism by the emergence of neo-Anabaptism as a pan-denominational phenomenon beginning in the 1990s but gaining greater visibility with the publication of Stewart Murray's *The Naked Anabaptist* in 2010.[4] How, indeed, does one construe a historical tradition to account for all of this—multiple movements within the tradition from its origins, expansion of the tradition beyond historic denominational lines to function as a movement shaping other ecclesial communities yet a Christian tradition that is identifiably distinct?

This chapter argues that the hermeneutical approach of Paul Ricoeur presents fruitful possibilities for theorizing Anabaptist tradition and a hermeneutics of tradition such that multiple, competing construals and their argumentation are constitutive of

---

[3]See, for example, J. Lawrence Burkholder, *The Problem of Social Responsibility from the Perspective of the Mennonite Church* (Elkhart, IN: Institute of Mennonite Studies, 1989); Gordon D. Kaufman, *Nonresistance, Responsibility, and Other Mennonite Essays* (Newton, KS: Faith and Life, 1979); John Howard Yoder, "Anabaptist Vision and Mennonite Reality," in *Consultation on Anabaptist-Mennonite Theology*, edited by A. J. Klassen (Fresno, CA: Council of Mennonite Seminaries, 1970); John Howard Yoder, "The Recovery of the Anabaptist Vision," *Concern* 18 (July 1971): 5–23; James M. Stayer, Werner O. Packull, and Klaus Deppermann, "From Monogenesis to Polygenesis: The Historical Discussion of Anabaptist Origins," *Mennonite Quarterly Review* 49 (April 1975): 83–121.
[4]Stewart Murray, *The Naked Anabaptist: The Bare Essentials of a Radical Faith* (Herald, 2010).

a tradition due to the pluriform and underdetermined nature of historical traditions and their texts and due to the perspectival locatedness of interpreters. Historical consciousness drives Ricoeur's paired hermeneutics of retrieval and suspicion, which are applied to interpreter, text, and tradition alike in a dialectic of understanding and explanation constituting the interpretive process.[5] Historical consciousness also requires individual and communal search for what Ricoeur terms "narrative identity," a self-understanding that, as we will see, works to address questions of changes in and permanence of identity across time.[6]

I begin by observing the central role texts and their interpretation play in Ricoeur's understanding of tradition, for whom textual interpretation provides the paradigm for encounter with historical traditions. It becomes clear that encounter with a tradition through its written texts is more active process than passive reception, and I draw out several implications for theorizing Anabaptist tradition that result. I then consider in greater detail two aspects of Ricoeur's interpretation theory (distanciation and the understanding-explanation dialectic) for the way they illuminate this engagement with traditioned texts as an encounter with tradition itself, sketching what this looks like in relation to biblical and historical texts in Anabaptist tradition. But each section also conducts a thought experiment, applying Ricoeur's hermeneutical approach to a broadened notion of a tradition itself as a "text." I argue that the plural, fluid, ongoing interpretation of the "text" of Anabaptist tradition constitutes its recognizable identity, accounts in some measure for its multiplicity, and requires a self-critical hermeneutics of suspicion now more than ever. Yet there are limits to the hermeneutical model, so in the final section I take up the question of change and recognizable continuity in a tradition's identity across time by exploring Ricoeur's "narrative identity" as a complementary concept.

---

[5] See Paul Ricoeur, "Hermeneutics and the Critique of Ideology," in *Hermeneutics and the Human Sciences*, edited and translated by John B. Thompson (Cambridge: Cambridge University Press, 1981), 63–100.
[6] See Paul Ricoeur, *Time and Narrative*, vol. 3, translated by Kathleen McLaughlin and David Pellauer (Chicago: University of Chicago Press, 1988), 244–49; Paul Ricoeur, *Oneself as Another*, trans. Kathleen Blamey (Chicago: University of Chicago Press, 1990), 113–25, 140–63.

Tradition and Text

"Every *tradition* lives by the grace of interpretation, and it is at this price that it continues, that is, remains living."[7] Ricoeur views textual interpretation as the paradigm for human encounter with historical traditions. So, for Ricoeur, interpretation of the written texts of a tradition constitutes an encounter with the tradition itself. Indeed, tradition requires the continual interpretation of its "deposit": "Our 'heritage' is not a sealed package we pass from hand to hand, without ever opening, but rather a treasure from which we draw by the handful and which by this very act is replenished."[8]

Defining Tradition

So what does Ricoeur mean by *tradition*? Ricoeur develops a threefold notion of the complex problem of tradition as the "condition of being-affected-by-the-past" using the terms traditionality, traditions, and tradition. Tradition as *traditionality* signifies the general structure of historical experience as a tension between the "efficacy of the past we undergo and the reception of the past we bring about," which lies at the heart of human experience marked by historicity.[9] Drawing on Hans-Georg Gadamer, Ricoeur explains that we find ourselves already situated within a horizon of view, already subject to the history of the effects of a tradition, of which we must become conscious. Engaging the horizon of the traditioned text from our present horizon may lead to a fusion of horizons, which includes testing our prejudgments, respecting the "otherness" of the text, and potentially receiving the heritage by refiguring it. Ricoeur summarizes: "effective-history, we might say, is what takes place without us. The fusion of horizons is

---

[7] Paul Ricoeur, *The Conflict of Interpretations: Essays in Hermeneutics*, edited by Don Ihde (Evanston: Northwestern University Press, 1974), 27, italic added.
[8] Ricoeur, *Conflict of Interpretations*, 27.
[9] Ricoeur, *Time and Narrative*, vol. 3, 220. For the full discussion, in which Ricoeur explicitly builds on Gadamer's historically effected consciousness, temporal distance, and fusion of horizons, see 207–21.

what we attempt to bring about."¹⁰ Hence, traditionality means both the "givenness" of our already being shaped by the effects of tradition and our choice to consciously engage, examine, and refigure its meaning in the present. Traditionality consists of an interplay between sedimentation and innovation. While born of a tradition's contents and paradigms (sedimentation), new works, meanings, and understandings emerge as the horizon of text and reader fuse (innovation). Innovation is also shaped by a horizon of future expectations, which may open up forgotten possibilities or unrealized potentialities.¹¹

The notion of *traditions* refers to the content of traditions plural. The plural flags the fact that neither tradition nor its texts are ever monolithic in the meanings communicated and that understandings are transmitted along the chains of interpretation and reinterpretation. Again, we are both heirs and innovators.¹²

The third aspect, *tradition*, also underscores the already situated nature of interpretation, this time in relation to the constructs of meaning and truth that we receive from the past. Here Ricoeur affirms Gadamer's rehabilitation of prejudice (or preunderstanding), authority, and tradition, observing that tradition-shaped preunderstanding makes understanding possible, for tradition preserves the possibility of our hearing voices of the past.¹³

Tradition Is a Verb!

The complexity of this description of tradition itself is already of help in conceptualizing Anabaptism as a tradition. One emphasis emerging across Ricoeur's three-part definition is the sense that tradition is verb—an ongoing action, a process. Here I make three observations to clarify the significance of this definition for theorizing Anabaptist tradition.

First, tradition is a verb—tradition*ing*—in the sense of being as much "operation" as deposit or heritage. Long chains of interpreters shape how we are affected by a tradition as well as

---

¹⁰Ricoeur, *Time and Narrative*, vol. 3, 221.
¹¹Ricoeur, *Time and Narrative*, vol. 3, 227; see also vol. 1, 68–70.
¹²Ricoeur, *Time and Narrative*, vol. 3, 221.
¹³Ibid., 222–23.

our conscious engagement with it. Anabaptism's "restitutionist" impulse has often ignored or at best short-circuited this reality, leapfrogging from the current context (whenever "current" is) to the sixteenth century and then (perhaps) to the first century. Tradition*ing* occurs across all of those gaps, and it occurs as part of the larger Christian tradition. Articulation of Anabaptist tradition is intelligible only when located in the larger context of Christian heritage and traditioning, historically and in the present. It is as a particular construal of Christian faith that Anabaptism first emerges and continues.

Second, tradition as a verb—tradition*ing*—is pluriform. Chain*s* (plural) of interpreter*s* (plural) historically and in the present, with various construals of meaning asserted, constitute a tradition. While Ricoeur insists that this is a given for any historical tradition, we find ourselves wrestling with it as a perceived challenge to the recognizable identity of Anabaptism. Here again reference to the larger Christian tradition is important: Anabaptism is itself a demonstration of the pluriform nature of Christianity, which, while sustaining multiple construals of meaning across varied streams internal to the tradition, has also retained a recognizable identity across time. Christianity is an identifiable historical tradition, albeit with significant internal diversity and arguments about the parameters. Anabaptism, as a tradition within this tradition, both has its own internal pluriformity and is itself one of the varied streams constituting the multiplicity of the larger diverse Christian tradition. We cannot lose sight of this "middle" position as we puzzle out questions of Anabaptist identity.

Third, tradition as a verb highlights the fact of human historicity—the situatedness of our experience—but as a point of potential opening rather than closure. This will become clearer in the discussion of distanciation that follows, but our locatedness—consciousness of the horizon of understanding from which we engage a tradition and its texts—is what makes possible a "refiguring" of tradition. Just as sedimentation reflects past contexts, innovation is (perhaps counterintuitively) born precisely of our locatedness. Tradition lives only as it is refigured and reembodied in the present: the fusion of horizons generating a "happening" of tradition can occur only via the open, intentional engagement of a situated interpreter. Tradition does not "live" in disembodied form.

Interpretation

"Every tradition lives by the grace of *interpretation*, and it is at this price that it continues, that is, remains living."[14] What does Ricoeur mean by *interpretation*, and to what extent is it a helpful model for thinking about Anabaptist tradition and engagement with it? At its simplest, for Ricoeur, in interpretation the reader moves from an initial understanding of a text through critical investigation, which produces understanding at a new level. What makes this possible is, perhaps surprisingly, the distance between the reader and the text itself; that gap makes space for a new understanding of the text and of the reader. I will next briefly explore Ricoeur's idea of distance as productive of meaning and then his understanding-explanation interpretive process. In each of those sections I also sketch some implications of this for treating Anabaptist tradition as a "text" more broadly construed.

Productive Distance

Textual interpretation provides the paradigm for human encounter with historical traditions for Ricoeur because communication in and through distance is characteristic of human historicity. This "distanciation" results in the text achieving semantic autonomy by which distance from the original author, context, and audience makes possible a new event of meaning in the interpreter's encounter with the text. The text's semantic autonomy is expansive; it expands readers to a potentially universal audience, expands the reference of the text to the world it projects, and expands the interpretive act to explication of "the type of being-in-the-world unfolded in front of the text" by the reader. This distance also allows for a critical examination of the interpreter's assumptions and the text's structure, content, and production.[15]

The "appropriation" or "refiguration" culminating the interpretive act thus forms the counterpart of semantic autonomy; we "make our own" the meaning of texts that lie at a distance from

---

[14]Ricoeur, *The Conflict of Interpretations*, 27, italic added.
[15]Ricoeur, "The Hermeneutical Function of Distanciation," in *Hermeneutics*, 131–44.

us in terms of original author, context, and audience (e.g., biblical texts). The previous discussion of traditionality clarifies that this "fusion" of the horizons of interpreter and text is possible for the historically conscious interpreter who recognizes the "givenness" of our already being shaped by the effects of tradition and who chooses to critically engage and refigure its meaning in the present. Thus, a kind of "participatory belonging" stands in tension with distanciation. The reader is both connected to and removed from the tradition they encounter in interpreting the text (for engagement with texts *is* an encounter with tradition for Ricoeur). Ricoeur describes reading as "the 'remedy' by which the meaning of the text is 'rescued' from the estrangement of distanciation and put in a new proximity."[16] The language of proximity is important. Distanciation makes possible new meaning but only if the text is interpreted; language has a reference only when used. The reader in a sense completes the meaning of the text by re-actualizing it as discourse referring to a world. This is "the grace of interpretation" by which tradition "remains living" for Ricoeur. The interpretive act culminates in an "appropriation" or "refiguration" that is a "happening" of tradition generating something new.[17]

Engagement with texts *is* an encounter with tradition for Ricoeur. But what happens if a tradition itself as a whole, such as Anabaptism, is construed as a "text"? What gains in theorizing tradition are made, and what limitations of this broadened hermeneutical present themselves?

The idea of productive distance in tension with a kind of "participatory belonging" reflects well the tradition*ing* process described in Ricoeur's threefold notion of tradition, including the ideas of sedimentation and innovation. The semantic autonomy born of distanciation provides a way of making sense of the potentially universal range of addressees a pan-denominational Anabaptism reflects—and of their appropriation as an embodied refiguring of the tradition. Limits, or at least questions, also arise: Does the sedimentation-innovation pairing functionally privilege

---

[16]Paul Ricoeur, *Interpretation Theory: Discourse and the Surplus of Meaning* (Fort Worth: Texas Christian University, 1976), 43. For one of many discussions on the dialectical relationship of participatory belonging and alienating distanciation, see Ricoeur, *Hermeneutics*, 53–62.
[17]Ricoeur, *Hermeneutics*, 177–78, 185.

traditioned understandings such that semantic autonomy is curtailed? Put another way, how fully can one speak of the semantic autonomy of the "text" of Anabaptist tradition as a whole when some measure of biblical and theological normativity is assumed as a Christian tradition? Ricoeur's interpretation theory includes critical examination of text and self-critical examination of interpreter, which, the next section will show, engage these issues at least in part from a different angle.

Understanding and Explanation

Interpretation consists of the movement from understanding to explanation and then from explanation to understanding at a new level. In this progression, Ricoeur's theory of the text grounds a dialectical (versus oppositional) relationship between understanding and explanation.[18]

From Understanding to Explanation

Initial *understanding* takes the form of "a naïve grasping of the meaning of the text as a whole."[19] But as a structured work of discourse, interpretation of the written text requires the reader to move from this initial "guess" to examine the features of organization, style, genre, and composition. This "detour" into *explanation* of the structural, organizational, and stylistic characteristics of the text informs construal of the work as a whole and judgments regarding the relation of the parts to the whole. The plurivocity of texts and perspectival location of interpreters results in multiple possible constructions regarding the import and configuration of parts and whole.[20] However, Ricoeur clarifies, "If it is true that there is always more than one way of construing a text, it is not true that all interpretations are equal. The text

---

[18]Ricoeur critiques Wilhelm Dilthey's opposition between explanation as the sphere of the natural sciences (the region of objects) and understanding as the sphere of the mind (the region of psychological individualities). See *Hermeneutics*, 150.
[19]Ricoeur, *Interpretation Theory*, 74.
[20]Ricoeur, *Hermeneutics*, 136–38, 211–15.

presents a limited field of possible constructions."[21] As a result, explanation functions as a process of validation following the logic of probability. A process of argumentation governs competing and conflicting interpretations, which must demonstrate the degree of their probability and adequacy as construals of the whole text in light of its structures. Ricoeur views this as an ongoing process of confrontation, arbitration, and even seeking agreement, though the latter may well remain beyond reach.[22]

It is worth noting, by way of illustration, that the reality of the interpretation of specific biblical and historical texts among Anabaptist communities reflects this movement from understanding to explanation—reflects Ricoeur's depiction of multiple, competing interpretations—though this history is sometimes told in a more monolithic fashion. In biblical hermeneutics one can point to diverse interpretations of biblical texts at any point past or present, changes in the understanding of biblical texts over time within a given community, differences in construals of the normativity of the biblical texts themselves and also of the authority claimed by any interpretation of them. Yet in a tradition that has long held communal consensus as a governing process and goal, such differences prove difficult to embrace. Divergent interpretation has been viewed more as a problem to be solved than a conversation to be had—a conversation, Ricoeur insists, made both possible and necessary by the nature of the biblical texts as polyvalent, historical texts with human interpreters situated in ever-changing contexts.

The reality of such a plurality of interpretations regarding the historical texts and beginnings of Anabaptism is also evident. Even at the height of its influence, Bender's "Anabaptist Vision" was not the only view twentieth-century Anabaptists held of their sixteenth-century origins. The embrace of polygenesis historiography affirmed a plurality of movements and beliefs at the birth of Anabaptism and has generated multiple interpretations and definitions of the tradition since. Here Ricoeur's model places multiple, competing interpretations in an intelligible framework, construing such conflict as a normal part of the process of interpretation and allowing for

---

[21]Ricoeur, *Interpretation Theory*, 79.
[22]Ibid.

movement toward (though not necessarily guaranteeing arrival at) agreement through argumentation.

What is gained by applying these interpretive insights to theorizing the "text" of Anabaptist tradition as a whole? The implications are significant: recognition of the perspectival and historically relative nature of theology expects multiple theological construals and their argumentation. Ricoeur's hermeneutical model offers a clearer and more comprehensive account of competing interpretations and their argument and arbitration as expected aspects of the ongoing, negotiated identity internal to a historical tradition. This plural, fluid, ongoing interpretation of the "text" of tradition constitutes its identity. The resulting multiple interpretations are "happenings" of tradition, born of the confrontation of the interpreter's world and the world disclosed by the "text" of tradition. This refiguration extends the tradition in dialogue with what has gone before but also as an event productive of new meaning—a "fusion of horizons." An altered topography results; what was there before remains but is added to in ways that may change how one makes sense of what was already there.

In the present context, a model in which plurality constitutes rather than threatens the identity of the tradition frees Anabaptist thinkers for the task of constructing understandings of the tradition and arguing their relative adequacy. Indeed, the questions of normativity and authority form part of the construal of tradition and judgments regarding the import and relation of parts and whole.

For example, Mennonite theologians describing Anabaptist tradition as a way of life entailing a radical ethic argue for this characterization on different grounds. J. Denny Weaver asserts this theological tradition must be "directed, guided, regulated, and limited by the assumption that the story of Jesus shapes all of reality," including "God's act in Christ to establish an alternative community as the beginning of the kingdom of God on earth, and the rejection of violence as the basis of the social relationships of that kingdom outpost in our real history."[23] For Weaver, then,

---

[23] J. Denny Weaver, "Mennonite Theological Self-Understanding: A Response to A. James Reimer," in *Mennonite Identity: Historical and Contemporary Understandings*, edited by Calvin Wall Redekop (Lanham, MD: Institute for Anabaptist and Mennonite Studies, 1988), 58.

lived expressions of Anabaptism from the sixteenth century to the present function authoritatively for the tradition and the explication of its theology to the extent that they reflect these three regulative principles—Jesus as norm, peace (including nonviolent love), community as alternative society—which are ultimately grounded in the normative biblical Jesus narrative.[24] In contrast, for Duane Friesen, the truth and authority of any narrative (biblical, historical, or otherwise) rests on whether it can empower us to make sense of our existence (its reasonableness) and whether it can empower us to live creatively and appropriately in the present world (its fruitfulness).[25] He employs criteria of adequacy, interpretive power, coherence, and practical implications to adjudicate the truth and authority of biblical and other narratives.[26] Friesen's debt to Gordon Kaufman is apparent; Kaufman rejects any presumed authority and insists that one assesses a historical tradition on its ability to orient life toward "humanization" (loving relationships fostering communities of reconciliation, justice and peace—a pragmatic criterion) in the current context in light of current historical, social, cultural, and scientific knowledge (a criterion of coherence).[27]

These variations reflect real differences in "ordering" the parts and their importance in the construal of the whole, demonstrating that divergent judgments, including those relating to normativity, need not mean divergent traditions. Ricoeur's construct offers a clearer and more comprehensive account of competing interpretations and their argument and arbitration as expected aspects of the ongoing, negotiated identity internal to a tradition.

---

[24]J. Denny Weaver, "Mennonites: Theology, Peace, and Identity," *Conrad Grebel Review* 6 (Spring 1988): 143; J. Denny Weaver, "Reading Sixteenth-Century Anabaptism Theologically: Implications for Modern Mennonites as a Peace Church," *Conrad Grebel Review* 16 (Winter 1998): 41.
[25]Duane K. Friesen, "A Critical Analysis of Narrative Ethics," in *The Church as Theological Community: Essays in Honor of David Schroeder*, edited by Harry Huebner (Winnipeg: Canadian Mennonite Bible College Publications, 1990), 235.
[26]Duane K. Friesen, *Artists, Citizens, Philosophers: Seeking the Peace of the City; An Anabaptist Theology of Culture* (Scottdale, PA: Herald, 2000), 272–73.
[27]Gordon D. Kaufman, "Doing Theology from a Liberal Point of View," in *Doing Theology in Today's World: Essays in Honor of Kenneth S. Kantzer*, edited by John D. Woodbridge and Thomas Edward McComisky (Grand Rapids: Zondervan, 1991), 398–99; Gordon D. Kaufman, *An Essay on Theological Method*, 3rd ed. (Atlanta: Scholars Press, 1995), 87.

Yet here a significant limitation of the hermeneutical model also presents itself. If the movement from understanding to explanation requires investigating the structure of a text as a means of validating and arguing for one's construal of the whole, what structures the "text" of a tradition as a whole? Written texts—biblical, historical, literary—all achieve closure and fixation in a way that a living tradition more broadly does not. To which "structural features" might one appeal in demonstrating the relative adequacy of one's construal of the theological tradition as a whole? Anabaptism's location as a tradition within a tradition perhaps helps some here. A hermeneutical model construes the emergence of sixteenth-century Anabaptism as a "happening" within the larger Christian tradition; sixteenth-century Anabaptism makes an argument for particular texts, understandings, and practices as determinative of Christian identity. Contemporary Anabaptist theologizing benefits from methodological consciousness of being a tradition within a tradition; it helps avoid a kind of insular self-referentialism and lands us squarely in the shared conversations and problems relating to norms, authority, privileging of sacred texts, sociology of knowledge, and the like that are part of doing Christian theology in our historically conscious, postmodern setting. I will return to this question of identity in light of the lack of closure achieved by a living tradition in the discussion of narrative identity.

From Explanation to Understanding at a New Level

The second movement of the interpretative process, from *explanation* to *understanding* at a new level, culminates in appropriation. For Ricoeur, textual interpretation requires moving from structural explanation to re-actualize the text as discourse referring to a world. A world unfolds in front of the text in the movement from explanation to understanding. But because self-understanding is mediated through interpretation of the "signs" of cultural works for Ricoeur, the interpreter's self-understanding also unfolds in front of the text. Ricoeur rejects the autonomous, self-positing ego. Receiving the disclosure of the text requires dispossession of the ego—a genuine openness to receiving an expanded self-understanding from the disclosure of the text. This dispossession of the ego includes the deconstruction of the illusions of the interpreting subject—a self-critical hermeneutic attending to elements of power, interest, and ideology shaping the interpreter's location and interpretation. Only in this way can self-understanding in front of the text be formed by the world of the text instead of deformed by the false-consciousness and unexamined prejudices of the interpreter. Ricoeur's debt to Jürgen Habermas is clear here: a hermeneutics of suspicion joins a hermeneutics of retrieval as central to his understanding-explanation dialectic.[28]

The practice of a self-critical, paired hermeneutics of suspicion and retrieval in the interpretation of Anabaptism's traditioned texts—biblical, historical, theological—is evident in the work of scholars wrestling with the role privilege, power, domination, and ideology play in textual interpretation, past and present. Yet the paired hermeneutics of retrieval and suspicion—the critique of illusions and ideology operational in and through the tradition—must be directed toward the "text" of tradition as a whole as well. For all traditions are ambiguous—marked, as David Tracy observes, by great good and frightening evil, by beauty and cruelty, by reason and error, by mutuality and domination, by belonging and interruption and otherness. There are no innocent traditions.[29] The dialectic of understanding and explanation helps conceptualize, in a historically conscious way, the plurality and recognizable identity of tradition. The movement from understanding to explanation helped account for the plurality of Anabaptist tradition both past and present; the movement from explanation to understanding addresses the ambiguity of this tradition and its texts, interpretations, and interpreters. Such ambiguity requires a hermeneutics of retrieval and of suspicion both. Deconstruction of the illusions and ideology operational in and through the tradition is part of the "price" by which tradition continues.

Growing scholarship over the past several decades calls attention to the ambiguous, mixed history of the Anabaptist tradition

---

[28]Ricoeur, *Hermeneutics*, 143, 186–87. This pairing and the understanding-explanation dialectic as a whole reflect Ricoeur's attempt to mediate the seemingly conflicting hermeneutical projects of Gadamer and Habermas; see Ricoeur, *Hermeneutics*, 63–100.
[29]David Tracy, *Plurality and Ambiguity: Hermeneutics, Religion, Hope* (San Francisco: HarperCollins, 1989), 66–81.

(including its biblical texts) regarding matters of gender, race, ethnicity, sexual orientation, class, power, and domination.[30] This work presents a challenge for a theological tradition that has often cast itself as a "contrasting alternative" to a Christendom marked by domination, violence, and oppression. While Anabaptist persecution and marginalization at the hands of religious authorities with greater power are undeniable historical realities, majority culture identity and accompanying elements of race and class privilege, for example, are equally an undeniable part of the experience of many Anabaptist-Mennonites of Western European descent in Canada and the United States, past and present. Even where some Anabaptists wish to draw sharp contrasts, Anabaptism shares in the mixed nature of the broader Christian tradition.

The self-understanding as "contrasting alternative" has also kept most discussions of power focused outside of the Anabaptist community, centered instead on a principled rejection of power as construed and wielded by the secular state and the call for a radical reconceptualization of power in light of Jesus's nonviolent way. While this theology and witness are terribly important, the need for critique and dismantling of ideologies of domination and abuse of power within the tradition remains great—in communities and congregations and institutions, in relationships between persons, and in systemic, institutional forms.[31] Deconstruction of the illusions and ideology operational in and through the tradition is part of the price by which tradition continues. Given the reality of power and ambiguity within Anabaptism, a hermeneutics of suspicion

---

[30]To name but a few: Gayle Gerber Koontz and Willard Swartley, eds., *Perspectives on Feminist Hermeneutics* (Elkhart, IN: Institute of Mennonite Studies, 1987); Lydia Neufeld Harder, *Obedience, Suspicion and the Gospel of Mark: A Mennonite-Feminist Exploration of Biblical Authority* (Waterloo: Wilfred Laurier University Press for the Canadian Corporation for the Studies in Religion, 1998); Steve Heinrichs, ed., *Buffalo Shout, Salmon Cry: Conversations on Creation, Land Justice, and Life Together* (Scottdale, PA: Herald, 2013); Drew Hart, *Trouble I've Seen: Changing the Way the Church Views Racism* (Scottdale, PA: Herald, 2016).

[31]Public disclosure of John Howard Yoder's sexual abuse, its theological underpinnings, and institutional failure to address it make this painfully evident (see *Mennonite Quarterly Review* 89 [July 2015]), though the call for Mennonite peace theology to explicitly address violence against women is decades old—for example, Elizabeth Yoder, ed. *Peace Theology and Violence Against Women* (Elkhart, IN: Institute of Mennonite Studies, 1992).

must inform the retrieval and reinterpretation of the tradition as well as the process of argumentation among the resultant multiple, competing construals. With a pairing of retrieval and suspicion, there is room both to affirm the truth about God, humanity, and the world disclosed through Anabaptism and to critique the ways the tradition has obscured such truth through the machinations of power, coercion, domination, and ideology, both conscious and unconscious.

To summarize, the concept of multiple interpretations and their argumentation resonates with contemporary attempts to make theological sense of the plurality within Anabaptism while also accounting for its recognizable identity across time. Ricoeur's hermeneutical model provides a construct for doing so, moving beyond a recognition of plurality to view such multiplicity as constitutive of the identity of a tradition, which emerges from the ongoing interpretation of its polyvalent but limited text in the present. Ricoeur's insistence on a paired hermeneutics of retrieval and suspicion supports efforts among some in Anabaptist circles to call attention to and address the ambiguity of the history of the tradition and its continued development. Yet Ricoeur's approach requires that such efforts constitute a part of all interpretive construals of the tradition and their argumentation. The critical moment must inform the dialectic of the efficacy of the past we undergo and the reception of the past we bring about; it must inform the way we are both heirs and innovators of tradition. The hermeneutical model situates construals of Anabaptism *as construals* of a tradition within a tradition; we share in the broader resources and the overwhelming ambiguity and fluidity of Christian tradition. Finally, the refiguration of tradition occurs at the intersection of the world of the text and the world of the reader, where interpretation becomes an event productive of new meaning. It is a "happening of tradition," an event that grows the tradition, creating a new horizon. Such a happening of tradition refigures both the interpreters' self-understanding and the tradition itself.

However, clear limitations also emerge in using Ricoeur's hermeneutical model to theorize a tradition as a whole. Traditioned understandings at least functionally seem privileged, even with a robust hermeneutic of suspicion. Which is to say the semantic autonomy—in the fullest sense—of traditioned texts and the "text" of tradition as a whole seems questionable. The approach also privileges written texts even though engagement with and the identity of a tradition cannot be limited to these; other disciplines are needed—cultural anthropology, theological aesthetics, and the like—for full-orbed description of and reflection on tradition. (Ricoeur would agree: The call for multiple approaches to anything characterizes his work.) And since a living tradition does not achieve closure or fixation in the way a written text does, the challenge of to which "structural features" one might appeal in demonstrating the relative adequacy of a construal of the theological tradition as a whole also remains. In the final section, I explore Ricoeur's concept of narrative identity as a helpful compliment for addressing change and permanence in a tradition's identity across time.

Narrative Identity

"Narrative identity is the poetic resolution of the hermeneutical circle."[32] Just as a living tradition never gains closure and fixation in the sense a written text does, personal identity reflects a parallel lack of closure. We answer the question, "Who am I?" by telling a story of our life. But we never do this from the final end point, death. Rather, at a given point in our lives we tell a story that answers the question, "Who am I?" from that point both backward and forward. The story we tell is selective. It makes connections between disparate events after the fact. We work to make some sense of the discontinuities, changes, differences; we work to narrate a whole. Doing this requires multiple versions of the story: When I answer the question, "Who am I?" for my daughters' water polo team and coaches, the story I tell is not the story of a professor but of a mother. And the stories we tell change over time; sometimes we even say things like, "I'm not the person I used to be." Articulating the nature of the continuous recognizable identity of a person across the span of their life presents a real challenge. We are a continuous self, but we aren't identifiable as such only on the basis of sameness.

---

[32]Ricoeur, *Time and Narrative*, vol. 3, 248.

For Ricoeur this is also true of communal identity, and the challenge is best addressed by the dialetic of narrative identity—a dialectic of identity as *sameness* and identity as (reflective) *selfhood*.[33] Sameness-only identity is inadequate to the varied stories we tell of our lives. It is reductionistic—as if the fullness of who we are or who our community is could be boiled down to a list of traits or distilled into a singular essence. I offer three brief observations demonstrating how narrative identity compliments Ricoeur's hermeneutical model in the task of theorizing tradition.

The "Self" of Selfhood

In the narrative identity dialectic, the "self" of selfhood is not the self-positing ego but rather "the fruit of an examined life." As stated earlier, self-knowledge is only possible indirectly for Ricoeur, as a self-reflective act mediated through the interpretation of the "signs" of cultural works. When I was talking about the movement from explanation to understanding, I noted that both the world of the text and the self-understanding of the interpreter unfold in front of the text. Receiving the disclosure of the text requires the dispossession of the ego (a hermeneutics of suspicion). And it requires a genuine openness to risk expanded self-understanding in the encounter with the world and way-of-being-in-the-world disclosed by the text. So, too, the dispossessed ego proves central to selfhood in the narrative identity dialectic. Indeed, Ricoeur asserts narrative identity as the "poetic resolution" of the hermeneutical circle.[34]

Identity as Sameness or Selfhood?

Ricoeur contrasts identity as sameness with identity as (reflective) selfhood. Identity as sameness accounts for similitude—numerical identity, interchangeability (this dress is the same as that dress)—but also for a stability across time born of acquired habits and dispositions. Ricoeur uses character "traits" or "distinctives" as a prime example of this type of recognizability. But this kind of permanence by

---

[33]Ibid., 245–49.
[34]Ibid., 247–48.

which a person is reidentified as the same via a set of "distinctives" provides an example of "sedimentation" for Ricoeur. In habits or distinctive traits, sedimentation has overcome the innovation that marks the dynamic, living identity of a person or a community. A list of traits or distinctives is not a self; it answers "what" but not "who," and the question of identity is not only a question of "what." Narrative identity requires sameness and selfhood both, for it is the self-reflective self that sets about answering the question "who" via emplotment and interpretive narration.[35] When we tell and retell the story of our lives, the significance of various events, ideas, and persons and the relationship between them is what we are drawing together. Ricoeur argues that this "interconnection of events constituted by emplotment" makes it possible to integrate sameness-identity (the list of "distinctives") with what seems to be its contrary: "diversity, variability, discontinuity, instability." The "what" of our lives becomes "transfigured" by the "meaning effect" born of the "configuring" narration. So, he concludes that the "narrative operation" develops "an entirely original concept of dynamic identity which reconciles . . . identity and diversity."[36]

Configuration

The process by which we configure a narrative whole that reconciles our own identity and diversity is ongoing. We tell and retell the story (stories, really) of our lives, configuring and reconfiguring the answer to the "Who am I?" question differently. It is not seamless, and it is never fully stable. The significance of events changes as we stand at different points and look backward and forward and engage in emplotment. (You don't know until well after the fact that you've fired the shot heard round the world.) Ricoeur employs a weaving image to describe the ongoing interpretive and dynamic nature of narrative identity, the dialectic of sameness and difference, of sedimentation and innovation, of permanence and change. New threads get added to the loom that change the pattern, including changing how we see the pattern that was previously visible. The dialectic of narrative identity produces imaginative variations on

---

[35]Ricoeur, *Oneself*, 115–25.
[36]Ibid., 140–43.

identity, not unlike imaginative variations on the world of text and on the self-understanding of the interpreter. Ricoeur summarizes the narrative identity of individual or community as "stemming from the endless rectification of a previous narrative by a subsequent one, and from the chain of refigurations that results from this."[37] Highly hermeneutical language, this is. It would seem what we are doing in historically conscious encounter with tradition and its texts is configuring and refiguring narrative identity, for ourselves as individuals and for our community, our tradition.

Conclusion

The discussion of narrative identity here underscores the methodological need for non-essentialist, non-reductionist conceptualization of Anabaptist tradition. A list of "distinctives" is inadequate to describe a living tradition whose story continues to unfold and be reconfigured in the present. One great strength of the hermeneutical model is this insistence that a tradition remains living only through its ongoing interpretation—through intentional engagement with it. At its best this means room for something new, born of dispossession of the ego and critique of ideology, born of historical consciousness and self-conscious argumentation, born of plurality and ambiguity and imagination.

---

[37]Ricoeur, *Time and Narrative*, vol. 3, 248.

4

Mennonite Women Doing Theology

A Methodological Reflection on Twenty-Five Years of Conferences

Carol Penner

Introduction

In 1991, I helped plan a Mennonite conference about feminist theology called Women Doing Theology (WDT), which turned out to be the first of an ongoing series of theology conferences. In this chapter, I explore the feminist and Anabaptist methodology of these conferences, focusing on the first eight, held between 1992 and 2016.[1] In the first section I outline the conferences, as detailed

---

[1] A ninth, "Talkin' Bout a Revolution: Dialogue, Practice and the Work of Liberation," was held November 8–10, 2018, at Anabaptist Mennonite Biblical Seminary, Elkhart, Indiana, sponsored by Women in Leadership Project of Mennonite Church USA, Mennonite Central Committee, Everence, and Mennonite Women USA. There

in Table 4.1. In the second section, I then outline commonalities the conferences shared. In the third section, I discuss how the theological methodology of the conferences was both feminist and Anabaptist. Finally, I conclude by offering suggestions for future research.

The Conferences

For ease of comparison, the basic details of the WDT conferences are outlined in Table 4.1.

The initiative for the first WDT conference came from the Mennonite Central Committee Women's Concerns staff person, Kathy Shantz. As Esther Epp-Tiessen recounts, "One of her dreams was to organize a conference which gave expression to women's perspectives on the Bible, the church, and Christian faith."[2] The planning committee created a purpose statement for the conference brochure: "This conference has been organized to provide a forum for Mennonite women to work on theological issues and to provide a meeting place for women and men who are interested in exploring the emerging theological voices of women." The goal was a binational gathering, and this first conference was a stand-alone event. We issued an invitation to attendees, hoping that women from another geographical area would plan a similar conference at a future date. Each of the subsequent five conferences emerged from a similar challenge.

The first six WDT conferences were held in Mennonite academic venues around Canada and the United States. The original purpose statement was used for the first six conferences, with a statement about diversity and racism added in 2003.[3] These six conferences

---

were over 200 participants at this event, including a small number of invited male participants.
[2] Esther Epp-Tiessen, *Mennonite Central Committee in Canada: A History* (Winnipeg: CMU Press, 2013), 183.
[3] "It is to be a place where all different women can come together to talk and learn with each other. The desire to be anti-racist came from the desire of the planning committee to have a conference where truly all women are welcome, and encouraged to use their voices." Pauline D. Aguilar and Sharon K. Williams, "Anti-Racism Audit Report, 'Gifts of the Red Tent: Women Creating, Women Doing Theology Conference,'" May 16–18, 2003, 2, web.archive.org/web/20060321034553/http:/www.mcc.org/womendoingtheology/audit/Audit_Report.pdf.

Table 4.1 Women Doing Theology Conferences

Date	Institution/Location	Attendees	Sponsors	Theme	Papers Published
April 30–May 2, 1992	Conrad Grebel College (CGC), Waterloo, Ontario	160 (including 9 men) (25% US)[a]	Mennonite Central Committee (MCC) Women's Concerns, CGC	In a Mennonite Voice: Women Doing Theology	*Conrad Grebel Review* 10, no. 1 (Winter 1992)
June 23–25, 1994	Bluffton College, Bluffton, Ohio	180[b]	MCC Women's Concerns, Bluffton College	Mennonite Voices in Dialogue	*Mennonite Quarterly Review* 68, no. 2 (April 1994)
May 9–11, 1996	Canadian Mennonite Bible College (CMBC), Winnipeg, Manitoba	215 (including 10 men)[c]	MCC Women's Concerns, Concord College, CMBC	Wind and Fire: Moving the Life among Us	*Conrad Grebel Review* 14, no. 2 (Spring 1996)
June 25–27, 1998	Bethel College, North Newton, Kansas	84[d]	MCC Women's Concerns, Kansas Mennonite Women in Ministry, Bethel College	Journey toward Healing: Women Doing Theology	papers not published as a unit
May 4–5, 2001	Conrad Grebel College, Waterloo, Ontario	160[e]	MCC Women's Concerns, CGC	Embracing Hope: Envisioning an Inclusive Theology of Service	*Conrad Grebel Review* 19, no. 3 (Fall 2001)

(Continued)

Table 4.1 (Continued)

Date	Institution/Location	Attendees	Sponsors	Theme	Papers Published
May 16–18, 2003	Eastern Mennonite University (EMU), Harrisonburg, Virginia	200[f]	MCC Women's Concerns, EMU	Gifts of the Red Tent: Women Creating	*Conrad Grebel Review* 23, no. 1 (Winter 2005)
February 20–22, 2014	Women in Leadership Project of Mennonite Church USA (WLP), Leesburg, Virginia	203 (3 men)[g]	WLP, MCC, Mennonite Mission Network, Eastern Mennonite Seminary, Mennonite Women USA	All You Need Is Love: Honoring the Diversity of Women's Voices in Theology	Jennifer Castro, ed. *All You Need Is Love: Honoring the Diversity of Women's Voices in Theology*. Elkhart, IN: Women in Leadership Project, Mennonite Church USA, 2016
November 14–16, 2016	WLP, Leesburg, Virginia	150 (no men)[h]	WLP, Everence, EMU, eight smaller organizations and individuals	I've Got the Power: Naming and Reclaiming Power as a Force for Good	Jennifer Castro, ed. *I've Got the Power! Naming and Reclaiming Power as a Force for Good*. Elkhart, IN: Women in Leadership Project, Mennonite Church USA, 2017

Table 4.1 (Continued)

[a] Women Doing Theology 1992 conference planning committee minutes, https://uwaterloo.ca/mennonite-archives-ontario/mennonite-organizations-and-institutions/conrad-grebel-university-college/miscellaneous-events.
[b] Cathleen Hockman, "Women Do Theology without the Stereotypes," *Mennonite Weekly Review* 72, no. 27, July 7, 1994, 1.
[c] Kathleen Epp and Aiden Schlichting Enns, "Women's Theology Conference Provides 'Hospitable Space,'" *Mennonite Reporter* 26, no. 11, May 27, 1996, 1.
[d] Gordon Hauser, "The Dignity of Doing Theology," *The Mennonite* 1, no. 19, July 7, 1998, 7.
[e] Cathleen Hockman-Wert, "Women Envision Theology of Service," *Canadian Mennonite* 5, no. 11, June 4, 2001, 18.
[f] Kristine Sensenig, "Women Share Talents, Theological Insights under a 'Red Tent,'" *Mennonite Weekly Review* 81, no. 24, June 16, 2003, 3.
[g] Kelli Yoder, "Women's Conference Asks 'Is Love Enough?'" *Mennonite World Review* 92, no.5, March 3, 2014, http://www.mennoworld.org/archived/2014/3/3/love-enough/.
[h] Becca Kraybill, "Second Women Doing Theology Conference Focuses on Power," Daily News/Updates, *The Mennonite*, November 7, 2016, https://themennonite.org/daily-news/second-women-theology-conference-focuses-power/.

each had organizational similarities. Over the years there was an increased effort to include the arts and to increase racial diversity among presenters and participants. With changes in technology, 2003 saw the event being advertised on the internet for the first time.[4]

The first six conferences were held on a fairly regular basis; then there was a break where no WDT conferences happened.[5] After a decade, another group of women through the Women in Leadership Project of Mennonite Church USA[6] picked up the concept and the name but with a national US focus[7] and a new mission statement:

> Mennonite women and women interested in Anabaptism, come. Pastors, academics, activists, students and members of the church, come. Women interested in doing theology—reflecting on God in relation to our lives—come. Come to listen to the stories of your sisters from all across the country and come to share your own. Come to build relationships. Come to nurture your soul, challenge your mind and find rest for your body. We all play a part in our shared theology. We all have experience, wisdom and insight to offer.[8]

These latter conferences are larger, with more funding, which has enabled the collected papers to be published in dedicated volumes.

---

[4] Mennonite Central Committee, Gifts of the Red Tent, web.archive.org/web/20030313130735/http:/www.mcc.org/womendoingtheology

[5] Accounts of the 2003 event reported, "The next Women Doing Theology conference is scheduled to take place in Canada in two years." See Kristine Sensenig, "Women Gather to Share under 'Red Tent,'" *The Mennonite* 6, no. 12 (June 17, 2003): 21. This proposed conference never happened. In 2004 Mennonite Central Committee Canada stopped funding a Women's Concerns staff person; that office had funded and encouraged every WDT event that had happened in Canada. Perhaps without that minimal staff oversight, the event did not have the momentum it needed.

[6] The Women in Leadership Project (WLP) began in response to a church-wide audit of Mennonite Church USA, which found that the number of women in church leadership was declining. One of the mandates of the WLP was to "host Women Doing Theology conferences biennially, creating spaces to honor and celebrate the diverse perspectives women bring to theology as well as to challenge the traditional and oppressive forms theology has taken." Women in Leadership Project Brochure, www.mennoniteusa.org/wp-content/uploads/2015/11/MCUSA_WLP_Brochure_2015_final.pdf.

[7] None of the invited speakers were Canadian, and I found no evidence that it was advertised to Canadians.

[8] Women Doing Theology Conference advertisement, www.mennoniteusa.org/wp-content/uploads/2015/12/IGP-Flier.pdf.

They emphasize diversity, include speakers from the Global South,[9] and address the inclusion of LGBTQ people.[10]

Commonalities

The eight WDT conferences spanned a period of twenty-five years. Even though six of the eight conferences were planned without continual institutional or organizational ownership, there were four striking commonalities across all eight.

Reclaiming Worship as Part of the Theological Enterprise

Most academic conferences do not include worship as part of their agenda. Academic discussions are generally seen as being intellectually rigorous and necessarily set apart from ritual faith practices. In contrast, every one of the WDT conferences included worship as an essential part of the conference agenda. The 1992 and 1994 conferences had five slots for plenary worship, while the 1996 conference had six slots. The 1998 and 2003 events had three periods of worship, one for each day of the conference. The 2014 event had five and the 2016 event had four periods of worship. Lydia Harder, a planner of one of the conferences, observed that in doing theology "worship is central."[11]

Overall, the worship at the WDT conferences often included women sharing stories. The Scripture and preaching often used feminine images for God. Creative methods of worship such as drama, dance, and visual artwork were often used. A great deal of effort went into worship at all of the conferences because worship was seen not as separate from the task of doing theology but as an essential part of it.

---

[9]Kelli Yoder, "Is Love Enough?" *Mennonite World Review* 92, no. 5 (March 3, 2014): 1.
[10]Anna Groff, "Women Are To Be 'Apostles to the Apostles,'" *The Mennonite* 17, no. 4 (April 2014): 32–33.
[11]Lydia Harder, "Guest Editorial," *Conrad Grebel Review* 14, no. 2 (1996): vi.

Diversity of Participants and Presenters

The WDT conferences began because women's voices have been marginalized. At the time of the first WDT conference, there were no women teaching theology in Mennonite schools in Canada, and women were only beginning to move into ministry positions. The first conference took place because women were interested in hearing what *women* had to say about theology. But there was an awareness of the need to listen to marginalized voices more broadly. The WDT conference organizers wanted to include participants embodying economic and cultural and racial diversity from the beginning stages. For example, every WDT conference made travel allowances and scholarships available based on need. The 2016 conference reserved these scholarships for people of color.[12] The planners for the first WDT conference tried to include resource people from diverse denominational, geographical, and age perspectives—women from Mennonite and Brethren in Christ backgrounds, from different parts of Canada and the United States, and from different age groups. We wanted to be sure to include women of color, so we invited African American Old Testament scholar Wilma Bailey to be one of the plenary speakers.

Looking back at this first conference, we had a very limited view of inclusion. I am white, as was everyone else on the planning committee. White privilege and the centering of white voices were not things we fully understood. April Yamasaki, one of a group of four on a listening committee for the conference, observed, "Many also noted the conference's own limitations, since participants were predominantly North American, middle-class, white women."[13] Tragically, it took eight conferences over twenty-five years to see voices of women of color more equitably included and to achieve significant diversity among participants.[14]

---

[12] Mennonite Church USA Staff, "Daily News Posts," *The Mennonite*, August 23, 2016, www.themennonite.org/daily-news/women-theology-conference-speakers-announced

[13] April Yamasaki, "In Search of Wholeness," *MCC Women's Concerns Report* 105 (November–December 1992): 4.

[14] For example, by the 2003 event, "About 20 percent of the participants, planners and leaders were women of color, and a variety of ages were represented." Groff, "Women Are To Be 'Apostles to the Apostles,'" 32–33.

The planners of the 2003 event tried to move away from the tokenism of a largely white group of resource people with a few women of color sprinkled in. Instead, they decided that each presentation would be discussed by two women of color and two white women.[15] The planners of this conference also requested that MCC do an anti-racism audit of the event to determine how well it was able to be an inclusive, anti-racist gathering.[16] These changes show a commitment to hearing the voices of all women; subsequent conferences maintained this commitment.

The Expansion of Theology beyond Academia

From the first WDT conference in 1992, the hope was to extend the circle of theological conversation outside the academy. People without academic degrees were invited to speak alongside those with academic degrees.[17] At WDT conferences no honorifics such as Prof. or Dr. were used to distinguish people. While people with academic degrees often presented at plenary sessions, in lists of resource people, the plenary presenters were not put at the forefront but were included with all of the people who responded and did workshops.

Everything did not always go smoothly. The language that academics are accustomed to use in theological discussions was not always accessible to the average person. Katie Funk Wiebe reflected on this after the first conference:

> What public language do we use as women theologians? Language has the power both to bind and to loose. At this conference it did both, bringing together but also separating. Theological jargon separated the academicians from the lay women at times. I asked myself, are women any better than the male theologians if by our

---

[15]Aguilar and Williams, "Anti-Racism Audit Report," 4.
[16]Women Doing Theology: Gifts of the Red Tent, web.archive.org/web/20061120190844/www.mcc.org/womendoingtheology.
[17]For example, "Pastors and professors were joined by graduate students, artists, missionaries, and social workers to talk together, worship, attend workshops, and listen to paper presentations punctuated by a baby's occasional hiccup." Cathleen Hockman, *Gospel Herald* 87, no. 28 (July 12, 1994): 9.

use of academese we exclude those who are not scholars to the same degree?[18]

While there was sometimes tension, reserving theological events for academics only was always rejected because the conferences were committed to hearing marginalized voices.

An Emphasis on Creative Dialogue

Mennonite academic conferences often follow a common academic format: a keynote address by someone literally reading an academic paper, with two or three scholars giving a response. The WDT conferences mostly rejected this model, opting instead for one that allows for more in-depth interactions for each participant.

At the 1992 conference, the plenary session was called a roundtable: the person presenting the paper was to be in contact with the three other people ahead of time as they were researching to discuss ideas together. The paper would flow out of the discussion, and the discussion would continue in the public setting of the conference.[19]

In the first three conferences, all the papers were published ahead of time, making it possible for "conferees to come far more prepared for a rich discussion than is possible in many scholarly conferences, where most who attend must depend on their ad hoc responses to oral presentations."[20] The purpose of this approach was further explained by Lydia Harder:

> Prepublication of the papers accomplished two purposes: (1) they ensured that the conference could become truly participative by making the same primary discussion material available to all registrants; (2) by entering the public conversation as a group,

---

[18]Katie Funk Wiebe, "Responses," *Conrad Grebel Review* 10, no. 2 (Spring 1992): 213.
[19]Carol Penner, "Women Doing Theology: A Conference Report," *Women's Concerns Report* 105 (November–December 1992): 1–2.
[20]"In This Issue," *Mennonite Quarterly Review* 68, no. 2 (1994): 147.

they gained courage and confidence in their ability to make a significant theological contribution.[21]

Having papers prepared ahead of time meant that at the event papers did not have to be read, freeing up more time for discussion. Pre-publication of the papers also took into account the fact that digesting a ten-page oral presentation is neither the best way to present ideas if you want them fully understood nor something that the average person can easily do. People in academic life are used to doing this, but the conferences were aiming to include people who might not have those academic skills. After the third WDT conference, the model changed. For the 2001 and 2003 conferences, the plenary speakers gave an oral presentation of a preliminary draft of their paper. Their final papers were written after the events, drawing from reflections shared in small group discussions.[22]

The WDT conferences also promoted dialogue through their emphasis on exchanging stories. Sharing stories is a way of explaining our theological roots and commitments: "Many expressed a deep concern to relate our theology to life—in the way we participate in academic life and in the church and the way we raise our children."[23]

Using creative mediums to express theological perspectives was something that characterized each WDT conference. This broadened the scope of dialogue, as women communicated with each other through concerts, art exhibits, coffee houses, and creative movement. Lydia Harder, reporting on the 1996 conference, suggests, "For it is in the language of poetry, story, dance, music, and art that our innermost experiences of God are expressed."[24]

Further, all of the WDT conferences included designated time for attendees to share in small groups. In the 1992 conference, "As much time was given to personal interaction in small groups as to plenary presentations."[25] At the 2016 conference every registrant

---

[21]Harder, "Guest Editorial," iv.
[22]Cathleen Hockman-Wert, "Women Envision Theology of Service," *Canadian Mennonite* 5, no. 11 (June 4, 2001): 18.
[23]Yamasaki, "In Search of Wholeness," 4.
[24]Harder, "Guest Editorial," vi.
[25]Margaret Loewen Reimer, "Women Explore 'Doing Theology' in Their Own Voices," *Mennonite Reporter* 22, no. 10 (May 18, 1992): 1.

was placed into a circle group: "Our hope is that this will encourage new relationships to form, provide a space to process how what we are learning is relevant to our own lives, and help shape the conference into a series of conversations informed by the thoughts, experiences and contributions of all participants."[26]

Theological Reflection

As we saw already, the four commonalities of the WDT conferences were reclaiming worship as part of the theological enterprise, diversity of participants and presenters, the expansion of theology beyond academia, and an emphasis on creative dialogue. I turn now to the question of how these commonalities reflect both a feminist and an Anabaptist methodology.

Drawing on Feminist Methodology

The Mennonite WDT conferences were structured in a way that reflected feminist values. Mennonite women did not create these conferences in a cultural vacuum, but rather they borrowed heavily from feminist theology conferences that were taking place at the time. In this section I share some brief comments about the rise of feminist theology conferences and the characteristics they shared with WDT conferences.[27]

While many worked for equal rights for women through history, the twentieth century saw several waves of political action for women's rights in Western society. In the 1960s the push for equality started to be felt in religious organizations. While in some denominations women gradually moved into ordained leadership positions in the church, that did not happen in the Roman Catholic Church. Large groups of progressive Roman Catholic women

---

[26]Anabaptist Women Doing Theology Conference Program, February 20–22, 2014, 6, www.mennoniteusa.org/wp-content/uploads/2015/03/WomenTheologyConference_Program.pdf.
[27]These values could also be tracked in the work of feminist theologians, but for the purpose of this chapter a more direct comparison with feminist theological conferences is most relevant.

gathered together in the 1970s to talk about ordination and other issues.[28]

Catholic theologian Elisabeth Schüssler Fiorenza coined the term "Women-Church" to describe Christian groups that wanted to include rather than exclude women. This term was the title of an important conference in Chicago in 1983—From Generation to Generation: Woman-Church Speaks. A high percentage of attendees were not professional theologians or clergy.[29] Three subsequent Women-Church conferences were held,[30] all with a common agenda: "The common thread is the effort to link religious faith with everyday life on terms that take women's well-being seriously."[31]

Another separate series of women's conferences happened in conjunction with the World Council of Churches Decade in Solidarity with Women (1988–1998). Groups of women from different continents met internationally to share theological views. One such event planned in 1993 in Minneapolis was called Re-Imagining: A Global Theological Conference By Women: For Men and Women. This conference addressed global inequalities from the perspectives of women, with an emphasis on new ways of doing theology that took power differentials into account.

A number of methodological similarities can be seen between these conferences and the WDT conferences.

Reclaiming Worship as Part of the Theological Enterprise

The Women-Church conferences included worship alongside of academic presentations: worship was a way of doing theology. Catholic women were at the vanguard of planning these conferences. As women they were blocked from fully participating

---

[28]Mary E. Hunt, "Women-Church," *Encyclopedia of Women and Religion in North America*, vol. 3, edited by Rosemary Skinner Keller and Rosemary Radford Ruether (Bloomington, IN: Indiana University Press, 2006), 1243.
[29]"Role of Catholic Women Debated," *Sojourners* 13, no. 1 (January 1984): 7.
[30]"Women-Church: Claiming Our Power" held in Cincinnati, Ohio, in 1987, another conference in Hartford, Connecticut, in 1988, and "Women-Church: Weavers of Change" in Albuquerque, New Mexico, in 1993.
[31]Hunt, "Women-Church," 1248.

in leading worship during the mass, so worship here was central. At the Women-Church gathering in 1988, keynote speaker Rosemary Radford Ruether explained that feminism generates a crisis in women's relationship to the church. Feminism helps women become aware of their need for nurture and self-expression: "The church holds out the promise of nurture and community, so when it ignores or systematically denies women's humanity, it betrays a promise at a deep level."[32] Worship that included women's experience and voices offered nurture and community to women at these conferences.

The Re-Imagining conference in Minneapolis in 1993 also included worship as a central part of the conference. The worship, which included feminine imagery for God, was subsequently widely criticized as being heretical and became a scandal in a number of denominations, resulting in people losing their jobs. Countless articles were written critiquing the theology of specific speakers, but the greatest criticism was reserved for some of the creative worship rituals.[33]

The Re-Imagining conference was referenced in worship during the second WDT conference in 1994: "In the final worship service, pastor Paula Diller Lehman said the silencing of women continues. She cited the flurry of controversy around an ecumenical conference called 'Re-Imagining,' which included feminist viewpoints that some consider heretical, last November."[34] This comment signals a desire to connect what was happening at WDT with the larger feminist movement: because women are still being silenced, conferences like these are needed.

As someone who attended the Women-Church gathering in Cincinnati in 1987, I can attest that worship by women for women, using female imagery for God, with only women leading worship, playing music, and preaching, was a riveting experience. This was something we wanted to duplicate in the WDT conference we were planning. WDT worship always had feminist elements, including using biblical stories that centered women and using feminine

---

[32] Melinda Tuhus, "Conference Celebrates Women-Church Movement," *Sojourners* 18, no. 1 (January 1989): 11.
[33] See, for example, James R. Edwards, "Earthquake in the Mainline," *Christian Century* 110, no. 16 (May 12, 1993): 38–43.
[34] Cathleen Hockman, "Women Do Theology without the Stereotypes," *Mennonite Weekly Review* 72, no. 27 (July 7, 1994): 1.

imagery for God. Every WDT conference devoted substantial amounts of time to worship, demonstrating that worship was central to their theological methodology.

Diversity of Participants and Presenters

Diverse participation was high on the agenda in the Women-Church conferences. At the 1987 Cincinnati event, Sister Theresa Kane declared, "We must eradicate ignorance, oppression, violence, militarism, racism, sexism and classism."[35] To that end, the conference included speakers from Central and South America and was conducted in Spanish and English.[36] At the 1993 Women-Church conference in Albuquerque, organizers struggled to diversify. Wanting to be diverse did not always translate into being diverse: "The multiracial, multiethnic, multicultural reality of common life in the United States made for difficult dynamics in this mostly white, Anglo, middle-class Christian movement."[37] The participants and the presenters included a "mix of races, classes, ages, nationalities, religious backgrounds and sexual orientations," but presenter Chung Hyun Kyung described the difficulties of listening across these divides.[38] Mary Hunt comments on the dynamics of the Women-Church movement: "The conflicts helped to force a more conscious self-awareness and opened the way for Women-Church to become more diverse."[39] The 1993 Re-Imagining conference also attempted to feature diverse voices, and there were 2,100 participants from twenty-seven countries.[40]

The WDT conferences had a similar feminist trajectory of wanting to become more diverse and then gradually achieving that goal. In both Women-Church and WDT, what began as a series of events that were largely controlled by white, middle-class women

---

[35] Maureen Conlan, "Women Crossing Worlds: Women-Church Fuels Worldwide Movement," *Sojourners* 16, no. 11 (December 1987): 7.
[36] Ibid.
[37] Hunt, "Women-Church," 1244.
[38] "Women-Church and Diversity," *Christian Century* 110, no. 16 (May 12, 1993): 512.
[39] Hunt, "Women-Church," 1244.
[40] "Report on the Re-Imagining Conference," *Journal of Feminist Studies in Religion* 11, no. 1 (Spring 1995): 137.

eventually shifted to more diverse leadership and participation. The Mennonite conferences took several decades longer to address inequality. This may be attributed to a greater entrenchment of white privilege in Mennonite churches, although the smaller, more modest size of the WDT conferences certainly meant that there were fewer resources to reach this goal of diversity.

An Expansion of Theology beyond Academia

The Women-Church conferences were academic in the sense that theologians made academically rigorous presentations, but the conferences widened the understanding of what theological work looked like. Feminist scholars like Rosemary Radford Ruether and Elisabeth Schüssler Fiorenza were speakers, but they were not held up as the only people who had the authority to speak. Women-Church groups, out of which the conferences arose, were communities that strove for a "discipleship of equals."[41] It was a movement that was critical of hierarchical practice and wanted a more democratic way of organizing, where power was distributed more fairly.

At the 1987 Women-Church conference in Cincinnati, "Speakers included prominent 'secular' feminists, as well as religious feminists scholars, and activists."[42] At the Women-Church conference in Albuquerque in 1993, a participant commented, "Church does not consist of the hierarchy, or who is your pastor . . . . Church has to do with the people."[43] Inclusion of women from diverse backgrounds sharing their stories was an important part of every Women-Church event. Rooting theology in the lived experience of women's lives was essential to the feminist thrust of the Women-Church conferences.

This feminist methodology was mirrored in the WDT conferences. Academic credentials were not showcased, and women from various walks of life gave presentations. Giving significant amounts of time to small groups allowed all participants to speak and hear each other.

---

[41]Hunt, "Women-Church," 1243.
[42]Ibid., 1244.
[43]"Women-Church and Diversity," 513.

An Emphasis on Creative Dialogue

Dialogue was central to Women-Church and was fostered in creative ways. It is difficult to find evidence of this because reporting about the conferences tended to focus on the ideas and not so much on the activities or structure of the conference or the way that dialogue took place for the average attendee. I recall that at the Women-Church gathering in Cincinnati, small group discussion was included alongside plenary presentations. Drama, dance, music, crafts, and art also figured prominently. A report from the 1993 Women-Church conference in Albuquerque states that "those gathered expressed their mourning and rage over the exclusion of women from the patriarchal church, and they celebrated—in storytelling, theater, song, and the visual arts—the vibrant life of the 'Women-Church' movement."[44]

The 1993 Re-Imagining conference also used creative ways of fostering dialogue: "Re-Imagining was a mega-event for body, mind, and spirit. In addition to 34 plenary addresses, there were small groups, workshops, ritual and worship, music, dance, plays, and visual arts."[45]

Women-Church influenced Mennonite women who planned the WDT events. My attendance at Women-Church in 1987 certainly shaped the first WDT conference. We wanted to hear the theology of Mennonite women in whatever way they expressed that theology. Artists and practitioners were invited to present in whatever medium they felt most comfortable. This led to visual installations and storytelling being part of the theological milieu of WDT.

Planners of WDT saw themselves as part of an ecumenical feminist movement that was sweeping through the church in Canada and the United States. Reports about significant theological events like Women-Church and Re-Imagining were part of the feminist culture of that time. Mennonite women were attending these events or reading about them. Feminist methodologies from these conferences shaped the methodology of the WDT conferences.

---

[44]Tuhus, "Conference Celebrates Women-Church Movement," 11.
[45]Edwards, "Earthquake in the Mainline," 512.

Unlike the Re-Imagining event, the WDT conferences generated only a minimal amount of attention in the Mennonite press.[46]

Drawing on Anabaptist Methodology

The WDT conferences were planned by groups of women who were Mennonite. The word "Anabaptist" is sometimes used interchangeably with the word "Mennonite." In that usage of the word "Anabaptist," if Mennonite women are shown to be consistently using a methodology for conferences, it could now be called an Anabaptist methodology.

But the term "Anabaptist" has a complex and storied history in theological circles. Some theologians use it to refer to theologies from the sixteenth century. Others, like Harold S. Bender, used the term to articulate an identity for Mennonites in the mid-twentieth century. Numerous Mennonite theologians have attempted to define Anabaptism. For the purposes of this chapter, I use Ted Grimsrud's explanation of the word Anabaptism as "hermeneutic," meaning "an interpretive framework, a set of values and convictions that guide how we see our world."[47] He suggests that this hermeneutic is shaped by the sixteenth-century story (in all its complexity) but is also dynamically applicable to the identity and tasks of Christian communities today.[48]

More specifically, I want to focus on the idea of "hermeneutic community." John Roth describes this communal process as one element of the "standard scholarly consensus" of hermeneutical principles: "Scripture is best interpreted as a communal process, in the context of a body of believers who, with the help of the Holy Spirit, gather to study God's Word and to discern God's will."[49]

---

[46]I have not found a single instance of a male theologian commenting on anything that happened at any WDT conference. This could be attributed to male theologians not being threatened by the feminist agenda of the conferences, or it could be that the conferences were disregarded as unimportant because they involved only women.
[47]Ted Grimsrud, *Embodying the Way of Jesus: Anabaptist Convictions for the Twenty-First Century* (Eugene, OR: Wipf & Stock, 2007), 15.
[48]Ibid., 16.
[49]John D. Roth, "Community as Conversation: A New Model of Anabaptist Hermeneutics," in *Anabaptist Currents: History in Conversation with the Present*, edited by Carl F. Bowman and Stephen L. Longenecker (Bridgewater, VA: Penobscot,

"Hermeneutic community" is a term often used in discussions of the biblical text, in that the congregation reads Scripture together to discern the will of God. I am using a broader understanding of the term hermeneutic community to mean the community as the place where people work out their theology. People forge theology in the crucible of congregational life as they engage with the Spirit of God, Scripture, and tradition. Because a conference such as WDT is a place where theology is being discerned, it is a type of temporary hermeneutical community. It is a significant community because women had been excluded from sharing their voice equitably in other hermeneutical communities, such as denominational structures, and entirely, such as in Mennonite academic circles. Next I discuss how WDT functions as a hermeneutical community in the context of the categories used in previous sections: worship as theology, diversity, theology beyond academia, and the importance of dialogue.

Reclaiming Worship as Part of the Theological Enterprise

The early Anabaptists didn't just want to think new ideas about God; they wanted to worship in a new, more liberating way. The way they worshiped was a way of doing theology; the action of rebaptizing was a theological statement. Theology flowed out of their devotion to God as expressed in worship. Paul Miller suggests that Anabaptists did not separate the idea of worship from their lives; it was not something to be done at a certain hour or a certain place, but rather it was something that permeated their entire way of life.[50] Walter Klaassen claims that Anabaptists gave up sacredness or holiness in certain words, certain places, and certain times.[51] Worship was something that should happen naturally as believers got together to study Scripture.

1995), 53. For other discussions of hermeneutic community see Walter Klaassen, *Anabaptism: Neither Catholic nor Protestant*, 3rd ed. (Waterloo: Pandora, 2001), 86–87; Lydia Harder, *The Challenge Is in the Naming: A Theological Journey* (Winnipeg: CMU Press, 2018), 50; and Palmer Becker, *Anabaptist Essentials: Ten Signs of a Unique Christian Faith* (Harrisonburg, VA: Herald, 2017), 81–93.
[50]Paul Miller, "Worship among the Early Anabaptists," *Mennonite Quarterly Review* 30, no. 4 (October 1956): 245.
[51]Klaassen, *Anabaptism*, 12–13.

Dividing worship from discussion of God seems antithetical in the Anabaptist tradition. When people get together to work out their theology, it only makes sense to pray together for wisdom, to meditate on Scripture, and to invite the Holy Spirit's presence into this activity. However, worship has not been a central part of Mennonite academic conferences in recent decades.

The WDT conferences took the hermeneutic community seriously; if they were going to be talking about God, they wanted God to be invited into that space and time. A theology conference could not be a theology conference without worship. Using feminine images of God in worship, for example, is an expression of theological reflection on God.

Diversity of Participants and Presenters

The hermeneutical community of sixteenth-century Anabaptism consisted of gatherings of believers who were male and female. That is the context in which people often discussed Scripture. An example can be found in Michael Sattler's writing when he "included 'sisters' in this interpretive process, one of several indications that women participated actively in Anabaptist gatherings."[52] Court records and accounts in books like the *Martyr's Mirror* suggest that women were very familiar with the biblical text. Feminist scholars today are actively involved in uncovering the role of women in the early Anabaptist movement.

Women's voices have long been subdued in the Anabaptist theological tradition,[53] and this has impoverished Mennonite theology. Quoting Rosemary Radford Ruether, Lydia Harder suggests that it is not simply a matter of Mennonite theology not speaking to women's experience but also that it spoke in a way that worked against women.[54] The WDT conferences attempted to create space for women's voices to shape Mennonite theology.

Harder suggests that including women in the hermeneutical community will lead to changes in our theological thinking: "As

---

[52] Stuart Murray, *Biblical Interpretation in the Anabaptist Tradition* (Kitchener: Pandora, 2000), 169.
[53] For an example, see Lydia Harder, *The Challenge Is in the Naming: A Theological Journey* (Winnipeg: CMU Press, 2018), 25–35.
[54] Ibid., 57.

women have entered public life in their vocations, changes are also coming about in the life of the congregation. Women are no longer content to be on the periphery of the hermeneutical community. Therefore, central theological formulations are being re-examined in order to include women's experience."[55]

An Expansion of Theology beyond Academia

Early Anabaptists rejected the assumption that the "traditional discipline of theology was for experts only, the concern and preserve of an elite corps of scholars which none but the specially trained could enter."[56] They did not reject scholarship outright; many of the early leaders were scholars.[57] But scholarly expertise did not give one a mediating role in interpreting Scripture for the uneducated.

Stuart Murray suggests that it is "likely that anticlericalism and egalitarian impulses in both the movement itself and its surrounding context militated against restricting the teaching office to recognized leaders."[58] The practice of viewing the congregation as hermeneutic community enfranchised the uneducated and powerless in both the Anabaptist movement and the peasant's movement of the sixteenth century.[59]

In the WDT conferences, scholarship was valued. Women with doctoral degrees were invited to speak; however, they were not considered to be the only ones with something to contribute—or even the most important ones. Katie Funk Wiebe reflected on the first WDT conference and the challenge for Mennonite female scholars to be careful about the power and privilege of education:

> Are we true Anabaptists who submit to one another when we, in public discourse, whether in written or oral form, use language that is enigmatic, sometimes so abstract and general as to confuse rather than clarify? Can women do theology without shifting to a language that sounds like it comes from an alien country,

---

[55]Ibid., 80.
[56]Klaassen, *Anabaptism*, 45.
[57]Ibid., 40.
[58]Murray, *Biblical Interpretation*, 157.
[59]Ibid., 172.

which act is in itself a sign of intimidation? A little power is always appealing, regardless of what form it comes in.[60]

The WDT conferences provided spaces where women could share their theological views; academic women were part of that mix.

An Emphasis on Creative Dialogue

Palmer Becker describes dialogue as an essential part of a discerning hermeneutic community. He outlines how preaching, teaching, and Bible study are all ways that the community discerns the will of God. Using the example of the early Anabaptists, who met "face-to-face in small groups and house church settings,"[61] he encourages intimate dialogue through small group work. He quotes Jessica Reesor-Rempel, a pastor in Ontario who leads a feminist Bible study. She suggests that there are commonalities between the Anabaptist and the feminist approach to discernment:

> As we read [the Bible] we ask questions about power, privilege, gender roles, and the nature of God that we have not been encouraged to ask in a larger church setting. When we gather there are no authorities or experts, rather, each participant is invited to explore her own interpretation of Scripture with the group. Everyone has something to teach and everyone has something to learn.[62]

Ted Grimsrud speaks of contemporary Anabaptism as a movement that has a practice-oriented theology. This theology is connected to social life and concrete ethics; it applies the life and teaching of Jesus to our everyday stories of our present life.[63] Storytelling is an invitational way for people to share their faith stories.

The WDT planners chose formats that were intentionally dialogical, as the brochure for the 2003 conference shows:

> The intent of the dialogical approach is to be more inclusive and liberating. In addition, this form of response recognizes

---

[60]Katie Funk Wiebe, "Responses," *Conrad Grebel Review* 10, no. 2 (Spring 1992): 213.
[61]Becker, *Anabaptist Essentials*, 90.
[62]Ibid., 91–92.
[63]Grimsrud, *Embodying the Way of Jesus*, 31.

the founding beliefs of Anabaptists that the interpretation of the Bible should be done within a community and the non-hierarchical understanding of the priesthood of all believers. Early Anabaptists exhibited communal and dialogical models of biblical interpretation and preaching. It also honors the wisdom of women's experiences as well as their academic knowledge, when discussing theological matters.[64]

A variety of creative forums and types of dialogue was the foundation of the WDT conferences.

Significantly, the 2014 and 2016 organizers named their conferences Anabaptist Women Doing Theology instead of Mennonite Women Doing Theology. This associates WDT less with a denomination and more with a way of thinking.

Conclusion

Today, many Mennonite academic conferences have relatively small numbers of people attending, and the majority of attendees are men. If planners of academic conferences want to create an environment that is more appealing to women, it would be helpful to look at conferences that were planned by women. The WDT conferences show an alternative vision of conference planning. Reclaiming worship as central to the theological project, diversity of participants and presenters, the expansion of theology beyond academia, and an emphasis on creative dialogue were found consistently in conferences that women planned. The WDT conferences used a methodology that is consistent both with feminism and Anabaptism.

This chapter has just scratched the surface of the significance of the WDT conferences. I have looked primarily at methodology and not at the content of the conferences. Unpacking the theological insights of the WDT conferences will undoubtedly be the subject of future work by an Anabaptist scholar. It will also be important to research other Mennonite groups of women that were gathering at

---

[64]Mennonite Central Committee, Gifts of the Red Tent, conference schedule,web.archive.org/web/20030313130735/http:/www.mcc.org/womendoingtheology/schedule.html.

the same time as the WDT conferences such as African Anabaptist Women Theologians, Latin American Women Theologians, and Asian Women Theologians.[65] Women's voices have been gaining power and momentum over the past decades; comparing and contrasting their views will be fruitful.

The WDT conferences were significant for me and many Mennonite women, in helping us to find our theological voice. Hopefully the methods that WDT used for planning conferences can be informative for Mennonite theology moving forward.

---

[65] "Anabaptist Women Theologians," Mennonite World Conference, www.mwc-cmm.org/article/anabaptist-women-theologians.

5

Queering Anabaptist Theology

An Endeavor in Breaking Binaries as Hermeneutical Community

Stephanie Chandler Burns

Introduction

With the rise in the field of queer theory, it comes as no surprise that queer theology has emerged on the scene. With roots in apologetic theology, liberation theology, and relational theology, queer theology is based on the theoretical works of Michel Foucault, Judith Butler, and Eve Kosofsky Sedgwick.[1] Queer theory challenges concrete notions of sexuality and gender, proposing instead that our set categories are much more fluid than previous

---

[1] Patrick S. Cheng, *Radical Love: An Introduction to Queer Theology* (New York: Seabury, 2011), 35.

cultural understandings would dictate.² While queer theology has emerged and evolved over the past twenty years—and despite its rising significance—queer theology has not had much of a foothold within Mennonite communities.³ In this chapter, I attempt to change this by exposing points of dialogue between Anabaptist and queer theologies. After outlining some key terms and definitions, I share some stories and experiences of LGBTQ Mennonites. These stories inform a theological reflection on the gifts that queer theology may have to offer to the current atmosphere of Anabaptist theology.

Context

Brief Description of Queer Theology

My understanding of what constitutes queer theology comes from the work of Patrick Cheng in *Radical Love*. Cheng's work outlines a few important definitions, both for the term "queer" in general and for "queer theology" more specifically. For Cheng, the term "queer" consists of three definitions. First, it is an umbrella term for non-normative identities, which thus encompasses a variety of terms that describe both sexual orientation and gender identity.⁴ Second, queer is transgressive action, in that it twists around what is seen as normative, plays with boundaries, and disrupts a status quo of gender identity or sexual orientation.⁵ Finally, Cheng notes that the term "queer" erases boundaries, calling into question the very categories that are understood as natural.⁶ Queer theology, then, consists of theology that does any of these three things within theological discussion.⁷ Queer theology is queer people talking about theological concepts. Queer theology is theology done in a deliberately transgressive manner, especially when it comes to topics of gender and sexuality. Queer theology is theological work

---

²Cheng, *Radical Love*, 36.
³Alicia Dueck-Read, "Breaking the Binary: Queering Mennonite Identity," *Journal of Mennonite Studies* 33 (August 2017): 115.
⁴Cheng, *Radical Love*, 3–5.
⁵Ibid., 5–6.
⁶Ibid., 6–8.
⁷Ibid., 9–11.

that challenges binary categories, particularly of sexuality, sex, or gender, although not limited only to these categories.[8] In the next few paragraphs, I describe what I understand to be the queer context in Anabaptist discussions to begin to understand how queer Anabaptists might be talking about queer theological concepts.

Mennonite Church Canada, Assembly 2016

In July 2016 at the Mennonite Church Canada Assembly in Saskatoon, Saskatchewan, delegates were asked to vote on a recommendation that came out of a nine-year listening and discernment process known as "Being a Faithful Church 7" (BFC 7).[9] The proposed motion would allow room for individual churches within Mennonite Church Canada to discern for themselves how to respond to the question of LGBTQ welcome and affirmation in individual congregations. Each congregation would be given the freedom to discern whether, in their context, LGBTQ inclusion might be a move guided by the Holy Spirit. During the discussion leading up to the vote on the motion, a man stood up to offer his piece to the conversation.[10] He proceeded to read the passages that are known to LGBTQ Christians as "clobber passages," insisting that to allow such room in this motion would be allowing the church to abandon God. As he spoke, a group of LGBTQ Mennonites and allies gathered in the hall. They grouped together in prayer and lament, weeping and holding one another, reminding each other that all are loved by God. Many remained in the hallway long after the hurtful comments ended until the end of the discussion regarding the BFC 7 motion. Later in the day, the Listening Committee reported on the atmosphere they had observed among the delegate body,

---

[8]Ibid., 10.
[9]Mennonite Church Canada, "Being a Faithful Church 7 Summary and Recommendation on Sexuality 2009–2015," PowerPoint Presentation at Mennonite Church Canada Assembly, Saskatoon, July 7–9, 2016, www.home.mennonitechurch.ca/BFC.
[10]David Driedger, "Just Let Him Finish; Or, You Cannot Serve Both Process and Advocacy," David CL Driedger (blog), January 16, 2017, https://davidcldriedger.wordpress.com/2017/01/16/just-let-him-finish-or-you-cannot-serve-both-process-and-advocacy.

applauding the group for providing a safe and vulnerable space to have discussion. Many LGBTQ Mennonites present felt that this further erased and victimized their experiences, both of that day and of the church more broadly.[11]

This is just one story, but it is an important one in that it outlines the pain and difficulty of being LGBTQ and Mennonite at present within the Canadian Mennonite context. It is a recent story, experienced at a national church level by many LGBTQ-identified Mennonites. It is indicative of the current climate within the Mennonite church, and it provides an example of the types of alienating experiences and level of polarization that occur when one is the focus of church process. This dynamic is currently taking place within both the US and Canadian Mennonite contexts.

Queer Mennonite Experience

To date, few official academic works have been written by queer Anabaptists. According to Alicia Dueck-Read, "There is currently a lack of studies on diverse gender and sexual identities within Mennonite studies."[12] It is for this reason that Dueck-Read's work is so significant. In both works cited here, Dueck-Read (previously Dueck) attempts to bring more queer Mennonite voices to the forefront. In *Negotiating Sexual Identities*, Dueck-Read interviews nine individuals regarding their experiences as both queer and Mennonite.[13] Further, in "Breaking the Binary: Queering Mennonite Identity," Dueck-Read interviews another four individuals who identify as transgender or genderqueer.[14] Ultimately, Dueck-Read's works help Anabaptist queer experience to move away from the anecdotal and can help us identify trends among LGBTQ-identified Mennonites. Throughout both of Dueck-Read's works, she outlines how vital it is that queer stories and queer voices be central to dialogue.[15]

---

[11]Driedger, "Just Let Him Finish."
[12]Dueck-Read, "Breaking the Binary," 115.
[13]J. Alicia Dueck, *Negotiating Sexual Identities: Lesbian, Gay, and Queer Perspectives on Being Mennonite* (Zurich: Lit Verlag, 2012).
[14]Dueck-Read, "Breaking the Binary," 115.
[15]Ibid.

The pain and tension of being LGBTQ and Mennonite is also evident in the stories shared in Dueck-Read's works. In *Negotiating Sexual Identities*, Dueck-Read shares the story of Julia, a lesbian woman from Winnipeg, Manitoba. Julia grew up in a Mennonite community where her father was a pastor. Julia herself developed a passion for theology and before coming out was attending Mennonite institutions studying theology. During study for her PhD, Julia came out as lesbian and realized this would significantly hinder her goals of teaching biblical theology in a Mennonite institution. So she left her PhD program, returned to Winnipeg, and later left formal Mennonite communities altogether when her marriage with her partner was not supported by her congregation.[16] Although she felt supported by individual members of her church, she indicated that lack of institutional support made her feel like a second-class citizen. She and her partner left their formal involvement with the Mennonite church, telling Dueck-Read they were "tired of not being like that first class citizen [who] is heteronormative."[17] Despite having left officially, Julia still considers herself Mennonite, and she finds that Mennonite values of social justice, community, and ethical living shape her daily life.[18]

Another story shared by Dueck-Read has similar dynamics at play. While Jodi did not grow up in a Mennonite home, she became familiar with Mennonites through a placement with Mennonite Central Committee. Mennonite values of peace and justice, shared leadership, community responsibility, and accountability resonated with Jodi. She became deeply involved with Mennonite communities through studying for a master's degree in conflict transformation and peacebuilding at Eastern Mennonite University and further involvement with Mennonite Central Committee (MCC).[19] Before coming out, she worked with MCC for over a decade. Although she has found many Mennonite circles where she feels embraced and supported, she experiences sadness due to the rejection she feels due to MCC's hiring policies. She reflected with Dueck-Read, noting that she would not be able to work for MCC again and stating that

---

[16]Dueck, *Negotiating Sexual Identities*, 143–44.
[17]Ibid., 160.
[18]Ibid., 144.
[19]Ibid., 142.

it would not be a place where she could be herself due to MCC's hiring policies.[20]

In both Julia's and Jodi's stories, Dueck-Read points out how individuals often feel a tension between a strong commitment to Mennonite values and rejection by Mennonite communities. In her later work, "Breaking the Binary: Queering Mennonite Identity," Dueck-Read indicates that similar dynamics exist for transgender and gender nonconforming Mennonites. In this work, many interviewees indicated that silence regarding topics of gender and sexuality signified that these were tense topics with engrained rules and social norms attached. One participant, Peter, noted the lack of terminology present in Low German with which to discuss topics of gender and sexuality.[21] In this work, individuals noted that interacting with Mennonite communities always requires some level of self-censoring,[22] desexualization,[23] and dissociation with Mennonite circles.[24]

Dueck-Read argues that, as larger church structures and framers of official doctrine and church practice seek clarity on the topic of LGBTQ inclusion, queer Mennonite voices must be heard.[25] I agree in earnest. A good way to begin to hear these voices is to read both of Dueck-Read's works and to view the "Listening Church Project," a video created in 2015 that shares stories and reflections of more LGBTQ Mennonites from across Canada.[26] While I cannot begin to summarize each individual story, these works express themes that are important for understanding the current attitudes in the Mennonite church toward LGBTQ individuals.

Most notably, in both Dueck-Read's work and in the "Listening Church Project," many individuals indicate their dedication and love for the church. In the "Listening Church Project," one individual identified as Ben names his commitment to the church as a result of the commitment that he made through baptism. Despite

---

[20]Ibid., 160.
[21]Dueck-Read, "Breaking the Binary," 122.
[22]Ibid., 123.
[23]Ibid., 124.
[24]Ibid., 126.
[25]Ibid., 4.
[26]Darryl Neustaedter Barg and Irma Fast Dueck (producers), *Listening Church Project*, video documentary, 2015, www.listeningchurchproject.ca.

frustration and struggle, he remains a part of the church in order to follow through with the mutual commitment of baptism.[27] In her conclusion to *Negotiating Sexual Identities*, Dueck-Read summarizes queer Mennonite experience as discovered through her work, noting that LGBTQ Mennonites are present, active, passionate about community, and dedicated.[28] She also notes the existence of tension between identities of Mennonite and LGBTQ. This tension has caused many to leave and those who stay to face a risk of, or to experience, great personal pain.[29] She explains that, as we have seen in a few of her stories previously summarized, many individuals experience a degree of support on the personal level, whether from friends, family, or others within their congregations, but the lack of structural support and recognition remains painful for many who stay involved within the wider church.[30] Dueck-Read's conclusions ring true to my own experience as a bisexual Mennonite and resonate with the story of the Assembly in Saskatoon I shared here already. At minimum, I think we can tentatively conclude that the queer Mennonite experience is marked by tension: between love and pain, dedication and rejection, knowing ourselves to be loved by God and not being able to stay in the room. In these ways, the queer Mennonite experience finds itself within the tensions of binarized thinking.

Integrating Lived Experience and Theological Reflection

The Need for a Broad Narrative Base

Despite such stories, little has been done to center the voices of those who have the most at stake in such conversations: LGBTQ Mennonites themselves. While the "Being a Faithful Church" process attempted to gather insight from various stakeholders

---

[27] Barg and Dueck, *Listening Church Project*. This particular sentiment is present in many stories but is particularly well articulated by an individual named Ben.
[28] Dueck, *Negotiating Sexual Identities*, 170.
[29] Ibid.
[30] Ibid.

across the country, little attention has been paid to the insights that queer methods of doing theology might have for this current climate. How might LGBTQ and queer Mennonites do theology? How might queer theology and Anabaptist theology enter into dialogue with one another? Might queer theology breathe new life into Anabaptist theology? As a queer Mennonite myself, much of my work is filtered through the lens of my own queer experience. As far as I can find, the number of queer Anabaptists represented in academic contexts is few, and the number of those engaging in questions and topics of queer theology is even fewer. Thus, the field of academic queer Anabaptist theology is underdeveloped at best and almost absent at worst.[31] Certainly, there is a lack of coordinated, disciplined academic conversation regarding queer Anabaptist theology. Given the importance in Anabaptist circles of the hermeneutical community and the various identities represented under the umbrella term "queer," it is necessary to avoid framing one queer Anabaptist experience as a universal experience. I end up running the risk in doing Anabaptist work on queer theology of misrepresenting or appropriating queer stories through offering my own, limited perspective. In many ways, what I offer is simply one understanding of a queer Anabaptist theology. Indeed, it is one of likely many queer Anabaptist theologies (although I suspect that, perhaps, few of these have yet to be written down). More conversation is needed to determine which of my priorities from my queer Anabaptist theology might resonate with other queer or LGBTQ Mennonites.

In the final sections of this chapter I attempt to find dialogue points between queer and Anabaptist theology. Indeed, many of the things I am most drawn to in Anabaptist theology are things that I have grown to love about queer theology. I discuss some of the important factors of queer theology, suggesting a few meeting points that are ripe starting places for further dialogue and one corrective that may help the Anabaptist community as it continues to discern the importance of the contributions of queer-identified Mennonites. This work seeks to be a preparation for further work that can then

---

[31]For a deeper academic understanding of the identities and experiences of both LGBTQ-identified Mennonite individuals and groups, see Dueck, *Negotiating Sexual Identities*.

be done in bringing the priorities of queer and Anabaptist theology together into a more robust understanding of a queer Anabaptist theology.

Healy's Taxonomy

Although queer Anabaptist theology is currently rare in academic settings, queer-identified Anabaptists are certainly doing their own theology. Much of this theology happens at the level of ordinary theology, a term I borrow from Nicholas Healy. Healy describes three realms in which theology is created: (1) official theology, or that which is outlined doctrinally within tradition and institutional structures; (2) ordinary theology, or the type of theological reflection engaged in by all Christians as they work out faith within everyday life; and (3) professional (or academic) theology, the type engaged by theologians within the academy.[32] Although queer Anabaptist theology is largely absent from both the official and the professional conversation, queer theology—and especially queer Anabaptist theology—is currently engaged most often by the ordinary theologian. At the same time that queer Anabaptist theology is absent from the academy, ordinary queer Anabaptist theology happens in grassroots meetings and gatherings throughout Canada (and beyond) and has been active for many years. In Kitchener-Waterloo, my hometown, it happens in a group known as Queerly Christian, which serves as a safe place to reconcile experiences of faith, sexual orientation, and gender identity.[33] It happens through gatherings in Manitoba known as the Pilgrim Group at Bethel Mennonite Church or in queer-positive student spaces at Canadian Mennonite University.[34] Online, a group of queer Anabaptist pastors meets to support each other in sharing their gifts for ministry with the church. Queer Anabaptist

---

[32]Nicholas M. Healy, "What Is Systematic Theology?" *International Journal of Systematic Theology* 11, no. 1 (2009): 24.
[33]Queerly Christian is a joint program between Pastors in Exile and Erb Street Mennonite Church in Waterloo, Ontario. For more information, see http://erbstchurch.ca/program/queerly-christian.
[34]Dueck, *Negotiating Sexual Identities*, 127.

theology happens at Assembly and Convention,[35] through LGBTQ and family meetings and services, and through advocacy by Pink Menno[36] and the Brethren Mennonite Council for LGBT Concerns.[37] Queer Anabaptist theology happens while we weep and lament together in hallways and when we sing together as motions are passed. Occasionally, queer Anabaptist theology can happen in the *Canadian Mennonite* and *The Mennonite* magazines. In the absence of official or academic queer Anabaptist theology, these are some of the ways theology is engaged by LGBTQ Mennonites.

Such dynamics of queer Anabaptist theology make it difficult to pinpoint a specifically Anabaptist way of doing queer theology, if only because those engaging the topic are so diverse and widespread. Indeed, I will not attempt to concretely solidify a queer Anabaptist theology before having more of a chance to engage with other LGBTQ Mennonites regarding the ways their faith and their sexual orientations or gender identities might mix.

Cheng and Queering the Quadrilateral

Cheng reimagines the Wesleyan Quadrilateral to provide four sources of queer theology. For Cheng, queer theology is found and created through interaction with Scripture, lived experience, reason, and tradition.[38] Each source must draw on the others, providing corrective to one another and reigning in extreme interpretations.[39] It is through Cheng's reimagining of the Wesleyan Quadrilateral that queer and Anabaptist theology can enter into dialogue with one another. On their own, queer and Anabaptist theology each draw on each of these four sources of theology to varying degrees. When brought into dialogue, queer and Anabaptist interactions with Scripture, lived experience, reason, and tradition can bring new insights to one another.

---

[35] Assembly and Convention are two of the common terms used to refer to annual or biannual denominational meetings.
[36] Information about Pink Menno can be found at http://www.pinkmenno.org.
[37] See https://www.bmclgbt.org.
[38] Cheng, *Radical Love*, 11.
[39] Ibid.

Scripture: Suspicion and Reclamation

In my own works elsewhere, I interact most often and deeply with queer interpretations of Scripture and the relationship of Scripture to queer experiences. In attempting to retrieve a bisexual hermeneutic, I apply two hermeneutical principles: suspicion and reclamation.[40] My preference is to begin the task of biblical interpretation with suspicion to the hetero- and cis-normative systems and assumptions present in the text. It is not enough, however, to read the texts with suspicion. According to Deryn Guest, reading with suspicion allows for the reimagining of the interpretation of certain texts, reclaiming them by providing the space to enter into more liberative readings.[41] In many ways, these are the dynamics I see happening within my own experiences with queer Christian and queer Anabaptist communities. Such suspicion and reclamation is happening in practical settings and informal "ordinary" theological conversations with friends who are LGBTQ and Mennonite. While many would never use the terms suspicion or reclamation to define their readings of Scripture, suspicion is nonetheless applied as we ask what the point might have been to the household codes in Paul or the laws in Leviticus. Reclamation happens as we ask what was going on with Naomi and Ruth or why Paul seemed to have a negative view of women.

Indeed, it could be argued that such suspicion and reclamation is very much an Anabaptist move. Just as the current group of Anabaptist queer individuals would not necessarily name their theological moves as "suspicion" and "reclamation," the early Anabaptist thinkers—and even Protestant forebears such as Martin Luther—viewed other readings of Scripture with suspicion and reclaimed new readings of texts based on their new commitments. Even before the Anabaptist movement began in earnest, Luther wrote to Pope Leo X, "I acknowledge no fixed rules for interpretation of the Word of God, since the Word of God which teaches freedom in

---

[40]Steph Chandler Burns, "Non-Binary Identity in Ruth and the Re-Structuring of Power," Presentation at the Women Doing Theology Conference, Leesburg, Virginia, November 4–6, 2016.
[41]Deryn Guest, *When Deborah Met Jael: Lesbian Biblical Hermeneutics* (London: SCM, 2005), 219–20.

all other matters must not be bound."⁴² Here, in 1520, early in the Protestant Reformation, Luther sets the stage for suspicion toward traditional interpretations of Scripture.

In a recent article, Dennis D. Martin notes that the Anabaptist-Mennonite attitude that has remained most steadfast over the centuries is their enduring attitude toward the Catholic period of history—that is, Anabaptists present and past look at the history of Christendom with an eye of suspicion. This suspicion, he claims, is a common thread running through Mennonite groups, allowing for a rejection of the continuity of church history and of certain Catholic forms of tradition, including readings of Scripture.⁴³

Lived Experience: Queer Hermeneutic Community

In the grassroots, "ordinary" level of queer Anabaptist theology, conversations are happening within hermeneutical communities. While "gaydar" is a term often used in jest on television sitcoms, in my own lived experience, whether at conferences or online, LGBTQ Anabaptists tend to find one another, eager to explore together the ways our faith has a place within God's kingdom. We may sit quietly closeted in the back or meet up after regular programming for drinks and reflect together on our unique experiences of Anabaptist community. Our lived experiences are thus interpreted together, in light of Scripture, reason, and tradition, within a hermeneutical community not unlike the communities of early Anabaptists. It is significant that queer Anabaptist theology (again, within my own lived experience) has seemed to naturally form hermeneutical communities within which to engage with Scripture and tradition. We are, in this way, quite Anabaptist in our approach. While such communities still have learning to do to make space for a multitude of voices, LGBTQ spaces have in my overall experience been safer places in which more voices can be heard.

---

⁴²Martin Luther, "The Freedom of a Christian (1520)," in *A Reformation Reader: Primary Texts with Introductions*, edited by Denis R. Janz (Minneapolis: Fortress, 1999), 106.
⁴³Dennis D. Martin, "Nothing New under the Sun? Mennonites in History," *Conrad Grebel Review* 5 (1987): 2.

In my learning about early Anabaptist history, I am often told that early Anabaptist circles were much more egalitarian and inclusive than many other groups of the time and that women were instrumental.[44] In this line of witness, the queer community offers a means of returning to this inclusive and radical early vision of the Anabaptist hermeneutical community. The postures surrounding informal, ordinary, and marginalized theological discussion have something to teach the wider Anabaptist community of the twenty-first century about a return to or reimaging of the community as the authority. Queer Mennonites thus pick up on some of the strengths and priorities of early Anabaptists, reclaiming them for more liberative readings.

Reason: Rejecting Binaries

Anabaptist communities have been dialoguing together to reclaim texts for more liberative readings since the beginning. In its conception, Anabaptism was understood as breaking binary assumptions, leading to the self-identity as "neither Catholic nor Protestant."[45] Such a self-identity points to a time when Anabaptists sought to break down categories that were seen as oppressive in other contexts and lived experiences. The early Anabaptists claimed what they could claim and what they needed from various traditions while breaking with what did not mix with their experience of God. Indeed, Mennonite historian John Roth confirms this tendency, reminding us that Anabaptists and Mennonites have historically rooted their identities in being distinctive, holding a defensive posture toward other traditions. This posture, Roth notes, has always been stated in oppositional terms such as "neither Catholic nor Protestant."[46] Much like my Anabaptist queer friends today, Anabaptist thinkers have long held suspicion toward more "traditional" readings and have instead, through reading and studying together in community,

---

[44]Troy Osbourne, "TS 640: The Mennonite Tradition in the Historical Context," course at Conrad Grebel University College, Waterloo, Ontario, spring 2017.
[45]Walter Klaassen, *Anabaptism: Neither Catholic nor Protestant* (Scottdale, PA: Herald, 2001), 1–10.
[46]John D. Roth, "The Challenge of Church Unity in the Anabaptist Tradition." Lecture at Conrad Grebel University College, Waterloo, Ontario, 2012.

sought new "clarity of Biblical vision that [gives] birth to its own purer, truer, more faithful understanding."[47]

Today Anabaptist theology, informed by queer theology, can continue to critically examine other oppressive binaries. Not only would queer Anabaptist theology address binaries present in understandings of sexual orientation, sex, or gender, but it would also recognize the oppressive systems upheld by other binary views of the world, including race, socioeconomic status, and even perhaps conceptions of Christianity or God in binary terms. Perhaps the queer tendency to break binaries might even breathe new life into peace theology by requiring deeper engagement with the false dichotomy created between peace and violence and engaging a larger spectrum between the two. Such queer critiques of Anabaptist and other peace theologies may eventually make way for a more robust understanding of violence and the ways it manifests spiritually and emotionally as well as physically.

Tradition: Peace Theology

My temptation is to not engage with Anabaptist peace theology in this chapter but to leave it out of the conversation risks leaving the quadrilateral incomplete. For Anabaptists, peace theology is the historical tradition that can provide a lens through which queer Scripture readings, lived experiences, and reason are interpreted. While peace theology is central to the Anabaptist perspective, in my queer experience and opinion, peace theology has been largely absent from the wider Anabaptist conversations surrounding the topic of LGBTQ inclusion. Despite this, many of the individuals interviewed in Dueck-Read's works noted that one main resonance for them with Anabaptist theology is the Anabaptist commitment to peace and justice. Indeed, many such individuals mentioned their own LGBTQ advocacy as part of their specifically Anabaptist commitment.[48] Whereas the rest of the Wesleyan Quadrilateral provides dialogue points between queer and Anabaptist theology, it is in the case of peace theology that queer theology has a specific corrective that can be offered. Through queer readings of Scripture,

---

[47]Roth, "The Challenge of Church Unity."
[48]Dueck, *Negotiating Sexual Identities*, 148–53.

queer lived experience, and queer reason in the form of breaking binaries, queer theological insights can encourage a return and recommitment to what is arguably one of the central pieces of Anabaptist tradition: the historical peace stance. By widening the circle of who is allowed to be a part of the hermeneutical community, a fuller picture of God's justice will emerge.

Conclusion

This is, in many ways, an incomplete conclusion. While I have established that queer Anabaptist voices have something to offer to the Anabaptist community at large, the details of what that offering might be is still a work in progress. This is necessary if we are to pay heed to the diverse voices that have the potential to contribute to the discussion. Further work by other LGBTQ and queer-identified Mennonites and Anabaptists is needed in order to more fully flesh out the implications and visions of a uniquely queer Anabaptist theology. Nonetheless, such a theology exists already, in small, grassroots hermeneutical communities of queer Anabaptists.

6

On the Need for Critical-Contextual and Trauma-Informed Methods in Mennonite Theology

Melanie Kampen

Introduction

I was recently at a Mennonite college doing some research.[1] All around me were display cases filled with archival materials related to Mennonite conscientious objectors. The collective memory curated by this display was one of risk, hardship, perseverance, and most of all faithfulness. Ten years ago this display would have

---

[1] I want to begin by acknowledging the land on which the conference that spawned this volume took place. The Trinity Western University (TWU) main campus is on the ancestral and unceded territory of the Stó:lō people and Kwantlen First Nation. TWU's Richmond Campus is on land that has been cared for by the Musqueam Coast Salish people, and the Tsawwassen, and Kwantlen families for over 9,000 years. The Coast Salish people have experienced genocide through smallpox blankets and cultural genocide through Indian Residential Schools. Let us pause to remember this history of violence and to honor the work for trauma healing and right relations that peoples are working toward today. See here: http://www.richmond-news.com/news/weekly-feature/the-first-people-of-richmond-1.2281754.

resonated with me, elicited reverence for my forefathers, awe at the depth of their commitment to nonviolence and their absolute refusal to take up arms. But now the display rings hollow for me. An absence haunts me. Absent in this display of nonviolence are the Mennonite conscientious objectors who worked as teachers in Indian Residential Schools in Canada. Absent in this display of nonviolence are the Mennonite conscientious objectors who abused and assaulted women and children in their own communities. The maintenance of this form of nonviolence, this conscientious objection to violence, has long silenced women, people of color, and queer people, drowning out their experiences of violence—silence in the name of peace.

In what follows, I critique contextual and inclusionary peace theology approaches for their failure to attend to various forms of privilege, violence, and oppression *within* Mennonite communities and institutions. I contend that what is needed for Mennonite theology today is not a new and better peace theology that includes marginalized voices but critical-contextual and trauma-informed methodologies, imperative to which is a recognition that forms of violence are intertwined and compound one another. In this chapter, critical contextualization involves a deep understanding of social relations of power and how various forms of oppressions interlock and compound one another. Additionally, a trauma-informed approach privileges the experiences of those who are suffering within because of unjust social relations of power. With a critical-contextual and trauma-informed orientation toward violence, the task of theology is no longer to provide the church with an increasingly inclusive peace theology that simply widens around a stable center. I recommend that Mennonite peace theology must rather adopt a posture of continuous self-reflexivity, critical contextualization, harm reduction, and trauma healing amid ongoing violence. I suggest some elements of this methodology at the end of my chapter.

Mennonite Theological Violence

The Limits of Contextualization and Inclusion

Mennonite theology and discipleship have often been characterized by a desire for purity—an idealized ecclesiology that Menno Simons referred to as a church without spot or wrinkle, quoting Eph 5:27. This desire has played itself out in a number of ways in Mennonite theologies, which have benefited a particular demographic—namely, white, middle-upper class, cisgender, heterosexual, able-bodied, neurotypical men—while harming others who do not fit this norm. I suggest that the crux of this problem is not one theological debate or another but a common methodological approach in Anabaptist and Mennonite theologies.

Mennonite theology generally conceives of itself as historically situated and geographically contextualized. Theologies are in turn understood and evaluated against the backdrop of these diverse contexts. The contextual approaches of Mennonite theologies are often characterized as, and sometimes romanticized as, a source for liberating (i.e., nonviolent or peace) theologies, radical ethics, and discipleship. However, a contextual methodology can still assert oppressive regimes of truth. Indeed, the privileging of certain contexts, perspectives, and experiences for Mennonite theology has not and does not account, for example, for unjust Mennonite relations with Indigenous Peoples in Canada and the United States, other people of color, LGBTQ people, and women, to name a few. Critical social theorist Sherene Razack writes that "interlocking systems need one another, and in tracing the complex ways in which they secure one another, we learn how women are produced into positions that exist symbolically but hierarchically."[2] Following Razack's notion of interlocking oppression and the use of trauma theory in theology, I contend that Mennonite theology, though it is often contextual and has avoided some harmful methodological approaches because of that, has failed to situate its peace theology in the context of multiple and interlocking oppressions. Thus, a trauma-informed, critical-contextual methodology is needed. Peace theology that takes these approaches as its starting points destabilizes a supposedly inclusive expanding center. It recognizes instead that forms of violence are intertwined and compound each other, necessitating the pursuit of a peace theology marked by critical analysis of social relations of power, harm reduction, and trauma healing amid ongoing violence.

---

[2]Sherene Razack, *Looking White People in the Eye: Gender, Race, and Culture in Courtrooms and Classrooms* (Toronto: University of Toronto Press, 1998), 13.

The Bender-Yoder Trajectory

The definition of violence and nonviolence (or peace) of Mennonites in Canada and the United States has been dominated by the refusal to take up arms—a specific form of violence rooted in the refusal of the sixteenth-century Schleitheim Anabaptists to take up the sword.[3] Harold Bender's influential treatise *The Anabaptist Vision*, published during the Second World War, reiterated the primary definition of violence in terms of war, weapons, and bloodshed.[4] Calling Mennonites back to what he perceived as the essence of Anabaptism and the early church (read "authentic church"), his emphasis on love and nonresistance as the refusal of war contributed immensely to the ongoing script of peace and violence among Mennonites, including many Mennonites today. Later, with John Howard Yoder's publication of *The Politics of Jesus* in 1972, this narrow pacifist script was further solidified.[5] Although Yoder's work includes minimal analyses of power structures, because these were framed as the world over against the church, these analyses are never applied to Mennonite churches, colleges, or communities. As we now know, Yoder's own conduct fit his theology: his definitions of peace and violence and the work of the church conveniently never come into conflict with the sexual abuse he perpetrated on more than 100 women.[6]

Both Bender's and Yoder's theologies are historically rooted and deeply contextual, in the sense that they draw on and take Mennonite history seriously as well as respond to some of the ecclesial and political struggles of their time. However, both Bender and Yoder are also writing from a deeply patriarchal and white settler context, in which they hold the most social, economic, and even ecclesial power. Because of this, it is no surprise to the people of color, queer folks, and women who have critiqued them that Bender, Yoder, and the dominant Mennonite

---

[3] "The Schleitheim Confession of Faith (1527)," in *The Protestant Reformation*, edited by Hans Hillerbrand (London: Macmillan, 1968), 129–36.
[4] See https://www.goshen.edu/mhl/Refocusing/d-av.htm.
[5] John Howard Yoder, *The Politics of Jesus* (Grand Rapids: Eerdmans, 1972).
[6] See Rachel Waltner Goossen, "'Defanging the Beast': Mennonite Responses to John Howard Yoder's Sexual Abuse," *Mennonite Quarterly Review* 89 (2015): 7–80, and other articles in the same volume.

peace theology has failed to attend to the violence of racism, anti-blackness, Indigenous genocide and assimilation, homophobia, anti-queerness, sexism, and misogyny. For example, critics of Yoder and other Mennonite church leaders and theologians who have perpetrated sexual violence have never seen this as a problem of someone's theology conflicting with their personal behavior but see it rather as a problem rooted in their theology itself. Inattentive to their white-heteropatriarchal-cisgender social location, Mennonites continue to promote a peace theology in which certain forms of violence are overtly neglected. The result of this is that the trauma experienced by those most affected is compounded through the refusal of individual churches and national bodies to attend to the aforementioned forms of violence and likely many more that have gone unnamed.

Other Voices

Despite the dominant soteriological script of Mennonite peace theology, many unacknowledged theologians, community activists, and church leaders have spoken out about their experiences of violence and harm in their Mennonite churches, colleges, and communities, deconstructing the aforementioned structure and model for Mennonite peace theology and discipleship and imagining more liberating ways of relating across difference. Women like Ruth Krall, Lydia Harder, Gayle Gerber Koontz, Carol Penner, Stephanie Krehbiel, Jennifer Yoder, Hilary Scarscella, and Kim Penner (to name only a few of hundreds) have put countless hours in churches and classrooms working with Mennonites to identify and deconstruct sexual and gender violence both systemically and interpersonally. Black theologians Nekeisha Alexis, Malinda Berry, and Drew Hart and Latina/o/x theologians Felipe Hinojosa, Nancy Bedford, and Juan Martinez have worked on addressing various forms of racism in Canada and the United States. Indigenous Mennonites Lawrence Hart, Iris de León-Hartshorn, Harley Eagle, and Erica Littlewolf continuously remind Mennonites of the violent history of the land they walk on and the need for truth-telling for peace and justice. To be sure, Mennonites have also learned much from non-Mennonite and non-Christian community members, leaders, and teachers.

Unsettling Mennonite Theology

Interlocking Forms of Violence

The people I have named and their many unnamed teachers, mentors, and accomplices have been absolutely vital for reducing harm in Mennonite communities, supporting victim-survivors of sexual, racial, and gender violence, and working to transform unjust social relations of power. However, both institutionally and academically, work against sexual, racial, and gender violence tends to be siloed. At best, this allows people affected by specific forms of violence in specific contexts to work together and support one another. At worst, it turns traumatic experiences of individuals into "hot button issues" for church administrators and theologians to debate ad nauseum at the expense of victim-survivors, as "due process" takes the place of deep social, ecclesial, and theological transformation (as Harder and Krehbiel have demonstrated in their own work and experiences). I want to suggest that what is missing from the current analysis of peace and violence among Mennonites in Canada and the United States is attention to the ways sexual, racial, and gender violence compound one another and how each of these forms of violence constitute elements of the broader term "colonial violence," or simply "colonialism." Space does not permit me to trace all the ways sexual, racial, and gender violence have functioned and continue to operate as interlocking oppressions in the maintenance of a settler-colonial state. Considering the hyper-sexualization of women of color, the number of missing and murdered Indigenous women and girls, and the rising attacks on black trans women, my claim shouldn't be a stretch of the imagination. I want to talk instead about what might constitute a methodology that attends to the interlocking nature of violence and how trauma theory can help us move toward more liberating and healing theologies, churches, schools, and other communities.

As I already suggested, an interlocking methodology is needed to disrupt the impasse that individual churches, national bodies, and schools face as they attempt to address sexual, racial, and gender violence in their constituent communities. This is an unsettling methodology even for progressive Mennonites who are used to approaching difference by widening the circle of inclusion.

The problem with an inclusionary approach, however, is that it simply widens the boundaries of a stable center that continues to be maintained. In an inclusion model, debates about inclusion and exclusion will go on the same way with minor changes in process; in other words, the center that makes it possible to include and exclude in the first place continues to govern the whole. The critical-contextual and trauma-informed methodological approaches that I propose here aim to address different forms of violence and unjust social relations of power by looking at how they are intertwined and compound each other. As a result, it also questions the relationship between a center and a periphery. Adding approaches from trauma theory, a critical-contextual methodology is less concerned with a current center or tradition than it is with the experiences of victim-survivors of settler colonialism and patriarchy—of sexual, racial, and gender violence. Instead of asking the traditional theological questions, "As Mennonites, as followers of Christ, how do we understand peace and violence? And what is our role with regard to these?" a decolonizing methodology begins by asking, "Who is suffering? Who is experiencing violence and trauma? And why? How is power distributed? What is at stake and for whom?" The starting point is not tradition or Scripture but the experience (personal, interpersonal, and structural) of those most affected and harmed by the traditional starting points, practices, and theologies. Critical contextualization can be practiced by developing not another peace theology that tries to take all forms of violence into account (replicating the desire for purity) but one that addresses unjust social relations of power on personal, interpersonal, and structural levels (which are also interlocking) and takes on the practices of harm reduction, informed by trauma theory—a trauma-informed theology.

Trauma-Informed Theology

Sexual violence, racial violence, gender violence—more often than not, these are deeply traumatic experiences. Trauma and violence are not the same thing. Violence is the nonconsensual crossing of a relational boundary, which can occur at interpersonal and structural levels. Violence names the cause of harm. Trauma is what remains in the aftermath of violation, when a person cannot cope with or make sense of the violation. In her book *Spirit and Trauma*, theologian Shelly Rambo describes trauma as elusive and enigmatic. Digressing from notions of trauma as an event, she reconceptualizes the structure of trauma as spectral, characterized not by a moment of violence in the past but by the continuous invasion of fragments of the past into the present. She argues that "the central problem of trauma is a temporal one . . . . The trauma is not located in the past but instead is located in the gap between the occurrence of the traumatic event and a subsequent awakening to it . . . . Death returns in an unrecognizable and ungrasped form; life then becomes a perplexing encounter and continual engagement with death."[7] What remains in the aftermath of trauma, then, is a different constitution of life, in which death is irreducible to life yet indissociable from it. What remains in the aftermath of trauma is survival, or what Christian ethicist Traci West has called victim-survivors.[8] Rambo draws on the notions of witness and testimony. Taking her cue from Holocaust survivors Dori Lau and Elie Wiesel, Rambo emphasizes witness and testimony as crucial in the prevention of further violence.[9] In her theology, "'Witness' is an accompanying term to 'remaining'; it describes a way of being oriented to what remains, to the suffering that does not go away."[10] Furthermore, "'witness' becomes a term describing the complex relationship we have to persons and events, given the realities of the suffering that remains."[11] Thus, to witness is not merely to observe or to offer observational insights into what took place in an event (the juridical use of the term); rather, a witness is, "first, a person positioned in respect to suffering in such a way that she can see truths that often escape articulation, that emerge through the cracks in the dominant logic. Second, this tenuous placement also means that the witness is subject to the continual elisions that make it impossible to see, hear, or touch clearly. In order to witness, one must enter into the elisions

---

[7]Shelly Rambo, *Spirit and Trauma: A Theology of Remaining* (Louisville: Westminster John Knox, 2010), 19–20.
[8]Traci C. West, *Wounds of the Spirit: Black Women, Violence, and Resistance Ethics* (New York: NYU Press, 1999).
[9]Rambo, *Spirit and Trauma*, 17.
[10]Ibid., 24.
[11]Ibid., 26.

at the heart of suffering."[12] Rambo develops a similar notion of testimony as a mode of speaking as a witness.[13]

Rambo's work offers a framework that enables theology to proceed from a place of being trauma informed. Drawing on trauma theory, Rambo emphasizes the need to "think in terms of the traces of the events, the marks they leave in their wake. The challenge in addressing trauma is to continually resist the temptation to cover over—to elide—the suffering in an effort to witness to it. The challenge is to attend to the ways in which violence continues to mark persons and communities long after the violent event. The work of resisting and attending is the work of the Spirit."[14] Key to this trauma-informed theology is the recognition of experiences of victim-survivors as a primary sites of knowledge about systems of violence, harm reduction, and social, ecclesial, and theological change.

Conclusion

Returning to the display of conscientious objectors at the Mennonite college I started this chapter with, I think about the maintenance of this specific narrative of peace and nonviolence and wonder how my own work intersects with this. I think about the experiences of Mennonite refugee women settling in Canada during the twentieth century, whose experiences of sexual violence, rape, and ostracization by their communities was silenced and condemned. I think about the experiences of Indigenous children in Indian Residential Schools (three of which were operated by Mennonites) and the families from which they were taken. I think of the sexual violence within our churches and universities, continuously covered up by administrators, community members, and church leaders—people in positions of power and socio-ecclesial authority. I think about the violence perpetrated daily against people of color, especially Indigenous, Black, and Latina/o/x people. I think about the violence against women, girls, transgender people, and those

---

[12]Ibid., 28.
[13]Ibid., 164–72.
[14]Ibid., 13.

who identify as lesbian, gay, bisexual, or other non-normative sexualities. Mennonite theological methodology in its current forms does not have the capacity to attend to the interlocking and traumatic nature of these violations. Rambo's framework, along with the aforementioned critical contextualization, can help us to trace the complex and multifaceted dynamics and affective dimensions of violence and trauma that our communities endure today.

7

The Ecumenical Vocation of Anabaptist Theology

Jeremy M. Bergen

The Anabaptist tradition ought to be regarded as a reforming movement *within*, and *for the sake of*, the (capital-C) Church identified by the Nicene-Constantinopolitan creed as one, holy, catholic, and apostolic. Several implications follow from this claim. Anabaptism ought to seek not its preservation or advancement per se, nor that of particular denominations, but Christ and the faithfulness of Christ's church, a body in perpetual need of reform and renewal.

Anything that might characterize Anabaptism as distinctive (a term I will problematize in this chapter) ought to be distinctive specifically in relation to other Christians and be oriented toward the unity and integrity of the church. This means that for a Mennonite like myself, who identifies with the Anabaptist tradition (and I will discuss the tensions with Mennonite and Anabaptist identities as well), I ought to regard myself simply as Christian in relation to the wider world. My Anabaptist identity has integrity only to the extent that I am engaged in genuine dialogue with other Christians about Christian faithfulness and mission. As Christians, our mission is to the world; as Anabaptists, our mission is in relation to other Christians.

Within this framework, the mandate of Anabaptist theology is to enable those who are affiliated to hold and engage this tradition both deeply and lightly: deeply because movements of reform and renewal are profoundly concerned with the faithfulness of the whole church and with giving and receiving necessary correction within the body; lightly because Anabaptist identity is not a basic or ultimate identity, like Christian identity, but a secondary and provisional one oriented to a larger purpose.

I first develop the connections between reform, unity, and particular traditions such as Anabaptism. Second, I position Anabaptism within a practical-prophetic mandate. Third, I contend that any so-called distinctives of an ecclesial tradition such as Anabaptism must be gifts for the whole church, not claims for one group. Fourth, I draw a connection between the reforming function of contemporary Anabaptist discourse and actual churches, such as Mennonite churches. Finally, I argue that under the conditions of division, a vocation of reform requires discerning the work of the Spirit in the Anabaptist movement. Since I identify with the tradition to which I address my argument, I use "we" to refer to contemporary members of the Anabaptist movement.

Ecclesial Traditions and Reform in Service of Unity

The unity of the church is both a gift and a calling.[1] The church at Ephesus was called to "make every effort to maintain the unity of the Spirit in the bond of peace" (Eph 4:3) precisely because these bonds could be broken. At the same time, Paul affirmed that *there is* one body, one Spirit, one Lord, one faith, one baptism (Eph 4:4-6). Without the divine giftedness of unity, there would be no orientation, basis, or even motivation to seek unity, to pray for it, and to celebrate it once received.[2] In recent decades, ecumenical

---

[1] This phrasing was given prominence at the seventh assembly of the World Council of Churches (WCC) in Canberra, especially "The Unity of the Church—Gift and Calling: The Canberra Statement" (1991). Unless full bibliographic information is given, WCC documents are available at www.oikoumene.org.

[2] Here I echo the Joint Working Group of the World Council of Churches and the Roman Catholic Church, "The Nature and Purpose of Ecumenical Dialogue" (2004), no. 32, in *Growth in Agreement III*, edited by Jeffrey Gros, Thomas F. Best, and Lorelei F. Fuchs (Grand Rapids: Eerdmans, 2007), 593.

texts have articulated how the nature and mission of the church, including its unity, are grounded in God's mission. One succinct articulation is in the Canberra Statement: "The purpose of God according to Holy Scripture is to gather the whole of creation under the Lordship of Jesus Christ in whom, by the power of the Holy Spirit, all are brought into communion with God (Eph 1). The church is the foretaste of this communion with God and with one another."[3] The reconciliation and fellowship that characterize the church's true unity are at the same time the church's mission.

While unity does not mean uniformity, it does mean a visible unity in contrast to the present state of affairs and to partial expression of unity.[4] In the words of a recent conciliar statement, visible unity entails "communion in the fullness of apostolic faith; in sacramental life; in a truly one and mutually recognized ministry; in structures of conciliar relations and decision-making; and in common witness and service in the world."[5] That all Christians cannot presently commune around the Lord's Table is but one sign of the lack of visible unity. Recognizing that unity is not merely the heroic mandate of humans, the Holy Spirit is nevertheless discerned in the movement from enmity and separation to reconciliation and unity.

I do not presume to specify the form or concept of unity to which the Anabaptist tradition might contribute (and in light of which it may be rendered superfluous); concepts of unity are themselves important matters of ecumenical debate. One concept, organic unity, emphasizes agreement in matters of doctrine and unified ecclesiastical structures, perhaps through mergers. It highlights the unity of all

---

[3]"Canberra Statement," no. 1.1. See also "Called To Be the One Church: The Porto Alegre Statement," adopted by the ninth assembly of the World Council of Churches (1996), no. 10; and World Council of Churches, *The Church: Towards a Common Vision* (2013), nos. 1–10.
[4]One bilateral dialogue helpfully outlined four models of "partial unity," which are inadequate but may play transitional roles: (1) spiritual unity in which ecclesial structures are irrelevant; (2) fellowship-in-dialogue in which the process of dialogue is taken as the goal; (3) fellowship-in-action such as common service; and (4) intercommunion, or Eucharistic hospitality between otherwise visibly divided churches. Lutheran-Roman Catholic Dialogue, "Facing Unity," (1984), nos. 9–12, in *Growth in Agreement II*, edited by Jeffrey Gros, Harding Meyer, and William G. Rusch (Grand Rapids: Eerdmans, 2000), 446.
[5]World Council of Churches, *The Church: Towards a Common Vision*, no. 37.

in each place—that is, beginning with the local. Another concept, unity in reconciled diversity, highlights the valuable contributions made by the diversity of Christian expression. The identities of various traditions need not be erased as existing churches reconcile and act together in profoundly new ways. A third concept, conciliar fellowship, resonates with organic unity but places emphasis on the global character of the relationships.[6] These models of unity are best understood as means not ends and are therefore not mutually exclusive. Rather, they help Christians to define and focus on the call to unity (and holiness, catholicity, apostolicity) and recognize the Spirit's work for unity, on the way to a goal that cannot yet be described in all its contours. Communion/*koinonia*/fellowship, which has emerged as perhaps the key ecumenical concept, is not a distinct model for unity but refers to the quality of relationships that must characterize any unity.[7]

Despite the foregoing discussion, it is not necessary that much Anabaptist theology be invested in technical ecumenical debates. The key is rather an orienting posture about the nature and calling of the Anabaptist tradition in light of a unity that must be discerned together with other Christians and the vocation of theology that emerges in all its multiplicity from within that tradition.

I advance the thesis that the Anabaptist tradition be regarded as a tradition of reform as a normative claim because it is not necessarily true descriptively.[8] A historical assessment of whether the earliest Anabaptist leaders understood themselves to be acting for the reform of the entire church or to be visibly separating the true church from false churches is beyond what I can do here.[9] The defining action of the early Anabaptists, adult baptism, clearly had the effect of

---

[6] My description follows Lukas Vischer, Ulrich Luz, and Christian Link, *Unity of the Church in the New Testament and Today* (Grand Rapids: Eerdmans, 2010), 18–27. See also Lorelei F. Fuchs, *Koinonia and the Quest for Ecumenical Ecclesiology* (Grand Rapids: Eerdmans, 2008), 49–69, especially her extensive bibliography.

[7] Fuchs, *Koinonia and the Quest for Ecumenical Ecclesiology*, is the definitive work on the ecumenical development and deployment of the concept of *koinonia*.

[8] For example, the word "reform" is not used in the *Confession of a Faith in a Mennonite Perspective* (Scottdale, PA: Herald, 1995), a document of Mennonite Church Canada and Mennonite Church USA.

[9] By 1560, it is clear that they are part of neither Protestant nor Catholic churches. See C. Arnold Snyder, *Following in the Footsteps of Christ: The Anabaptist Tradition* (Maryknoll, NY: Orbis, 2004), 28.

separating them out as subject to capital punishment apart from whatever intention they have may had. The Anabaptist call for the restitution or restoration of the primitive church typically assumes a fall of the church and thus much greater discontinuity between Anabaptist congregations and other Christians than reform would imply.[10] Even if my argument is not supported by early Anabaptist sources, I submit it as a correction to the tradition.

In contrast to sectarianism, the idea of Anabaptism has recently functioned as a basis for a more complacent denominationalism. Harold Bender's massively influential "Anabaptist Vision"[11] served, in part, to claim the Anabaptist movement as the foundation for contemporary Mennonite denominations and related institutions. Mennonites could take their place alongside others within American religion, confident that their Anabaptist tradition contributed to that landscape itself, especially freedom of conscience and separation of church and state.

In his programmatic vision, Bender also had a reforming agenda, but it was primarily an intra-Mennonite one. The recovery of an Anabaptist identity served, in part, to transcend the fundamentalist-modernist debate that was ripping apart Mennonite churches and institutions. It was a reform of identity with a particular agenda of internal unity.[12]

Dennis Martin criticizes the restitutionist motif in Anabaptism, arguing that

> the revolt against tradition and the advocacy of restitutionism as it was known in the sixteenth century presumed a sequential, one-dimensional, linear view of history and thus opened the way for the modern view of progress in history, a view in which progress is made by recovering the true Jesus or the true church. That was the only way the sixteenth-century reformers could

---

[10]For example, Palmer Becker explicitly contrasts reformation with restoration and identifies the Anabaptists with the latter. Palmer Becker, *What Is an Anabaptist Christian?* rev. ed. (Elkhart, IN: Mennonite Mission Network, 2010), 10–11.

[11]Originally published as Harold S. Bender, "The Anabaptist Vision," *Church History* 13 (March 1944): 3–24.

[12]Bender also sought to correct those Reformation historians who understood Anabaptism primarily through the lens of the apocalyptic, revolutionary, and theocratic Kingdom of Münster, 1534–35.

come to terms with their conviction that the church had spent centuries buried in the "dark ages," during which God seemed so absent from most of his church.[13]

The restitutionist hope of reestablishing the true church is deeply intertwined with the modern fantasy of the clean slate.

A hermeneutics of reform is profoundly different, argues Martin, as it is characterized by a basic assumption of continuity rather than discontinuity. "Reform rejects not by categories or blocks but examines each institution and each period of history for its own sake."[14] It therefore "accepts the past all the way down to the present while at the same time calling for reform of institutions where they have become deformed."[15] Reform "reads history in the reverse direction from the modern reading: backward toward the incarnation"[16] and "understands perfection in its pre-modern sense . . . as maturity, completion, fullness, rather than absolute, utopian perfection, which is the modern definition."[17]

However, Martin also argues that we can position the restitutionist motif within a framework of reform:

> Although radical outside challenges are undoubtedly part of God's providential guidance toward reform, seen from the reform perspective, they must not be reified and given permanent validity. If indeed their role was to push the mainstream to reform, then the adherents of the restitutionist groups must also recognize the limits of their role, recognize that they are instruments rather than ends themselves.[18]

Acknowledging such instrumentality ought to lead to repentance for aspects of past practice and to an embrace of contemporary reformist agenda.

---

[13]Dennis D. Martin, "Nothing New under the Sun? Mennonites and History," *Conrad Grebel Review* 5, no. 1 (Winter 1987): 6.
[14]Ibid., 19.
[15]Ibid., 11.
[16]Ibid.
[17]Ibid., 14.
[18]Ibid., 22.

Indeed, in international dialogues with Catholics and with Lutherans, Mennonites have recast sixteenth-century Anabaptism within a more reformist interpretation of history. The final reports of both dialogues include sections on "Considering History Together," which are oriented by a desire to heal memories of a painful past and observe that the process of reading this history together calls for further repentance and reconciliation. The overall reforming framework is especially pronounced in the Mennonite-Lutheran dialogue, which also acknowledges that separation from the emerging Lutheran movement was not so much an intentional split as an "evolving process of group formation within the complex, sometimes confusing, dynamics of religious convictions, political self-interest, and a basic struggle for survival."[19]

The interweaving commitments to read history together, heal memories, and share gifts are found in bilateral ecumenical dialogues of other traditions as well. For example, a new and shared reading of history has enabled Catholics to appreciate that Luther's "intention was to reform, not to divide, the church."[20] Thus, Luther may be understood as an abiding witness to the gospel whose words remain relevant for all Christians, not just those in churches that bear his name. A hermeneutics of reform may be a way of reframing a history often remembered with polemic and resentment as a story in which one also recognizes how another tradition pursues faithfulness and asks what might be learned and received from that perspective.

Reform is best understood and assessed in light of Tradition. Mennonite historian and theologian Walter Sawatsky recommends a definition of (capital-T) Tradition as "the activity of the Holy Spirit in the ongoing life of the Church."[21] Significant in this understanding is its trinitarian and ecclesial character, as well as its formulation in line with an emerging ecumenical discourse about tradition. One key World Council of Churches (WCC) document

---

[19]Ibid., 23.
[20]*From Conflict to Communion: Lutheran–Catholic Common Commemoration of the Reformation in 2017*, Report of the Lutheran-Roman Catholic Commission on Unity (Leipzig: Evangelische Verlagsanstalt; Paderborn: Bonifatius, 2013), no. 28.
[21]Walter Sawatsky, "Teaching Christian History in Seminary: A Declension Story," *Conrad Grebel Review* 30, no. 3 (Fall 2012): 271. He draws this definition from Orthodox sources.

called for continual discernment of whether and how particular traditions—one of which may be the Anabaptist tradition—reflect and embody the Tradition, which may be understood as the gospel itself. A WCC study from the 1990s notes, "The Holy Spirit inspires and leads the churches each to rethink and reinterpret their [particular] tradition[s] in conversation with each other, always aiming to embody the one Tradition in the unity of God's Church."[22] On the way toward such embodiment, vigorous theological debate about the gifts each tradition might offer and might receive, as well as whether and which reforms might be needed for the gifts to be shared, will be necessary.

These views of Tradition and traditions recognize the role of the Spirit not only in sustaining the church as it exists in its historically concrete particularity but also within a multiplicity and diversity that might well be deeply consonant with the church's unity. Therefore, a task of Anabaptist theology, in conversation with other Christian traditions, is to continually discern the relationship of the Anabaptist tradition to the Tradition—that is, "the activity of the Holy Spirit in the ongoing life of the Church." On one hand, theology's task is a receptive one—to perceive the Spirit in the life of the church, including the unity whose author is that Spirit. On the other hand, the form such theological reception may take will be, at times, creative, provocative, conflictual, exploratory, open-ended, interpretive, retrieving, conserving, and doxological (without intending any of these to be binaries). Regardless of which constituencies might be addressed, Anabaptist theology ought to occupy itself with the critical and constructive relation of the Anabaptist tradition with the Tradition.

Ecclesiological Discourse as Practical-Prophetic Intervention

Nicholas M. Healy claims that the purpose of ecclesiology as a discourse is to "help the church respond as best it can to its context

---

[22]World Council of Churches, *A Treasure in Earthen Vessels: An Instrument for an Ecumenical Reflection on Hermeneutics*, Faith and Order Paper 182 (Geneva: WCC, 1998), no. 32.

by reflecting theologically and critically on its concrete identity."[23] In that respect, ecclesiology is practical-prophetic discourse. Underlying this is a distinction between the believed, or "ideal," church and the experienced church.[24] When Christians say the church is "the community of disciples," the "Bride of Christ," or "the People of God," they are expressing a belief rather than a plain description of the church around the corner. Healy's insight is articulating how it is that the ideal accounts of church, or "blueprints," function in relation to the actual, concrete church in history, the faithfulness of which is ecclesiology's true intention. Ideal images of the church imply some diagnosis of the condition of the experienced church; some aspect of context, temptation, or failure; and thus also a prophetic proposal for reform and renewal where this is needed.

This is already evident in the New Testament writings, which contain dozens of images of the church. The church as People of God highlights continuity with Israel at a time when the newness of the Jesus movement might have obliterated this link. The church as Bride of Christ emphasizes loyalty and exclusivity to a community tempted otherwise. The church as Body of Christ also emphasizes the importance of the contributions of the diverse parts within the whole in contrast to a tendency to privilege one part. Buried within all of these images is an account of the experienced church and, in response, a contextually prophetic word.

The concept of Anabaptism works in an analogous way with such images of the church. It implies a diagnosis of a temptation or threat to the faithfulness of the church, as well as a correction. To invoke Anabaptism thus calls for response, for correction and renewal. But we also ought to be critical of its use as well and ensure that it is provisional, contextual, and malleable. Bender's "Anabaptist Vision" is best understood as a tactical intervention in mid-twentieth-century Mennonitism. Likewise, Stuart Murray's *Naked Anabaptist* is primarily addressed to particular Christians who are thinking about their mission and identities in contemporary post-

---

[23]Nicholas M. Healy, *Church, World, and the Christian Life: Practical-Prophetic Ecclesiology* (Cambridge: Cambridge University Press, 2000), 10.
[24]See also Fernando Enns, *The Peace Church and the Ecumenical Community: Ecclesiology and the Ethics of Nonviolence*, translated by Helmut Harder (Kitchener, ON: Pandora, 2007), 1–3.

Christendom Europe.[25] Neither are timeless statements of essence, nor are they comprehensive foundations for ecclesial identities.

So what might be the content of the reforms that Anabaptism seeks to embody and to which it calls other Christians? The answers given to this question have varied over time and space: believer's baptism; the priority of Scripture; the interpretation of Scripture by the local congregation; rejection of sword and oath; separation of church and state; church as community of disciples; nonconformity and simplicity; an ethics of the Sermon on the Mount; economic sharing; nonresistance, nonviolence, or peacemaking. All of these and more are realized, and idealized, within the multiplicities of Anabaptist theology. The Catholic-Mennonite dialogue emphasized the potential for collaboration and cooperation in witnessing for peace.[26] For the Lutheran-Mennonite dialogue, which took the condemnations of the Anabaptists in the Augsburg Confession as a point of departure, outstanding points of difference were identified as baptism and relation of Christians and civil authority.[27] On these points of difference, we may have something to offer but also much to learn; Anabaptist theology must seek to do both. Having identified a range of possibly distinctive features (none of which are really distinctive), I develop an essential qualification.

Distinctives as Gifts, Not Claims

To engage Anabaptism as a tradition of reform in relation to the church catholic calls on theologians to tread lightly around the question of "distinctives," let alone "essences." The dangers in the quest for "distinctives" are several. First of all, there is a documented tendency under the conditions of church division to identify difference with essence. Already in the sixteenth century,

---

[25]See Stuart Murray, *The Naked Anabaptist: The Bare Essentials of a Radical Faith* (Scottdale, PA: Herald, 2010).
[26]Roman Catholic-Mennonite International Dialogue, "Called Together to be Peacemakers" (2003), in *Mennonites in Dialogue*, edited by Fernando Enns and Jonathan R. Seiling (Eugene, OR: Pickwick, 2015), 19–114.
[27]Lutheran World Federation and Mennonite World Conference, "Healing of Memories, Reconciling in Christ" (2010), in Enns and Seiling, *Mennonites in Dialogue*, 187–307.

the puzzling existence of more than one church gave rise to the question of which was the true church that led to salvation. As each gave account of its existence, those things that might be marginal to identity but were unique, such as office of the papacy, became the wedge upon which a claim to be the true church could be based.[28] One would not appeal to Jesus Christ because a claim about him does not, on the surface, help distinguish true from false churches.

Ecumenist Lukas Vischer argues that identifying permanent characteristics of a confessional tradition is

> sectarian because, as a rule, they are self-congratulatory and tend the minimize the darker sides of the . . . tradition; even more dangerously, they enclose the churches in preconceived perspectives and force them to be what they are supposed to be. Therefore, the search for identity as it is pursued today in many churches is utterly uninteresting and even counterproductive. It almost inevitably leads to spiritual impoverishment and to the continuation of existing division. At the same time it closes minds to new spiritual contributions.[29]

Gerald Schlabach articulates this temptation more specifically in relation to traditions of protest and reform. However valid the correctives may be, once a tradition "elevate[s] impulses of 'protest' into identity markers for entire Christian communities, those impulses tend to undermine the very bonds of Christian community" because the principles supersede accountabilities to particular communities and thus the stability required to embody and sustain the reforming impulse is undermined.[30]

More recently, Mennonite theologian Alex Sider has charged that the language of Mennonite distinctives characterizes a "brand

---

[28]R. R. Reno, "The Debilitation of the Churches," in *The Ecumenical Future: Background Papers for "In One Body through the Cross: The Princeton Proposal for Christian Unity,"* edited by Carl E. Braaten and Robert W. Jenson (Grand Rapids: Eerdmans, 2004), 46–72.

[29]Lukas Vischer, "The Reformation Heritage and the Ecumenical Movement," in *Towards a Renewed Dialogue: The First and Second Reformations*, edited by Milan Opočenský (Geneva: World Alliance of Reformed Churches, 1996), 163.

[30]Gerald Schlabach, *Unlearning Protestantism: Sustaining Christian Community in an Unstable Age* (Grand Rapids: Brazos, 2010), 33.

of white heteropatriarchal Mennonite theology and ethics," which marginalizes those who are made to "prove their bona fides vis-à-vis the normative vision" and fosters a superiority complex for those at its center.[31]

However, to hold what we might think of as distinctives as gifts is to offer them and to give them away. To see the Anabaptist tradition as one of reform is to be reminded that where we differ in belief or practice from other Christians, especially on matters that appear to be "church dividing," we hold such convictions, however deeply, not as possessions. If we are referring, for example, to our convictions around the relationship between the church and civic authorities—an issue identified in the Lutheran-Mennonite dialogue as a real difference—we must be prepared to articulate and contend for our position in a way that might result in successful persuasion. We must, in other words, be prepared to engage so deeply in the unique contours of our traditions that we are prepared to lose the justification for remaining divided. At the same time, holding our convictions in humility as we engage with other Christians in the attempt to speak truly about God, we must be open to being challenged, corrected, and called to renewal. We will almost certainly find that we have stereotyped views of others and have not truly and charitably heard the accounts that other Christian traditions give of their faithfulness to the gospel. We will see how our idealized accounts of ourselves have created harmful blind spots.[32] We will have more to receive than to give. Nor should we think of giving and receiving as either/or. Part of the task is discerning catholicity as expressed in "right diversity"; seemingly incompatible positions may in fact be held together within new theological frameworks, sustained by practices of charity and communion. None of this will be easy by any means, in part because we remain divided often not due to principled differences of doctrine or ethics but because we have developed ecclesial and theological cultures that are characterized by soft triumphalism.

A consideration of how several Mennonite theologians have developed Mennonite, or Anabaptist, theology in the context of and

---

[31] J. Alexander Sider, "Self and/as Victim: A Reflection on 'Mennonite' Ethics," *Conrad Grebel Review* 34, no. 3 (Fall 2016): 27.
[32] See the chapter by Melanie Kampen in this volume.

in dialogue with the broader Christian tradition reveals dangers as well as opportunities. Central to A. James Reimer's program was the development of what he called "dogmatic foundations" for Mennonite theology, rooted in the classical theological tradition and trinitarian orthodoxy. In his chapter "Mennonites and the Church Universal," Reimer proposes a catholicity that consists of the gifts of the Spirit given to a range of local churches, denominations, and church traditions. The diverse gifts that Paul understands to be given to a congregation may be applied to the relationship of particular Christian traditions within the universal church. Each has a gift to offer the whole. Thus, Roman Catholicism may offer apostolic succession and sacraments, Lutheranism the emphasis on justification by grace through faith, Anglicanism worship and liturgy, Mennonites discipleship and peace witness.[33] While his laudable goal is "diversity without relativism and unity without dogmatism,"[34] there is a substantial problem.

Reimer draws an analogy between various Christian confessional traditions and individual persons within a congregation—each gifted by the Spirit. This means that the catholicity with the church is imagined to exist at the universal level but not at more local levels. So, even though Roman Catholicism may be guardians of sacraments for the sake of the whole, since Mennonites and Lutherans cannot partake of a Roman Catholic Eucharist nowhere would actual sacramental practice instantiate the catholicity of this vision. A catholicity without location is not a mark of the church as a concrete body. It is an abstract catholicity and, despite Reimer's intentions, an invisible church. Thus, as a unity realized, albeit abstractly, this proposal will neither highlight the failures of the churches in their disunity nor foster lament and repentance and conversion.

Thomas Finger is also interested in an exchange of gifts, and he engaged productively with the Orthodox and as well as the Reformed traditions. The problem with his approach is captured in the title of his article "Appropriating Other Traditions While

---

[33]A. James Reimer, *Mennonites and Classical Theology: Dogmatic Foundations for Christian Ethics* (Kitchener, ON: Pandora, 2001), 549–50.
[34]Reimer, *Mennonites and Classical Theology*, 551.

Remaining Anabaptist."³⁵ Although Finger affirms that theology is always particular—it emerges from one perspective even as it makes universal claims—and ought to be in critical dialogue with other theological traditions and receive from them as appropriate, he is driven by anxiety that Anabaptists remain Anabaptists. I counter that this ought not to be a foundational concern. Finger gives a broader and more inclusive answer to how much we can appropriate while remaining who we are than does J. Denny Weaver,³⁶ but both share a concern about contamination and therefore loss of Anabaptist identity.

Even more influential than Reimer and Finger is John Howard Yoder, whose participation in a variety of scholarly and ecumenical settings, vigorous and critical engagement with important ecumenical texts and theologians from other traditions, and influential writings on peace theology, ecclesiology, and mission well beyond Mennonite circles, especially *The Politics of Jesus*,³⁷ would appear to make him an ideal representative of what I am advocating. Indeed, it is largely because of his contributions that Anabaptist theologizing has significant intellectual respectability in the theological academy. However, among the many failures that his pattern of sexual predation of women has revealed are the deeply problematic blind spots in this theology, particularly around power and openness to receiving correction.³⁸ Moreover, the virtual identification of his theology with Anabaptist theology—a volume on the engagement with Anabaptism by Catholic and Protestant scholars turns out to be, in just about every case, an engagement with the work of Yoder³⁹—has limited the depth and development of the tradition. It has also fostered the view that Anabaptism is

---

³⁵Thomas Finger, "Appropriating Other Traditions While Remaining Anabaptist," *Conrad Grebel Review* 17, no. 2 (Spring 1999): 52–68.

³⁶Weaver argues that the difference between Anabaptist theology and "general" Christian theology ought to go all the way down. See J. Denny Weaver, "The General versus the Particular: Exploring Assumptions in 20th-Century Mennonite Theologizing," *Conrad Grebel Review* 17, no. 2 (Spring 1999): 17–51.

³⁷John Howard Yoder, *The Politics of Jesus*, 2nd ed. (Grand Rapids: Eerdmans, 1994 [1972]).

³⁸See Rachel Walter Goossen, "'Defanging the Beast': Mennonite Responses to John Howard Yoder's Sexual Abuse," *Mennonite Quarterly Review* 89 (2015): 7–80.

³⁹John D. Roth, ed., *Engaging Anabaptism: Conversations with a Radical Tradition* (Scottdale, PA: Herald, 2001).

a position rather than a thick and dynamic tradition of multiple perspectives and approaches with the capacity to contend in wider theological debates for a variety of positions.

More promising is the work of Fernando Enns and Gerald Schlabach. (As I write this, I recognize that they are, like Reimer, Finger, and Yoder, white men. This is a profound problem.) Enns roots his engagement with Anabaptist theology in the concrete ecumenical encounters and exchanges of Mennonite dialogues that begin by taking the fact of church division as a scandal. Furthermore, he tracks in some detail the reciprocal relationship between the Anabaptist-Mennonite peace witness and the broader ecumenical movement. He argues that engagement in the ecumenical movement has allowed Mennonites to broaden our understanding of peace while in turn enabling the ecumenical movement to make peace much more central to its work than would otherwise be the case.[40]

Schlabach gets even more particular in his development of a just policing model that he believes can be a vision toward which both Mennonites and Catholics may genuinely contribute. Regardless of the substantive question about the viability or faithfulness of the just policing model, he makes an important case for how Mennonites can offer their gifts concretely for the reform and renewal of the church and proposes how war need not be a church-dividing matter between Mennonites and Catholics.[41] Mennonites are challenged to recognize and learn from Catholicism's long, deep, and theologically rich tradition of social teaching oriented toward justice and peace. Schlabach's own personal movement toward reception into Roman Catholicism can complicate this picture[42]—such movement between traditions is not what I am advocating. Yet the mission of Anabaptism, rightly understood, is to act on the basis of its own identity but to be so engaged that its separate identity may become unnecessary.

---

[40]See Enns, *The Peace Church and the Ecumenical Community*.
[41]See Gerald Schlabach, "Just Policing: How War Could Cease To Be a Church-Dividing Issue," *Journal of Ecumenical Studies* 41 (2004): 409–30; and Gerald Schlabach, ed., *Just Policing, not War: An Alternative Response to World Violence* (Collegeville, MN: Liturgical Press, 2007).
[42]See Gerald Schlabach, "You Converted to What? One Mennonite's Journey," *Commonweal* (June 1, 2007): 14–17.

Anabaptism and Actual, Concrete Churches, or What Do We Do with Denominations?

As a contemporary point of reference, as opposed to a description of a sixteenth-century movement, Anabaptism has tended to be ideological. The term picks out certain theological and ecclesial emphases believed to be important. It is also allegedly more inclusive, since anyone subscribing to its program can be Anabaptist, as opposed to the more ethnically, culturally, or denominationally defined "Mennonite."[43]

An ideological center may have a useful and critical function, but it does so by extracting any such center from a complex, ambiguous, and embodied tradition. It may also function to shut down diversity, even legitimate diversity, in the quest for an essence. Harold Bender was accused of doing this with reference to his sixteenth-century sources.[44] Walter Sawatsky criticizes Mennonite church leaders for their implicit rejection of the polygenesis thesis and their concomitant devaluing of diversity.[45] Stuart Murray's project in *The Naked Anabaptist* may be read in a way that also forecloses on the diversities, ambiguities, and tensions that might

---

[43]This point is emphasized in Gilberto Flores, "Church as an Instrument of Hope," in *Anabaptist Visions for the New Millennium*, edited by Dale Schrag and James Juhnke (Kitchener, ON: Pandora, 2000), 43–48. The cultural and ethnic dimensions of Mennonite identity are complex. For one account of some issues in Canada, see Royden Loewen, "The Poetics of Peoplehood: Religion and Ethnicity among Canada's Mennonites," in *Christianity and Ethnicity in Canada*, edited by Paul Bramadat and David Seljak (Toronto: University of Toronto Press, 2008), 330–64. The discourse that most directly engages the complex relationships between Mennonite identity, culture and faith, including lack of faith, is that of Mennonite literature and its critics. See Robert Zacharias, ed., *After Identity: Mennonite Writing in North America* (Winnipeg: University of Manitoba Press; University Park, PA: Pennsylvania State University Press, 2015).

[44]Most notably in the landmark article James M. Stayer, Werner O. Packull, and Klaus Deppermann, "From Monogenesis to Polygenesis: The Historical Discussion of Anabaptist Origins," *Mennonite Quarterly Review* 49 (1975): 83–121.

[45]Walter Sawatsky, "20th Century Anabaptist-Mennonites Re-shaped by Context: First, Second, and Third Worlds," in *Prophetic and Renewal Movements: The Prague Consultations*, edited by Walter Sawatsky (Geneva: World Alliance of Reformed Churches: 2009), 178.

emerge from a consideration of twenty fully clothed and embodied Anabaptists rather than of a single naked one.

A tradition of reform must become adept at discerning right diversity—which gifts to give and which to receive—or, in a word, how to embody "catholicity." And this must be done not on a theoretical level but at a concrete, embodied one. The church whose faithfulness is our concern is not an abstract or ideal entity but the actual Body of Christ in history. This brings me, at least, to attend to Mennonite congregations and denominations as well as to those whose relation to "Mennonite" is marked by ambivalence, resentment, or rejection. We know that congregations and denominations often disappoint us. Denominations are consumed with bureaucratic self-preservation, and they multiply disunity through splits. But this is all the more reason to attend to the concrete and resist the temptation to talk only about ideal categories, such as Anabaptism. Indeed, it is often the disillusionment that accompanies the disconnect between the ideal church and the experienced church that leads one group or another to separate and try to get it right this time.

Barry Ensign-George argues that a denomination "provides a form in which new insights into the faith, or new applications of old insights to changing contexts and circumstances, can be tested by being lived out."[46] As "intermediary, contingent, partial, interdependent, and permeable," denominations mediate between the most local and the universal.[47] At their best, they rest on the assumption that there is more than one faithful response to consider and they foster theology and structures of community that might service this insight.

At the same time, the turn to *Mennonite* theology requires attention to the contradictions, failures, and compromises of a people and their institutional life. This requires a style of thinking about reforms not in an abstract way, for an imagined church "out there," but only ever for the actual churches, Mennonite and non-Mennonite, in their concrete particularity.

---

[46] Barry Ensign-George, *Between Congregation and Church: Denomination and Christian Life Together* (London: T&T Clark, 2018), 5–6.
[47] Ibid., 198.

In a recent article on Mennonite relations with Indigenous people in a church magazine, Robert Zacharias describes a conversation he had with friends he grew up with in a small predominantly Mennonite town in southern Manitoba. These friends did not identify with Christian faith and claimed they were no longer Mennonites—and maybe never were. Zacharias writes, "But here's the thing about [their] story: It's not true. Our past is not that easily dismissed. What's more, it is never simply ours to dismiss. After all, these friends of mine, like me, are in Canada precisely because of our Mennonite identities."[48]

These identities cannot be so easily disowned because they have emerged from a history that has both received harm and harmed others. And those identities now make particular demands for justice and reconciliation with Indigenous people, just as they also require that a Mennonite like me wrestle with how our tradition could fall short in so many other ways.

Ethnicity, family, and connection to particular lands are in tension with the story we may tell ourselves as Anabaptists about being a religious movement characterized by believer's baptism. The complex relationship between Anabaptism and Mennonites is not one I can begin to reconstruct here, other than to say that if Anabaptism seeks reform for the sake of the wider church it cannot ignore the concrete communities that have attempted to give it expression or that have emerged from its sojourns. Anabaptist theology will reject the idea that one can simply jettison one's history, especially sinful history, and start with a blank slate. The Spirit has been shaping Anabaptist communities in complex ways, often in spite of the ambiguities of our historical experiences. At the same time, we should not imagine an easy continuity with historical Anabaptism such that Mennonites are its happy culmination. Such a view assumes the Spirit has simply blessed what is and thereby may fail to see how the Spirit might be interrupting us and troubling our views of who we are.

I could have developed my entire argument around the theme of Anabaptist martyrs, which continue to have an important role in

---

[48]Robert Zacharias, "Ceremonies of Belief: Unsettling Mennonite Stories," *Canadian Mennonite*, April 19, 2017, http://www.canadianmennonite.org/stories/ceremonies-belief.

the shaping of Mennonite faith identity, including through critical response to that heritage.[49] What I am saying does indeed seek to receive the gifts of Anabaptists, including martyrs, when they point to Christ; it also recognizes how many aspects of this history can perpetuate a separative logic. Thus, in dialogue with Lutherans, Mennonites acknowledged and confessed that we "have sometimes claimed the martyr tradition as a badge of Christian superiority and have sometimes nurtured an identity rooted in victimization that has fostered a sense of self-righteousness and arrogance and has blinded us to the frailties and failures that are also deeply woven into our tradition."[50] What happens in practice, even if it is not recognized in theory, is that patterns of seeing ourselves and the wider church are shaped by resentment, superiority, or complacency. These dynamics are perpetuated in our theological imaginations. To fulfill its ecumenical vocation, especially one shaped by calls to repentance and reform, Anabaptist theology must dive into these realities and contradictions.[51]

A final note on denominations: From an ecumenical perspective, denominations embody a profound tension. They are agents capable of being ecumenical actors, of allocating resources to reflect a commitment to seek relations with other Christian traditions, and of articulating effectively and at times authoritatively the gifts on offer for the whole church. Yet their very existence as denominations ought to be at stake if that ecumenism is to be a profound one—that is, if it is to facilitate a shared movement toward a common center, Jesus Christ. While they can take action, they are also typically motivated by self-preservation rather than an openness that may result in the end of their distinctive existence. Thus, they tend to foster a tepid ecumenism underwritten by an invisible church account of unity.

---

[49]See David Weaver-Zercher, *Martyrs Mirror: A Social History* (Baltimore: Johns Hopkins University Press, 2016), especially chapters 8–12.
[50]"Healing of Memories, Reconciling in Christ," in *Mennonites in Dialogue*, 291.
[51]I have proposed ways of reframing the legacy of Anabaptists killed by Catholics—and by Lutherans—in light of acts of reconciliation between Mennonites and these traditions. See Jeremy M. Bergen, "Problem or Promise? Confessional Martyrs and Mennonite–Roman Catholic Relations," *Journal of Ecumenical Studies* 41 (2004): 367–88; Jeremy M. Bergen, "Lutheran Repentance at Stuttgart and Mennonite Ecclesial Identity," *Mennonite Quarterly Review* 86 (2012): 315–38.

The Holy Spirit and Anabaptism within the Presently Divided Church

The presently divided church is a state of affairs ultimately contrary to Christ's prayer for the unity of his followers (John 17:21). Yet often movements of reform have resulted in schism—further impeding the call to unity—and Anabaptism is no exception. As we discern the relationship of this tradition to the Tradition as the life of the Holy Spirit in the church, we might find that a schismatic tradition comes up short. So how do we understand our ecumenical vocation in light of this reality?

Here I turn to how particular Christian traditions engaged in bilateral ecumenical dialogues understand the Spirit to be at work in their history of church division.[52] As expected, there is a strong association of the Holy Spirit with the movement to unity, including the imperative of dialogue. When reconciliation or union occurs, that is understood as the work of the Spirit. However, a number of dialogues also assert that the Spirit has accompanied a history that was marred by the sinful disobedience that led to schism and division. This may allow some further nuance in considering the continuities and discontinuities in the life of the church.

The international Anglican-Catholic dialogue acknowledged that the Spirit gives gifts to the whole people of God for the sake of the church's mission. These gifts rightly reflect a diversity of perspectives; although diversity of gifts is not the direct cause of division, it is the occasion from which divisions may develop.[53] That dialogue noted that some impulses that contributed to separation were sinful while other impulses that so contributed were not. A dialogue between Catholics and Evangelicals goes further and claims that the Spirit may have mandated some ruptures in communion, though these must be understood as temporary. "Evangelicals insist (as do Roman Catholics) that . . . 'Church discipline, biblically based and under the direction of the Holy Spirit, is essential' and that 'church discipline may demand the curtailing of concrete forms

---

[52]This section draws on work I have done with dialogue texts. See Jeremy M. Bergen, "The Holy Spirit and Lived Communion from the Perspective of International Bilateral Dialogues," *Journal of Ecumenical Studies* 49 (2014): 193–217.
[53]Anglican-Roman Catholic International Commission, "Church as Communion," nos. 29–30, in *Growth in Agreement II*, 336.

of fellowship even in cases where offenders against the apostolic teaching are acknowledged as brothers and sisters.'"[54]

The international Methodist-Catholic dialogue acknowledged that while there are "faith-filled risks and discontinuities" in history, these may be "embraced by the reforming, renewing and indeed recreating power of the Holy Spirit as the Church journeys through history."[55] That same dialogue issued a report in 2006 that built on the Catholic conviction that the Holy Spirit uses traditions separated from the Catholic Church as means of salvation.[56] The Spirit may be there, despite division. The dialogue report even raises the question of whether the Spirit may have permitted these divisions so that various traditions would discover and nurture particular gifts ultimately for the sake of the whole. The report continues, "A review of past history suggests that God has led each of our churches in new ways that came through the separations."[57] The gifts that each tradition has been developing must be shared, for the benefit and blessing of all Christians. The dialogue reiterates that separation is not, in itself, acceptable. Yet, within God's providential ordering, such separations may enable Christians to see in new and vivid ways gifts that otherwise may not have been discerned and received. This is to say that we ought not to simply regret the sojourn of Anabaptism, even as it has fostered sectarianism, division, and animosity within the body; there are gifts that have been held by this tradition that will reform and truly build up the one, holy, catholic, and apostolic church. At the same time, Anabaptism is not an unalloyed triumph, nor should its existence be understood as an end in itself. The aforementioned dialogues draw attention to the difficult but essential work of discerning the Spirit through all such particular traditions.

---

[54]Roman Catholic Church and World Evangelical Alliance, "Church, Evangelization, and the Bonds of Koinonia" (2002), no. 18, in *Growth in Agreement III*, 274.

[55]International Methodist-Catholic Dialogue Commission, "Encountering Christ the Saviour: Church and Sacraments" (2011), no. 24, www.vatican.va/roman_curia/pontifical_councils/chrstuni/meth-council-docs/rc_pc_chrstuni_doc_20110612_durban-document_en.html.

[56]Second Vatican Council, *Unitatis Redintegration: Decree on Ecumenism* (1964), no. 4.

[57]International Methodist-Catholic Dialogue Commission, "The Grace Given You in Christ: Catholics and Methodists Reflect Further on the Church" (2006), no. 14, www.vatican.va/roman_curia/pontifical_councils/chrstuni/meth-council-docs/rc_pc_chrstuni_doc_20060604_seoul-report_en.html.

In the mid-twentieth century, Yves Congar developed a theology of reform in the church that helped pave the way for the Second Vatican Council. His discussion of conditions or attitudes of reform are broadly applicable here. Prophets and reformers, whether individuals or communities, bear a crucial message. However, in the name of clarity and urgency, they tend to simplify. Thus, the perspective of the wider church and historical tradition is vital for testing and integration and to prevent the prophetic-critical insight from becoming its own self-contained system. Moreover, the virtue of patience is essential to the realization of true reform.[58] Although this may sound deeply conservative—and I break with Congar on the recognition that there may be providential roles even for "schismatic" movements that arise when, from a human perspective, rupture seems to be required by faithfulness—patience is good advice for an Anabaptist tradition that can be self-assured.

The early Anabaptists called attention to the biblical themes of repentance and conversion as implying the death of the old self and regeneration by the power of the Holy Spirit, which manifests in holiness of life. New birth is preceded by repentance and yieldedness to God's will, a yieldedness that entails offering one's life for Christ's sake, whether or not such an offering would culminate in martyrdom per se. The theme of death has also been invoked ecumenically. From the World Council of Churches' landmark 1961 New Delhi Statement on Unity:

> We all confess that sinful self-will operates to keep us separated and that in our human ignorance we cannot discern clearly the lines of God's design for the future. But it is our firm hope that through the Holy Spirit God's will as it is witnessed to in Holy Scripture will be more and more disclosed to us and in us. The achievement of unity will involve nothing less than a death and rebirth of many forms of church life as we have known them. We believe that nothing less costly can finally suffice.[59]

This, I submit, is a profoundly unsettling but necessary methodological framework for Anabaptist theology. It may be that one

---

[58] Yves Congar, *True and False Reform in the Church*, translated by Paul Philibert (Collegeville, MN: Liturgical Press, 2011), esp. 251–340.
[59] World Council of Churches, "New Delhi Statement on Unity" (1961), no. 3. The theme of death and the unity of the church is developed, in different ways, by Ephraim

of the gifts Anabaptists offer to the wider church is precisely the recognition that Anabaptism as a tradition may need to die to fulfill the calling to which it is called.

Conclusion

I once heard one of the famous pioneers of liberation theology, Gustavo Gutierrez, give a talk at the University of Toronto. It was the early 2000s, and John Paul II was pope. One person from the audience rose to ask a question about the future of liberation theology given that the Vatican seemed to be clamping down on it. Gutierrez's response: "I do not care about so-called liberation theology; I care only about the gospel." What I heard him say was that he did not need to promote himself or any particular institution or movement. Rather, his task is to point to the gospel of Jesus Christ. Of course, Gutierrez is convinced that the gospel *is* a message of holistic liberation, but that is different from being invested in the success of "liberation theology" per se. Similarly, Anabaptist theology's mandate is to develop its gifts in such a way that it mediates Jesus Christ and helps Christians turn ever again to Christ. In so doing, it will seek the unity of Christ's church. But it ought not be concerned with the success of Anabaptism alone or its institutions. To hold deeply to the reforming impulse that ought to be central to Anabaptism is precisely to hold this identity lightly.

My argument here is not about advocating an institutional ecumenism. Formal ecumenical dialogues have their place, perhaps necessary but never sufficient, in the pursuit of the calling to unity. Rather, I propose that theologizing out of the Anabaptist tradition ought to take a particular posture. Engaging with the full range of theological themes (not just ecclesiology and ecumenism), it should be theology that is characterized most especially by openness to the Holy Spirit, deep and searching humility about its place in the providential ordering of history, and unsettledness about its very existence. "Anabaptist" may well name one context from which

---

Radner, *The End of the Church: A Pneumatology of Christian Division in the West* (Grand Rapids: Eerdmans, 1998); Peter J. Leithart, *The End of Protestantism: Pursuing Unity in a Fragmented Church* (Grand Rapids: Brazos, 2016).

contemporary theologians speak, but each will also speak from a range of gendered, economic, social, and political contexts. Insofar as it is self-consciously though only provisionally Anabaptist, such theology will rigorously examine what it has to offer, and to receive, from other Christians. Finally, and most basically, it will allow itself to be continually reoriented by the Spirit toward the living Christ, a reorientation that from a human perspective entails ongoing reform and renewal.[60]

---

[60] I am grateful for research assistance from Zacharie Klassen.

8

Dialogue as Theological Method

Mennonite Missionaries, West African Churches, and Twenty-First-Century Anabaptist Identity

R. Bruce Yoder

Introduction

In 1994 Wilbert R. Shenk convened a gathering of people involved in relationships within the worldwide Anabaptist-Mennonite movement and suggested the writing of a history that would include the diverse voices that made up that movement.[1] This

---

[1] John A. Lapp, "The Global Mennonite History Project: The Vision and Process," *Mission Focus Annual Review* 19 (2011): 41–45; Wilbert R. Shenk, "A Global Church Requires a Global History," *Conrad Grebel Review* 15, no. 1 (1997): 3–18.

project became the Global Mennonite History Series of Mennonite World Conference.² Within the wider community of missiology and church history scholars, Shenk articulated a similar vision for a world Christian history.³ Indeed, dialogue among multiple voices has been both a theme and a method in Shenk's work.⁴ In the 1970s, as Secretary for Overseas Ministries of Mennonite Board of Missions (MBM), he outlined a dialogical method of theological discernment and missionary engagement with African Independent Churches (AICs), churches that were not aligned with Western missions or churches.⁵

This chapter argues that its twentieth-century engagement with AICs led MBM to implement a dialogical mission approach and suggests that this approach provides a precedent for discernment about Anabaptist theology among worldwide Anabaptist communities in the twenty-first century. Since the approach grew out of the missionary values of indigenization and self-theologizing, the narrative outlines the development of those concerns. Shenk and his colleagues developed a dialogical approach that allowed them to respect AICs' self-theologizing and the theological diversity that it implied as well as remain faithful to their own Mennonite heritage.

---

²John A. Lapp and C. Arnold Snyder, eds., *Global Mennonite History Series* (Intercourse, PA: Good Books, 2006).
³Wilbert R. Shenk, "Toward a Global Church History," *International Bulletin of Missionary Research* 20, no. 2 (April 1996): 50–57; Wilbert R. Shenk, ed., *Enlarging the Story: Perspectives on Writing World Christian History* (Maryknoll, NY: Orbis, 2002).
⁴See Shenk's leadership in the publication of Mennonite Board of Missions, *A Theology of Mission in Outline* (Elkhart, IN: Mennonite Board of Missions, 1978) and correspondence in IV-18-13-05, Box 4, A Theology of Mission in Outline; Wilbert R. Shenk, ed., *The Transfiguration of Mission: Biblical, Theological, and Historical Foundations* (Scottdale, PA: Herald, 1993); Wilbert R. Shenk, "'Go Slow through Uyo': A Case Study of Dialogue as Missionary Method," in *Fullness of Life for All: Challenges for Mission in Early 21st Century*, edited by Inus Daneel, Charles Van Engen, and Hendrik Vroom (New York: Rodopi, 2005), 329–40. In 1972, Shenk initiated the journal *Mission Focus* to stimulate thought and discussion. See also his development of MBM's policy of work with AICs "Ministry among African Independent Churches," January 30, 1980, IV-18-16, Folder 4 West Africa Program Docs, 1974–86. Unless otherwise noted, archival material cited in this chapter is from the Mennonite Church USA Archives in Elkhart, IN.
⁵Researchers have referred to these churches alternatively as African Independent, African Indigenous, African Initiated, or African Instituted Churches.

This chapter suggests that the diversity found in the twenty-first-century worldwide Anabaptist community is, in measure, analogous to the situation that MBM faced in West Africa and that a dialogical approach might be fruitful for theological discernment today.

A dialogical approach assumes that there is theological diversity within the Christian movement and seeks to encourage discernment that identifies and cultivates shared theological identity. Anabaptist communities located in different historical, cultural, and religious contexts express their theological convictions with respect to those unique contexts, even as their theology is informed by their engagement with the Anabaptist tradition and the larger contemporary Anabaptist community. Given such diversity, a dialogical approach attempts to assist Anabaptists across different contexts to name commonalities as well as differences and to increase shared theological understanding.

The Growing Importance of Local Contexts

As MBM missionaries became convinced of the importance of historical and cultural contexts for Christian belief and practice, they sought to encourage local expressions of the faith and capacitate church leaders for theological discernment that would take historical and cultural particularities seriously. Indigenization was a key concept that described such concerns, in opposition to practicing a simple transfer of belief and practice from mission-sending nations. In Africa, decolonization in the post–Second World War decades reinforced the theological agency of Christian leaders. This section describes the influence of indigenization and decolonization on MBM's approach in West Africa to help explain the emergence of the dialogical method outlined in the following section.

Indigenization

The missionary value of indigenization prepared the way for missionaries to expect the churches they planted to be self-theologizing churches. This section draws from MBM's early twentieth-century experience in India to show how understandings of indigenization evolved to become a primary concern by the time missionaries began working with AICs in Nigeria in 1958. Missiologists understood an indigenous church to be one that was self-financing, self-administering, and self-propagating and that embodied the exigencies and circumstances of its context—precepts that early MBM missionaries embraced.⁶

Mennonite missionaries sought to better understand the Indian context. They learned local languages, studied Indian culture and Hindu religion, and wrote articles about what they learned for their home church press.⁷ In its schools the mission sought to adapt curriculum to the students' environment.⁸ MBM's 1939 mission study course described India and addressed the challenge of applying North American Mennonite doctrines, suggesting that while they were the same in principle, the application of doctrines was to be "governed in each country by conditions and necessity."⁹ An increasing attention to the importance of local contexts for Christian belief and practice became characteristic of the mission's work in India.

During the same period the North American Mennonite community was undergoing stresses that would threaten to inhibit indigenization in India. Some leaders moved to reinforce Mennonite identity by strengthening nonconformity with the world and regulating certain markers of the faith—Mennonite distinctives such as "plain" patterns of dress.¹⁰ Missionaries understood the

---

⁶Wilbert R. Shenk, *Henry Venn: Missionary Statesman* (Maryknoll: Orbis, 1983); Peter Williams, "'Not Transplanting' Henry Venn's Strategic Vision," in *The Church Mission Society and World Christianity, 1799–1999,* edited by Kevin Ward and Brian Stanley (Grand Rapids: Eerdmans, 2000), 147–72; John A. Lapp, *The Mennonite Church in India, 1897–1962* (Scottdale, PA: Herald, 1972), 97, 165, 173–77; Wilbert R. Shenk, *By Faith They Went Out: Mennonite Missions 1850–1999* (Elkhart, IN: Institute of Mennonite Studies, 2000), 57.
⁷Lapp, *Mennonite Church in India, 1897–1962,* 69, 77–78; Theron F. Schlabach, *Gospel versus Gospel: Mission and the Mennonite Church, 1863–1944* (Scottdale, PA: Herald, 1980), 158–59; George J. Lapp, "India and the Missionary," *Gospel Herald,* March 1, 1917.
⁸Lapp, *Mennonite Church in India, 1897–1962,* 71, 119.
⁹M. C. Lehman, *Our Mission Work in India* (Elkhart, IN: Mennonite Board of Missions and Charities, 1939), 108.
¹⁰Paul Toews, *Mennonites in American Society, 1930–1970: Modernity and the Persistence of Religious Community,* vol. 4, Mennonite Experience in America

limits of transferring distinctive markers of faithfulness to India and struggled to balance an appreciation for the Indian context with the home church's expectations.[11] They enforced prohibitions of polygamy, jewelry, mustaches, and life insurance and stressed the importance of nonconformity and the prayer veil for women but did not adhere to all dress regulations.[12]

Mennonites also sought to reinforce theological identity by codifying theological doctrines. From 1898 to 1928, Daniel Kauffman published three versions of a manual of biblical doctrines.[13] Kauffman was editor of the *Gospel Herald*—the closest thing to a Mennonite Church official church paper—from 1908 to 1943 and exerted considerable influence.[14] The move to solidify doctrine and visible markers of the faith corresponded with the Fundamentalist movement and the critique of ostentatious dress from the holiness movement. Some among MBM's constituency urged the mission to send only missionaries who affirmed Fundamentalist doctrines.[15] Others aligned such concerns with distinctives such as the head covering for women and the prohibition of moustaches and neckties.[16] Such movements were a timely resource for those who sought to protect the Mennonite faith community from worldly

---

(Scottdale, PA: Herald, 1996), 62–63, 72–76; Lapp, *Mennonite Church in India, 1897–1962*, 59–60.

[11]Lapp, *Mennonite Church in India, 1897–1962*, 167; Schlabach, *Gospel versus Gospel*, 162, 164.

[12]Lapp, *Mennonite Church in India, 1897–1962*, 60, 167, 169.

[13]Daniel Kauffman, *Manual of Bible Doctrines: Setting Forth the General Principles of the Plan of Salvation, Explaining the Symbolical Meaning and Practical Use of the Ordinances Instituted by Christ and His Apostles, and Pointing out Specifically Some of the Restrictions Which the New Testament Scriptures Enjoin upon Believers* (Elkhart, IN: Mennonite Pub. Co., 1898); Daniel Kauffman, ed., *Bible Doctrine: A Treatise on the Great Doctrines of the Bible, Pertaining to God, Angels, Satan, the Church, and the Salvation, Duties and Destiny of Man* (Scottdale, PA: Mennonite Pub. House, 1914); Daniel Kauffman, ed., *Doctrines of the Bible, a Brief Discussion of the Teachings of God's Word* (Scottdale, PA: Mennonite Pub. House, 1928).

[14]Schlabach, *Gospel versus Gospel*, 111.

[15]Ibid., 117.

[16]"Proceedings of the Mennonite Board of Missions and Charities, 1930," (Beech Church, Louisville, Ohio: Mennonite Board of Missions and Charities, May 3, 1930), point no. 3, IV-06-02 MBM Exec Committee Documents and Mtg Minutes 1906–71, Box 2, Minutes 1927–33; Lapp, *Mennonite Church in India, 1897–1962*, 62.

influences and dangerous social changes, at home or on the mission field.[17]

In 1933 the faithful transfer of Mennonite distinctives and doctrines to mission fields was an issue at MBM's annual meeting. Kauffman posed a rhetorical question, "To what extent should the home Church project its standards into the Church on the field?"[18] His answer was, "One hundred percent."[19] While allowing for the characteristics of individual workers and diverse environments, he opposed different standards for different regions of the world.[20] Kauffman did not spell out what standards he had in mind, but in the context of efforts to reinforce Mennonite distinctives and orthodox doctrine his audience likely understood implicitly markers of nonconformity as well as doctrinal orthodoxy.

As the mission was engaging Indian thought patterns and religious assumptions, the home church was solidifying its doctrinal expressions. Correct belief was being standardized according to North American assumptions at the same time that MBM missionaries were, for the first time, in a long-term encounter with religious expressions that were vastly different from those of the church that sent them.

Missionaries had to balance their appreciation for the importance of local contexts with North American assumptions about Mennonite identity. For example, George Lapp argued that Western traditions, policies, and methods were not sufficient to establish the church in India since the goal was a church that would be "wholly Indian in tradition, policy and expression."[21] Lapp's appreciation for the Indian context, however, did not diminish his desire to share the Mennonite heritage. He kept current on Mennonite scholarship,

---

[17]Toews, *Mennonites in American Society, 1930–1970: Modernity and the Persistence of Religious Community*, 70–76; C. Norman Kraus, "American Mennonites and the Bible, 1750–1950," *Mennonite Quarterly Review* 41, no. 4 (October 1967): 309–29.
[18]Daniel Kauffman, "How Far Should the Home Church Project Its Policies into the Church on the Field?" in *Twenty-Seventh Annual Report of the MBMC*, edited by Sanford C. Yoder (Elkhart, IN: Mennonite Board of Missions and Charities, 1933), 98.
[19]Ibid.
[20]Ibid., 98–99.
[21]George Jay Lapp, *The Christian Church and Rural India: A Report on Christian Rural Reconstruction and Welfare Service* (Calcutta: Y.M.C.A. Publishing House, 1938), 4.

subscribing to the *Mennonite Quarterly Review* and lecturing about Mennonite convictions at ecumenical gatherings.[22] At the request of Indian Mennonites, he wrote a book about Menno Simons and Mennonite history and spearheaded the collaborative writing of another about Mennonite doctrines; both were in Hindi.[23] As they sought to encourage indigenization, missionaries had to navigate the influence of local contexts and the home church's expectations about Mennonite identity.

Self-Theologizing in the Context of Decolonization

If tension arose in India between fidelity to North American Mennonite distinctives and indigenization, during the post–Second World War years decolonization reinforced the move toward indigenization. Missionaries Edwin and Irene Weaver arrived to Nigeria in November 1959, and a month later Nigerians voted to choose their representatives in the first independent government, although the formal transfer of power would happen the following October.[24] Nigerian churches, too, expected to gain independence.[25] The Weavers had experienced similar dynamics in India where

---

[22]George J. Lapp to Harold S. Bender, September 8, 1936 and George J. Lapp to Harold S. Bender, August 23, 1933, HM 1–278 H. S. Bender, General Corr., 1931–38, Box 7, L—Miscellaneous, Mennonite Historical Library, Goshen, IN; George Lapp to Family, February 22, 1933, HM 1–143, Box 1, Corr. November 1930–31, folder 7.

[23]Fannie Lapp to Family, August 2, 1926, HM 1–143, Box 1, Corr.—1925, folder 2; George Jay Lapp, *[Menno Simons and the Mennonite Church]* (Jabalpur, India, 1929); George J. Lapp, "Report of Meeting Held at East Chestnut Street Mennonite Church, July 22, 1929" (East Chestnut Street Mennonite Church, Lancaster, PA, July 22, 1929), IV-7-1 Executive Office, Correspondence 1900–45, Box 10, Lapp, George J. 1921–45; George J. Lapp to Harold S. Bender, August 23, 1933.

[24]Edwin and Irene Weaver to J. D. Graber, December 13, 1959, IV-18-13-02, Box 11, Nigeria—Edwin Weaver 1959; Toyin Falola and Matthew Heaton, *A History of Nigeria* (New York: Cambridge University Press, 2008), 155–56.

[25]Matthew Ekereke et al., "Welcome Address from the People of Ibiono to Mr. and Mrs. Hostetler," February 15, 1959, HM 1–563, Box 3, Folder 21, Nigeria Church, 1958–60; A. G. Somerville and E.A. Onuk, "Announcement of the Presbyterian Church of Nigeria," Public Announcement (Abakaliki, Nigeria: Presbyterian Church of Nigeria, July 29, 1960), HM 1–696, Box 4, Folder 12, Somerville, Rev. A. G.

political independence had corresponded with Indian Mennonites' push for a transfer of mission and church structures to Indian hands.[26] In Nigeria the AICs warned the missionaries not to follow the example of "colonialist missionaries" but to accompany them as they embarked on their new journey of independence.[27] These African churches would not submit to the authority of foreign missions and would not accept belief and practice with which they disagreed.[28] The Weavers affirmed the existence of these African Christian movements and the legitimacy of their theological agency.

The focus on indigenization naturally highlighted the question of the relative importance of North American assumptions about theology for the churches with which missionaries worked. If indigenization underlined the significance of local contexts and precluded a simple transfer of North American Mennonite distinctives, one needed to clarify appropriate methods of discernment about Christian belief and practice. This section shows that MBM missionaries and their supervisors in the home office added self-theologizing to the characteristics of an indigenous church, encouraging church leaders to formulate teaching and practice that would be faithful in their particular contexts. MBM's subsequent dialogical approach was a way for it to engage in mission with self-theologizing churches whose faith expressions emerged from diverse religious histories and contexts.

Self-Theologizing

In India, Edwin Weaver highlighted the principle of self-theologizing already in 1949. He argued for Christian faith embodied in Indian ways and for Indian agency in theological discernment.[29] Although

---

[26]"Remarks on Indianization," March 1950, and D. A. Sonwani to J. D. Graber, April 14, 1950, IV-18-10, MBM Office of the Secretary 1941–57, Box 2, India—Church-Mission Relations 1947–51; Lapp, *Mennonite Church in India, 1897–1962*, 181–88.
[27]Ekereke et al., "Welcome Address from the People of Ibiono to Mr. and Mrs. Hostetler."
[28]I. U. Nsasak, "Minutes of Meeting of Leaders of Independent Churches" (Uyo, Nigeria: Independent Churches Leaders, February 18, 1967), HM 1–696, Box 2, Folder 19, Independent Churches 1966–67.
[29]Edwin I. Weaver, "This Year in the Church," in *Report of the Forty-Third Annual Meeting of the MBMC*, edited by Joseph D. Graber (Elkhart, IN: Mennonite Board of Missions and Charities, 1949), 104–8.

the principles of the Word of God were unchanging, the church had to "find for itself the meaning and application of these principles for her own life and her own setting."[30] Weaver suggested, "We Western Christians may not be the best interpreters of these principles for India."[31] He continued to advocate for the agency of local actors in the development of Christian faith expressions and doctrines in the years that followed.[32] Prioritizing Indian agency did not mean that Weaver considered Mennonite faith tradition irrelevant for the Indian church. He sought to understand how recent Western scholarship on Anabaptism might inform the life of the church in India and conceived a project to have Indian leaders engage works about Mennonite history and peace teaching to produce literature for the church.[33]

J. D. Graber, MBM general secretary and Weaver's supervisor, agreed that it was up to Indians to make decisions about faith and doctrine in their context but still envisioned a role for missionaries.[34] In a 1956 letter to all MBM missionaries, he affirmed the importance of making cultural adaptations in different contexts.[35] They were to plant the church of Jesus Christ and not the church of their homeland. Graber cautioned, however, that the North American Mennonite church held certain values that should not be forgotten, such as the doctrines of separation from the world and nonconformity.[36] Half a century of missionary engagement had convinced MBM of the need for the faith to be embodied in diverse ways, but the values of separateness, nonconformity, and the rejection of worldliness were still strong in the mid-1950s.

---

[30] Ibid.
[31] Ibid.
[32] Edwin Weaver, "Some Principles To Be Considered in Charting the Future Course of the Church," April 25, 1951, IV-18-10, MBM Office of the Secretary 1941–57, Box 3, India—Unification Commission 1950–53; Edwin Weaver to J. D. Graber, September 19, 1954, IV-18-10, Box 5, Weaver, Edwin and Irene 1951–55.
[33] Ibid., Edwin Weaver to J. D. Graber, January 5, 1953 and Edwin Weaver to J. D. Graber, May 20, 1954, IV-18-10, Box 5, Weaver, Edwin and Irene 1951–55.
[34] J. D. Graber to Edwin Weaver, October 22, 1954, IV-18-10, Box 5, Weaver, Edwin and Irene 1951–55.
[35] J. D. Graber to Overseas Representatives of the Mennonite Board of Missions and Charities, July 5, 1956, IV-18-03-02, Box 4, Executive Committee 1956–64.
[36] J. D. Graber to Nelson Litwiller, September 22, 1956, IV-18-13-02, Box 2, Argentina Field Secretary 1956.

Both Weaver and Graber assumed that the Indian church would express the Christian faith in ways different from that of the home church but that the Mennonite faith tradition had something valuable to share. Weaver highlighted Mennonite history and peace teaching, although interpreted by Indians, and Graber identified the doctrines of nonconformity and the rejection of worldliness.

The Home Office and AICs in Nigeria

Work in India provided missionaries with crucial experience that shaped their approach with AICs in Nigeria, but the legitimization of that approach via the support of MBM administrators was necessary for it to eventually become institutional policy. Veteran India workers Edwin and Irene Weaver, who were committed to indigenization and self-theologizing, pioneered the Nigeria work. J. D. Graber and his assistant John H. Yoder supervised the Weavers and encouraged their approach. Graber had been a missionary in India and oversaw MBM's work around the world. Yoder had not worked in India but had advised MBM missionaries in Europe. This section shows MBM administrators' earlier commitment to indigenization in Europe and demonstrates how that value continued to guide MBM's work in Nigeria, eventually preparing the way for its dialogical approach.

Before supervising MBM's Nigeria engagement, Yoder had helped MBM missionaries reflect on the relevance of North American faith and practice for the European context.[37] Questions arose about the appropriateness of North American Mennonite distinctives and

---

[37] Yoder advised missionaries in Europe and later in West Africa to set up or respect indigenous accountability structures instead of automatically assuming they should apply North American norms in foreign contexts. The advice he gave is consistent with indigenization theory. Yet he strongly resisted efforts by his own church community to hold him accountable to its norms for the sexual violence that he perpetrated on dozens of women over a period of two decades starting in the mid-1970s. See Rachel Waltner Goossen, "'Defanging the Beast': Mennonite Responses to John Howard Yoder's Sexual Abuse," the *Mennonite Quarterly Review* 89, no. 1 (2015): 7–80. Given the discordance between his advice and his behavior, Yoder's thought and work as well as its use in mission theory and practice needs further evaluation to identify errors or misjudgments that may well need to be corrected or simply rejected.

about how missionaries should address nonresistance in countries where there was no civilian alternative to military service.[38] In North America, Mennonite Church conference rules often mandated discipline for those who served in the military, but Yoder argued that missionaries and service workers should not assume that the North American experience would be normative.[39] J. D. Graber agreed, noting that missionaries in Japan were dealing with a similar issue, whether to require North American practices of nonresistance or simply teach and trust that the Holy Spirit would lead the new church to its own scriptural position.[40]

Mennonite leader and historian Harold S. Bender, however, responded to Yoder by resisting the implication that different contexts required different faith expressions.[41] Such an approach, he contended, might encourage an unhelpful focus on national identities within the worldwide Mennonite community, a legitimate concern in the post–Second World War years. Apart from allowing for minor differences, he argued for maintaining a common standard around the world. Bender's argument echoed the concerns of Daniel Kauffman who two decades earlier had asked the rhetorical question, "To what extent should the home Church project its standards into the Church on the field?"[42] The issue was no longer Mennonite distinctives such as dress or the battle against modernism. Instead, it was the faithfulness of North American embodiments of nonresistance, such as church discipline of those who accepted military service, for the European context. Bender likely argued out of the conviction that some European Mennonites'

---

[38]John H. Yoder to J. D. Graber, January 19, 1953 and John H. Yoder to J. D. Graber, March 10, 1953, IV-18-10, Box 5, Yoder, John Howard 1951–55.
[39]Toews, *Mennonites in American Society, 1930–1970*, 173–80; John H. Yoder, "Report on Conscientious Objection and Medical Service," March 3, 1953, IV-18-10, Box 5, Yoder, John Howard 1951–55; John H. Yoder to J. D. Graber, March 10, 1953.
[40]J. D. Graber to John H. Yoder, January 14, 1954, IV-18-10, Box 5, Yoder, John Howard 1951–55.
[41]Harold S. Bender, "Comments on John Yoder's Paper Regarding Non-Resistance in Mennonite Churches in Europe" (Goshen, IN, March 5, 1954), IV-18-10, Box 5, Yoder, John Howard 1951–55.
[42]Kauffman, "How Far Should the Home Church Project Its Policies into the Church on the Field?"

compliance with the militarism of Second World War was at least partly the result of weak theological commitments.

Graber and Bender's responses to Yoder's proposal show the significance of ministry in diverse contexts for MBM. Both were products of the twentieth-century North American Mennonite Church and its increasing engagement with the world, and they shared much common ground. They responded differently, however. Bender, a guiding force in working out North American Mennonite and Anabaptist identity that included a strong focus on peace, argued for a fairly strict application of North American standards of enforcement of objection to war. MBM General Secretary Graber, who had missionary experience in India and supervised mission work around the world, was familiar with the challenges of crossing national and cultural borders with assumptions about Mennonite faith in a way that Bender was not. Graber doubted that the faithful embodiment of nonresistance would look the same everywhere. Five years after the discussion about enforcing standards of nonresistance in Europe, it was not Bender but MBM administrators Graber and Yoder who helped Edwin and Irene Weaver discern how to engage AICs in Nigeria. They encouraged the Weavers to take the AIC's and their embodiment of Christianity seriously.

The importance of indigenization continued in Nigeria as it had in India and Europe. The churches that had invited MBM to Nigeria in 1958 seemed to meet the three-self criteria of the indigenous church and wanted to become Mennonite.[43] The Weavers, in consultation with Yoder, sought to reinforce the indigenous nature of the church, forming a conference-like structure that could decide matters of doctrine and practice.[44]

Edwin Weaver's concern for self-theologizing continued. He argued that indigenous churches had to understand and interpret

---

[43] S. J. Hostetler, "Report of Visit of S. J. and Ida Hostetler to the Church in the Calabar Province," (Accra, Ghana, November 28, 1958) and S. J. Hostetler to J. D. Graber, December 19, 1958, IV-18-13-02, Box 10, Nigeria 1956–59; J. D. Graber to S. J. Hostetler, December 31, 1958, IV-18-13-02, Box 4, Ghana 1958.
[44] Edwin Weaver to John H. Yoder, December 9, 1959, IV-18-13-02, Box 11, Nigeria—Edwin Weaver 1959; John H. Yoder to Edwin Weaver, December 18, 1959 and John H. Yoder to Edwin Weaver, February 1, 1960, HM 1–696, Box 4, Folder 39, Yoder, John Howard, 1959–60; Edwin Weaver to John H. Yoder and J. D. Graber, March 28, 1960, IV-18-13-02, Box 10, Nigeria Jan–May 1960.

the gospel message for their own times and cultures.⁴⁵ The Weavers discontinued the practice of accepting new congregations into the church on confession of a list of Mennonite doctrines from North America.⁴⁶ Instead they imported and subsidized the sale of Mennonite and general Christian literature, initiated regular Bible teaching conferences, and enrolled some leaders in Bible colleges.⁴⁷ For AICs that did not desire to become Mennonite or join another Western denomination, the Weavers affirmed their autonomous status and provided the same assistance. They continued the practice of reinforcing indigenous agency for theological discernment as they had in India.

The AICs that welcomed the Weavers to Nigeria already had a history of theological discernment. They belonged to the Ibibio people in Calabar province who had opted for Christianity in large numbers but carried traditional religious sensibilities into their new religion.⁴⁸ In some cases they treated church buildings as shrines or found themselves possessed by the Holy Spirit and demonstrated ecstatic activity that resembled spirit possession of the ancestor cult. There was a sense that the Christian God was engaging the Ibibio in ways that they understood. Continuity with traditional religious expressions did not mean that they were not loyal to their new religion. They fought against the traditional religion, attacking

---

⁴⁵Edwin Weaver to S. J. Hostetler, January 1960, HM 1–563, Box 3, Folder 22, Nigeria Mission, Personal, 1959–60; Edwin Weaver to John H. Yoder, January 5, 1960, IV-18-13-02, Box 10, Nigeria Jan–May 1960.

⁴⁶Edwin and Irene Weaver to John H. Yoder, December 24, 1959, IV-18-13-02, Box 11, Nigeria—Edwin Weaver 1959; Edwin Weaver to S. J. Hostetler, January 1960.

⁴⁷Edwin Weaver to John H. Yoder, April 30, 1960, IV-18-13-02, Box 10, Nigeria Jan–May 1960; "A Suggested Literature Program for Nigeria," March 1961, HM 1–696, Box 1, Folder 13, Urie Bender; "Books Abroad—For Nigeria," December 1961, IV-18-13-02, Box 11, Nigeria—Elizabeth Showalter 1959–65; Edwin Weaver to S. J. Hostetler, January 22, 1960, HM 1–563, Box 3, Folder 22, Nigeria Mission, Personal, 1959–60; A. Griffiths to Edwin Weaver, October 27, 1960, and Principle of Methodist Church Lay Training Centre to Edwin Weaver, October 29, 1960, HM 1–696, Box 1, Folder 42, Misc.

⁴⁸Nigeria and Department of Statistics, *Population Census of the Eastern Region of Nigeria, 1953* (Lagos: Census Superintendent [the Govt. statistician], 1955), 36, 42; Monday B. Abasiattai, "The Oberi Okaime Christian Mission: Towards a History of an Ibibio Independent Church," *Africa: Journal of the International African Institute* 59 (1989): 496, 500–01; John Cowan Messenger, "Anang Acculturation: A Study of Shifting Cultural Focus" (PhD diss., Northwestern University, 1957), 248–61.

its shrines and claiming that it was Satan who inspirited its beliefs and rituals.[49] Indigenous expressions of Christianity and their fierce loyalty suggest that Ibibio Christians sought a way to express attachment and fidelity to Christianity in forms that made sense and felt familiar within their religious framework.

As the Weavers engaged this dynamic, indigenous Christian movement, they found that Western ecclesiological categories were not meaningful to many AICs. There were well over a dozen Western denominations represented in southeastern Nigeria at the beginning of the post-colonial era.[50] Congregations changed their loyalty between them easily, without much regard for or knowledge of the traditions they represented.[51] Instead, spiritual assistance, fellowship, ministries of healing, and the provision of schools seemed to be far more relevant concerns. Edwin Weaver wrote to a missionary counterpart, "The historical events out of which we became 'Mennonite' and others became 'Lutheran,' etc. mean nothing to these people."[52] Christian identity was being transformed, and Western religious traditions did not hold the same significance in Nigeria as they did in Europe and North America.

Ibibio AICs were working out their understanding of Christianity, appropriating missionary teaching while retaining certain local religious assumptions. They read Western Christian literature but also articulated their own theological interpretations, sometimes publishing them for wider distribution.[53] The Weavers and their colleagues sought to assist by establishing a Bible school for AICs

---

[49]Abasiattai, "Oberi Okaime Christian Mission," 501; Messenger, "Anang Acculturation," 249; David Pratten, "Mystics and Missionaries: Narratives of the Spirit Movement in Eastern Nigeria," *Social Anthropology* 15, no. 1 (2007): 47–70.
[50]Edwin Weaver to John H. Yoder, December 9, 1959.
[51]Edet William Amamkpa, *A Short History of Ibesikpo* ([N.p.]: [Amamkpa], 1979), 26–33; Edwin Weaver to John H. Yoder, January 5, 1960; I. U. Nsasak et al., "The Abak Story," Research Report (Inter Church Study Team, February 1967), HM 1–696, Box 6, Folder 3, The Abak Story.
[52]Edwin Weaver to W. H. Graddon, March 9, 1960, HM 1–696, Box 2, Folder 6, Graddon, W. H.
[53]For example, E. J. Akam, *The Voice of Warning* (Uyo, Nigeria: Voice of Warning, 1970); E. J. Akam, *Fasting or the School of God* (Ibesikpo, Nigeria: The International Supreme Temple of Prayer Fellowship, n.d.); and E. J. Akam, "Are Pentecostal Manifestations Real and Scriptural?" n.d., HM 1–696, Box 6, Folder 4, I. U. Nsasak and D. U. Otong.

and arranging bursaries for advanced training for some church leaders.[54] When the matter of advanced training arose, however, some AICs were hesitant.[55] Such training was available only at select theological schools of foreign missions where they feared teachers would pressure students to modify theological convictions. AICs were willing to accept foreign assistance, but they reserved the right to articulate and defend their own theological commitments.

Dialogue as Theological Method

MBM's experience with AICs in Nigeria led to mission engagement across West Africa and a commitment to dialogue as missiological and theological method. Missionaries found AICs that valued their theological autonomy and desired opportunities for biblical training.[56] A focus on capacitating AIC movements was one way for MBM to meet a felt need and maintain mission engagement in the post-colonial era. This section shows how MBM appropriated its experience with Nigerian AICs to articulate a dialogical approach that both encouraged self-theologizing in African churches and recognized the value of the theological identity and contributions of missionaries. The argument is that a dialogical approach might well be helpful for theological reflection among the churches of the worldwide Anabaptist community in the twenty-first century.

African Agency and Theological Discernment

In 1969 Wilbert Shenk called for a theology of mission that would demonstrate to churches and other mission agencies the legitimacy

---

[54]Darrel and Marian Hostetler to Supporters, March 1964, IV-18-13-02, Box 5, Hostetler, Darrel Marian 1960–64; Edwin Weaver to Lloyd Fisher, Earl Roberts, and N. Eme, March 31, 1964, IV-18-13-02, Box 10, Nigeria 1964; Darrel Hostetler to Wilbert R. Shenk, August 31, 1965, IV-18-13-02, Box 10, Nigeria—Darrell Hostetler 1964–65; H. W. Gensichen to Edwin I. Weaver, December 5, 1963, HM 1–696, Box 1, Folder 42, Misc.; J. Walter Cason to Edwin Weaver, June 11, 1964, and Edwin Weaver to Walter Cason, January 1, 1965, IV-18-13-02, Box 11, Nigeria—Edwin Weaver 1964–65.
[55]Nsasak, "Minutes of Meeting of Leaders of Independent Churches."
[56]HM 1–696, Box 4, Folder 36, West Africa Reports.

of MBM's AIC ministry.⁵⁷ This section describes how MBM personnel came to articulate their dialogical approach and shows that MBM's move to legitimize self-theologizing AICs was part of a growing recognition of the contextual nature of all theology.

Shenk initiated a process of discernment among MBM workers through which he hoped to elucidate the implications of the Believers' Church tradition for mission theology and clarify a helpful understanding of church.⁵⁸ Missionaries sought to take seriously both their theological heritage and the West African context and to articulate a conception of the church that would allow for self-theologizing African churches. Only a mission method that was consistent with these values would achieve the outcome they sought.⁵⁹ Highlighting MBM's concern with African agency in theological discernment, Shenk noted, "There are some concepts of church which encourage and foster integrity in the way the young church develops in contrast to other approaches which inherently demand that the new church develop within a prescribed doctrinal polity framework."⁶⁰

MBM missionaries suggested that their Believers' Church heritage provided a theology of the church. They argued that from an Anabaptist perspective the indigenous congregation—one that was not dependent on a foreign mission or church but embodied a certain level of theological and administrative autonomy—was the normal form of the church.⁶¹ This affirmed "the theological

---

⁵⁷"Summary of Dec. 1, 1969 Discussion of West Africa Strategy" (Accra, Ghana: Mennonite Board of Missions and Charities, December 1, 1969), HM 1–696, Box 5, Folder 10, Background Material for "Among Indigenous Churches . . . . chapter 6"; Wilbert R. Shenk, "A Problem of Understanding," April 1970, IV-18-1, Overseas Committee Official Records, Minutes 1970–71; "Continuing West Africa Agenda," June 6, 1973, HM 1–696, Box 5, Folder 9, Background for "Among Indigenous Churches . . . ."

⁵⁸The Believers' Church focus arose in the post–Second World War decades among churches that shared the heritage of the radical reformation. See Donald F. Durnbaugh, "Believers Church," *Global Anabaptist Mennonite Encyclopedia Online*, 1987, http://gameo.org/index.php?title=Believers_Church&oldid=128086.

⁵⁹Shenk, "A Problem of Understanding"; Wilbert R. Shenk to Edwin Weaver, July 4, 1970, HM 1–696, Box 5, Shenk, Wilbert, 1970; Wilbert R. Shenk to Mr. and Mrs. Edwin Weaver, May 27, 1970, HM 1–696, Box 5, Shenk, Wilbert, 1970.

⁶⁰Wilbert R. Shenk to Edwin Weaver.

⁶¹John H. Yoder to Wilbert R. Shenk, February 16, 1970, IV-18-16, Folder 2 Mennonites in West Africa, 1958–81; Marlin Miller, "A Mennonite Statement of

legitimacy of the distinct existence of church bodies which do not stand in any direct juridical relationship to a specific 'mother church' in Europe or North America."[62] Shenk's interlocutors warned that MBM should not insist that African churches adopt the Believers' Church theology of the missionaries.[63] African churches needed to have the freedom to adopt theological positions for their own contexts.

Shenk outlined theological assumptions and method. The assumptions were that the gospel has to be applied afresh in each situation, that theological reflection takes place in a community of faith, that all members of the community participate even though some lead, and that the objective of the process is discipleship.[64] The concept of the church would be consistent with the Believers' Church model, which placed significant authority for defining belief and practice with the voluntarily gathered community of believers. Shenk proposed a dialogical method that would address the question, "What does it mean to be faithful to Jesus in this time and place?"[65] Respect among participants would be fundamental. The purpose of the dialogue would not be to convince participants of a particular view but to provoke the church to faithfulness. Shenk suggested that this approach might be "superior to others because it is committed to taking the 'other' seriously, giving him [or her] the benefit of the doubt so long as he [or she] affirms the lordship of Jesus and takes the Bible as the starting point."[66]

MBM instituted a policy for work with AICs in January 1980. It affirmed the local church as the place to "discern how God is speaking in the present based on the Word, the living Lordship of

---

Policy on Cooperation with African Independent/Spiritual Churches," February 7, 1975, IV-18-13-05, Box 5, West Africa Discussions—73–75.

[62]John H. Yoder to Wilbert R. Shenk.

[63]Edwin Weaver to Wilbert R. Shenk, June 13, 1970, HM 1–696, Box 5, Shenk, Wilbert, 1970; Marlin Miller, "Further Reporting on West Africa Trip—April/May 1970," May 1970, HM 1–696, Box 3, Folder 19, Miller, Marlin E.

[64]Wilbert R. Shenk to Marlin Miller, February 13, 1974, IV-18-13-04, Box 3, Miller, Marlin and Ruthann 1970–74.

[65]Wilbert R. Shenk to Marlin Miller, February 13, 1974, IV-18-13-04, Box 3, Miller, Marlin and Ruthann 1970–74.

[66]Wilbert R. Shenk to Marlin Miller, July 6, 1974, IV-18-13-04, Box 3, Miller, Marlin and Ruthann 1970–74.

Jesus Christ, and the continuing prompting of the Holy Spirit."[67] The policy identified dialogue as the method for theological reflection and missionary engagement.[68] It highlighted the accompanying value of respect for AICs and their cultures, mission churches, the history of all dialogue partners, and MBM. Every culture was to be a context for the work of the Holy Spirit. The approach encouraged African theological agency, allowed for missionary contributions, and respected the MBM's Believers' Church heritage.

MBM's growing conviction of the importance of local contexts for theology was not unique. Shoki Coe, director of the World Council of Churches' Theological Education Fund, coined the term "contextualization" early in the 1970s.[69] Missiologists suggested that self-theologizing was the logical outcome of a multicultural Christian movement and argued that all theologies were local.[70] By early in the twenty-first century, European theologians practiced *intercultural theology*, analyzing and comparing Christian theologies from around the world.[71] The trajectory from missionary witness to self-theologizing and finally to theological engagement among diverse expressions of the faith was larger than one mission agency's experience. The world Christian movement has been part of an increasingly intense globalization, but it also gave rise to, indeed has depended upon, the articulation of local theologies that grew out of indigenous Christian communities around the world. In this case the global and local are interdependent.[72]

---

[67]"Ministry among African Independent Churches."
[68]Ibid.
[69]T. E. F Committee, "A Working Policy for the Implementation of the Third Mandate of the Theological Education Fund," 1972, HM 1–696, Box 5, Folder 7, Background Material for "Among Indigenous Churches . . . ."; Wilbert R. Shenk, "Theological Education in Historical and Global Perspective," in *Theology in Missionary Perspective: Lesslie Newbigin's Legacy*, edited by Mark T. B. Laing and Paul Weston (Eugene, OR: Pickwick, 2012).
[70]Paul G. Hiebert, "Contextualization's Challenge to Theological Education," *Occasional Papers of the Council of Mennonite Seminaries and Institute of Mennonite Studies* 2 (1981): 32–44; Robert J. Schreiter, *Constructing Local Theologies* (Maryknoll, NY: Orbis, 1985).
[71]Mark J. Cartledge and David Cheetham, "Introduction," in *Intercultural Theology* (London: SCM, 2011), 1–10; Benno van den Toren, "Intercultural Theology as a Three-Way Conversation: Beyond the Western Dominance of Intercultural Theology," *Exchange* 44 (2015): 123–43.
[72]Dana L. Robert, "Shifting Southward: Global Christianity since 1945," *International Bulletin of Missionary Research* 24, no. 2 (2000): 50–58.

Local theologies from the non-Western world have enriched wider theological discernment. In Latin America, socioeconomic inequality, theological agency in base Christian communities, attention to contextual realities, and new openness after the Second Vatican Council led to the articulation of liberation theology, a leaven that has inspired theologies of liberation in other contexts.[73] In Africa, theologians sought contextual formulations, understanding Christ as ancestor, healer, chief, or elder brother.[74] In Asia, where Christians are typically a religious minority, theologies of dialogue are one way they have embodied the gospel.[75] These and other local theologies enrich theological reflection beyond their communities of origin.

Dialogical Method in the Twenty-First Century

If MBM sought an approach that both encouraged African theological agency and allowed missionaries to affirm their own theological identity, a comparable vision of dialogue holds the possibility of enriching and stimulating theological exchange among the diverse streams of the Anabaptist movement in the twenty-first century. This section suggests that a dialogical approach might increase worldwide participation in formal theological exchange among Anabaptists, help identify the contribution North American Anabaptist theological formulations can make to that wider exchange, and constructively engage the diversity that exists among Anabaptists around the world.

A dialogical approach might help Western Anabaptists make more room for theological reflection from other regions of the world. In the early years of the post-colonial era, MBM had to be intentional about encouraging African agency because Western mission

---

[73]Volker Küster, "Intercultural Theology Is a Must," *International Bulletin of Missionary Research* 38, no. 4 (October 2014): 171–76; Ian Linden, *Global Catholicism: Diversity and Change since Vatican II* (London: Hurst, 2009).
[74]Agbonkhianmeghe E. Orobator, *Theology Brewed in an African Pot: An Introduction to Christian Doctrine from an African Perspective* (Nairobi: Paulines Publications Africa, 2008); Robert J. Schreiter, ed., *Faces of Jesus in Africa* (Maryknoll, NY: Orbis, 1998).
[75]Peter C. Phan, *In Our Own Tongues: Perspectives from Asia on Mission and Inculturation* (Maryknoll, NY: Orbis, 2003).

agencies had expected Western theology to suffice for churches around the world. The historical trajectory of indigenization, self-theologizing, and local theologies showed the error of that assumption. Western Anabaptists have a similar challenge. The bulk of Anabaptist theological reflection that results in publication or is shared in academic conferences originates in Europe and North America and addresses the needs and priorities of those regions. While theological reflection happens in other regions—both in academic settings and informally in the sermons, prayers, Bible studies, ministries, and lives of Anabaptists around the world—little of that reflection becomes part of global theological exchange. The relative abundance of theological material generated by Western Anabaptists risks overshadowing theology from other Anabaptist communities. A dialogical approach might provide a structure that welcomes new voices and additional modes of theologizing.

A dialogical approach might help North American Anabaptists discern the place their theological formulations have in global theological discernment. Arguably the most significant factor in North American Anabaptist theological identity has been the mid-twentieth-century Benderian "Anabaptist Vision."[76] Even for those who would modify or challenge Bender's formulation, it has provided an important baseline.[77] Bender identified the essence of Anabaptism with the triad of discipleship, voluntary church community, and love and nonresistance, a formulation that provided a "usable past" upon which North American Mennonites articulated a theological identity.[78] Bender's formulation and its embodiment in North American Mennonite and wider Anabaptist theological reflection is an example of a contextual or local theology. In the wake of two world wars, the challenge of military conscription, and the Cold War, the focus on love and nonresistance reinforced

---

[76]Karl Koop, "Anabaptist and Mennonite Identity: Permeable Boundaries and Expanding Definitions," *Religion Compass* 8, no. 6 (2014): 199–207.

[77]Laura Schmidt Roberts, "The Church in the World: Shifting Notions of Ecclesial Identity among North American Mennonites," *Dialog: A Journal of Theology* 51, no. 1 (March 2012): 53–61.

[78]Harold S. Bender, "The Anabaptist Vision," *Church History* 13, no. 1 (1944): 3–24; Paul Toews, "Search for a Usable Past," in *Mennonites in American Society, 1930–1970 Modernity and the Persistence of Religious Community* (Scottdale, PA: Herald, 1996), 84–106.

Mennonite resistance to war and the desire to cultivate peace. After the push to codify Mennonite doctrine during the early decades of the century, the emphasis on discipleship pointed to a reaffirmation of holy and ethical living. A focus on voluntary church community reinforced the importance of the faith community as Mennonites were becoming more assimilated into society. Bender's formulation drew on the Anabaptist religious heritage, but it has been especially important for the theological identity it provided.

Given the contextual nature of all theology, North American formulations (Bender's or those of others who would modify or challenge his proposal) likely will not be useful as a norm or definition for the global Anabaptist movement.[79] The challenges and issues that Anabaptists around the world engage are diverse, as will be the corresponding theologies that undergird their embodiment of the gospel. Nevertheless, the theological identity that developed in North America during the last century may well stimulate renewal and reflection in other Anabaptist communities.[80] Where that identity resonates, communities may appropriate something of it. In conversation with their own contexts, with Scripture, with the history of the sixteenth-century Anabaptist movement and the tradition that grew out of it, and with other Anabaptist communities, churches around the world will articulate their own Anabaptist visions. There will be, indeed likely already are, multiple Anabaptist visions.

Finally, a dialogical approach might be useful because the situation Shenk and his colleagues encountered anticipated, in some sense, an aspect of the current diversity within the world Anabaptist community. The importance of the religious history that AICs brought to their adoption of Christianity relativized Western

---

[79]Some proposals appear to suggest that a Benderian formulation will provide such a definition. See Palmer Becker, *What Is an Anabaptist Christian?* (Elkhart, IN: Mennonite Mission Network, 2008); Palmer Becker, *Anabaptist Essentials: Ten Signs of a Unique Christian Faith* (Harrisonburg, VA: Herald, 2017).

[80]For example, during the twentieth century, French Mennonites experienced their own renewal of Anabaptist identity, which the Benderian formulation influenced in important ways. See Neal Blough, "The Anabaptist Vision and Its Impact among French Mennonites," *Mennonite Quarterly Review* 69, no. 3 (July 1995): 369–88; Jean Séguy, *Les Assemblées Anabaptistes-Mennonites de France* (Paris: Mouton, 1977), chaps. 8, 9, and 10.

Christian traditions in unanticipated ways. African Christians embodied the faith in forms and with meaning that resulted in differences between their expressions of the faith and those of Western Christians. The policy statement that Wilbert Shenk developed gave churches in their particular contexts the responsibility to discern what it meant to live faithfully in their specific times and places. It anticipated, however, a wider theological conversation. Shenk and his colleagues affirmed the existence of a worldwide multicultural church that would engender diverse, authentic expressions of the Christian faith, of which Western Christian traditions would be part.

A similar diversity historically, culturally, and with respect to theological expression is evident within the worldwide Anabaptist community in the twenty-first century. The Mennonite World Conference felt the need to produce the Global Mennonite History Series, written from the perspective of historians from its diverse communities around the world and their respective religious histories.[81] Congregations of immigrant, first nation, or other communities that emerge from cultures and religious traditions quite different from those of traditional Anabaptist-Mennonite groups have become part of Western Anabaptist denominations.[82] The Institute for the Study of Global Anabaptism at Goshen College has completed a Global Anabaptist Profile and found that differences between Anabaptists in the Global North and Global South tend to follow patterns already well documented in the wider Christian tradition.[83] The Western Anabaptist theological legacy needs to make room for other Anabaptist faith expressions that emerge from a wider field of historical, religious, and cultural contexts.

A dialogical approach to theological discernment within the worldwide Anabaptist movement might be a way to recognize diversity and work toward a shared theological identity. Such an approach could draw on the discernment of Shenk and his

---

[81] Lapp and Snyder, *Global Mennonite History Series*.
[82] See, for example, Jeff Wright, *Urban and Anabaptist: The Remarkable Story of Rapid Growth Among Mennonites in Southern California* (Elkhart, IN: Mennonite Board of Missions, 2001).
[83] Conrad Kanagy, Elizabeth Miller, and John D. Roth, *Global Anabaptist Profile: Belief and Practice in 24 Mennonite World Conference Churches* (Goshen, IN: Institute for the Study of Global Anabaptism, 2017), 9, 19–31.

colleagues and the policy that resulted.[84] As such it would be characterized by respect for churches in diverse contexts and an expectation of a range of theological expressions. Faith in the guidance of the Holy Spirit, affirmation of the lordship of Jesus Christ, and a commitment to ongoing interpretation of Scripture as a source of authority would undergird the dialogue. The goal would be to increase faithfulness and shared theological identity but not doctrinal uniformity.

Extrapolating from MBM's AIC policy, one might add further commitments for theological reflection within the Anabaptist steam of the Christian movement in the twenty-first century. Discernment about how the Anabaptist theological heritage is best appropriated would be a logical concern. A dialogical approach would require trust in the good faith of all participants; commitment to ongoing discernment; and skills in deep listening, clear and sensitive articulation of theological understanding, and critical analysis of theological assumptions. Initiatives of mutual care and accompaniment would help build and maintain trust among the faith communities involved.

Conclusion

This chapter has drawn on the history of Mennonite missionary engagement with African churches to suggest a dialogical approach to Anabaptist theology. The historical trajectory that led Shenk and his colleagues to such an approach with AICs provides an impetus in an age when churches in the world Anabaptist movement emerge from diverse traditions and embody diverse faith expressions. Dialogical discernment could provide a way to encourage contextually helpful articulations of the faith as well as to identify points of common concern and theological identity without assuming that a particular theological formulation from one context is normative for all the rest. It is a method with the potential to accommodate diversity while cultivating shared theological identity.[85]

---

[84]"Ministry among African Independent Churches."
[85]I would like to thank the editors of this volume for their insightful questions and suggestions in response to earlier versions of this chapter.

9

Restlessness as Theological Method

Paul Doerksen

> We have but faith: we cannot know,
> For knowledge is of things we see;
> And yet we trust it comes from thee,
> A beam of darkness: let it grow.
> –ALFRED LORD TENNYSON[1]

Introduction

I begin by acknowledging generally the difficulties embedded within the task of theology, with attempting to speak about God. As Krister Stendahl has written, "To speak about God is wholly arrogant and holy arrogance. It is to think what cannot be thought . . . to think is to grasp, to hold in one's mind, to possess. But sin of sins and the flaw of flaws is to think we can possess God."[2]

---

[1] Cited in Kent Eiler, "Rowan Williams and Christian Language: Mystery, Disruption, and Rebirth," *Christianity and Literature* 61, no. 1 (Autumn 2011): 31.
[2] Krister Stendahl, "To Speak about God," *Harvard Divinity Bulletin* 36, no. 2 (Spring 2008): 8, 9.

Doing Mennonite theology specifically, therefore, is difficult, especially since such theology is often done in close connection with the shaping of Mennonite identity. Theology pursued for such a purpose can thus be understood as something that is "usable," as an instrument necessary in the perpetuation of the search for identity. Insofar as Mennonite theology is pursued in this way, it carries in its train the temptation of distorting the nature of the theological task—namely, giving it a certain "grasping" quality, even while purporting to pursue theology in the service of the church. Put another way, the task of forging identity may well shape Mennonite theology; identity formation acts as theological method.

The burden of this chapter is to begin to resist such a grasping, holding, and possessing impulse in theology, especially when that impulse is pressed into service for the purposes of solidifying Mennonite identity. It is important to recognize that to engage in such resistance is not equivalent to emptying theological work of constructive content. It is also not a call to abandon theological tradition (which in Anabaptism often takes the form of confessions of faith), and it is decidedly not a call to embrace relativism or some version of secular liberalism. I'm referring here to the kind of theological discourse that is described by Brad Gregory as "Whatever." Gregory argues that it was the widespread theological (and other) disagreements in the sixteenth century that led to fragmentation instead of certitude and then, unintentionally, to "Whatever," wherein people can and do believe whatever they want, holding personal opinion up as the arbiter of legitimate religious belief and practice.[3] Rather, I seek to identify a misplaced desire for certitude and stability within Mennonite theology by drawing on Stanley Hauerwas, a sympathetic non-Mennonite critic, as well as some of the internal Mennonite discourse that raises similar concerns. In response to these concerns, I argue for the ongoing pursuit of theological method that is both essentially and devoutly restless.

---

[3] Brad Gregory, *The Unintended Reformation: How a Religious Revolution Secularized Society* (Cambridge: Harvard University Press, 2012), esp. chap. 2.

Unmasking Mennonite Theology

Hauerwas on the "Anabaptist Vision"

Stanley Hauerwas, despite (or perhaps in keeping with) his many assertions of being a Mennonite camp follower and high church Mennonite, has leveled incisive criticism at Mennonite theology. Hauerwas is keen to strip Christians of illusions that we hold and especially those that we think are the most Christian of all. As he puts it, "The great task before Christians today is to unmask the invisibility of those stories that constitute our lives which we assume, wrongly, are commensurate with being Christian."[4] His pursuit of this task has been described as "one of his most important ways of serving the church—he works to unsettle those things that have no basis in, and that might well contradict, the gospel of Jesus Christ."[5] This penchant for revealing and stripping away masks and illusions produces a way of engaging interlocutors' arguments as if these views mask ends other than what they claim for themselves, thereby camouflaging an unannounced but nevertheless real political agenda.[6] Hauerwas is deadly serious in his belief that Christians desperately need each other in order to be cured of our own self-deceptions.[7]

Living out such a stance, the unmasking of self-deception, takes on variegated content depending on the interlocutor. When Hauerwas takes on his unmasking task with regard to Mennonites, he does so in very particular ways, hoping as he does so that, even though

---

[4] Stanley Hauerwas, "In Defense of Cultural Christianity: Reflections on Going to Church," in *Sanctify Them in the Truth: Holiness Exemplified* (Nashville: Abingdon, 1998), 165.
[5] Charles Pinches, Kelly Johnson, and Charles Collier, eds. *Unsettling Arguments: A Festschrift on the Occasion of Stanley Hauerwas's 70th Birthday* (Oregon: Wipf & Stock, 2010), xv. This quotation comes from a *Festschrift* published in honor of his seventieth birthday, wherein eighteen of his former students write essays that argue with Hauerwas, seeking to unsettle any of his arguments that seem out of step with the gospel—and so it goes.
[6] John Berkman and Michael Cartwright, eds., *The Hauerwas Reader* (Durham: Duke University Press, 2001), 662.
[7] Charles Pinches, "Considering Stanley Hauerwas," *Journal of Religious Ethics* 40, no. 2 (2012): 197. See also Pinches et al., *Unsettling Arguments*, xv.

an ecclesial outsider, he can nonetheless strengthen Mennonites' friendships with each other as we are pushed to reconsider what it means to be a faithful church.[8]

Hauerwas is clear that Mennonite theology harbors deeply held illusions, and nowhere is he clearer than in his essay, "Whose Church? Which Future? Whither the Anabaptist Vision?" which he presented as the keynote address for a 1994 conference at Elizabethan College marking the fiftieth anniversary of Harold Bender's seminal essay, "The Anabaptist Vision," an invitation that itself shows Mennonites' regard for Hauerwas. It is here that Hauerwas offers perhaps his most sustained criticism of Mennonites, hoping to capitalize on an opportunity to say to Mennonites what an "insider" would not say, and perhaps more to the point, *could* not say precisely because of that status.

Hauerwas's analysis of Bender's essay and its subsequent impact seeks to reveal to Mennonites that we have become largely unintelligible to ourselves, an insight that by its very nature is difficult to gain from inside that unintelligibility. More specifically, Hauerwas notes that Anabaptists have not been able to come to grips with the fact that the world is no longer dominated by "Christendom"—that relationship of church and state in symbiotic, mutually supportive roles. Even though such a post-Christendom world is ostensibly what Anabaptists have always wanted, "a world in which no one is forced either by government or societal expectations to be Christians,"[9] we are ill-prepared for such a world, so we labor to find our way in the world we struggled to bring into being and that came into being for reasons that were certainly beyond our control. As a result, claims Hauerwas, our unintelligibility takes the form of making a fetish of those aspects

---

[8]Stanley Hauerwas, "Whose Church? Which Future? Whither the Anabaptist Vision?" in *In Good Company: The Church as Polis* (Notre Dame, IN: University of Notre Dame Press, 1995), 66.

[9]Hauerwas, "Whose Church?" 73. One example Hauerwas offers to illustrate what he is referring to is the notion of "voluntary church membership," which at one time would have been a prophetic challenge to mainstream Christianity, "but once Christendom is gone the call for voluntary commitment cannot help but appear as a legitimation of the secular commitment to autonomy" (73).

of our lives that seemed important for the previous world in which we found ourselves.[10]

The Mennonite Turn to Theology as Identity Formation

In our attempts to make ourselves intelligible internally and externally, Mennonites have turned in several directions all at once, in interrelated ways. One of our turns is toward the embrace of and emphasis on distinctiveness and identity. "What makes Mennonites Mennonite?" we earnestly ask. What particular gifts do we bear in our body that we alone can offer to the rest of the church and world? How can we place ourselves as a distinctive minority voice that may help to keep the rest of the Christian world honest? The pursuit of these kinds of questions has been and continues to be commonplace among Mennonites.[11] Hauerwas draws this propensity to our attention to reveal to us that such pursuit may be a serious theological and spiritual mistake, a series of narcissistic exercises, misguided attempts at self-confirmation that by their very nature show that something has gone wrong, that we have somehow convinced ourselves that pursuit of distinctiveness and strong identity is part of the faithful work of church, not realizing that

---

[10]Hauerwas, "Whose Church?" 73.
[11]See, for example, the nuanced discussions in Chris Huebner, *A Precarious Peace: Yoderian Explorations on Theology, Knowledge, and Identity* (Scottdale, PA: Herald, 2006), especially the chapter titled "A Precarious People: The Ambiguity of Mennonite Identity." Huebner's book pursues questions of "Disestablishing Mennonite Theology," "Disowning Knowledge," and "Dislocating Identity" and is a fine example of the pursuit of questions of identity without succumbing to the grasping impulse with which this chapter is concerned. For another interesting discussion along these lines, see Travis Kroeker's interaction with Harry Huebner's ecclesiological emphases, wherein Kroeker suggests that the church in Huebner's theology is ultimately too externally visible and that the church world distinction in Huebner's work is just a bit too sharp. See P. Travis Kroeker, "Making Strange: Harry Huebner's Church–World Distinction," in *The Church Made Strange for the Nations: Essays in Ecclesiology and Political Theology*, edited by Paul Doerksen and Karl Koop (Eugene, OR: Wipf & Stock, 2011), 92, 93. For a related line of discussion and inquiry in the field of Mennonite literature, see Robert Zacharias, ed., *After Identity: Mennonite Writing in North America* (Winnipeg: University of Manitoba Press, 2015).

our pursuits may well be vain, prideful attempts at grasping control of the ecclesial landscape insofar as that is possible as a minority group. These pursuits may cause us to spend inordinate amounts of time and energy seeking to maintain distinctiveness that does very little real Christian work, and instead solidifies differences that don't matter in ways that we think they do. Further, the cultivation of distinctiveness may well support an understanding of the church that privileges the making of autonomous choices among groups with identifiably distinct characteristics above all other considerations. Put another way, the cultivation of distinctiveness may carry with it a deep desire for certitude and stability—this despite all of our sophisticated protestations of fundamental openness and embrace of ambiguity.

This desire for certitude and stability has been with us for a long time; Mennonites are not alone in this pursuit and never have been. If Susan Schreiner is right, this desire can be found in the middle of the ferment of the sixteenth-century Reformation era. She argues that the early modern era can be understood as a struggle centered on the recurring fear of deception, that the sixteenth century both proclaimed the need for certainty and attempted (unsuccessfully in many ways) to provide its own answers to that need. Schreiner claims that it was concern for certitude that determined the theology, polemics, and literature of that formative era, resulting in serious and lasting fragmentation of the church. She traces the attempt to realize such certainty on the part of the reformers in their treatment of Scripture, the understanding of the role of the Holy Spirit, and especially the role of legitimate authority.[12] Gary Kuchar cautions us to acknowledge that the sixteenth century cannot be understood *only* as a search for certainty; rather, he identifies competing impulses of certainty and mystery that remain in tension with one another, not only between and among reformers but also *within* specific thinkers.[13] It is precisely these kinds of impulses that I want

---

[12]Susan E. Schreiner, *Are You Alone Wise? The Search for Certainty in the Early Modern Era* (New York: Oxford University Press, 2011), 324. See also Gregory, *Unintended Reformation.*

[13]Gary Kuchar, "Sounding the Temple: George Herbert and the Mystery of the Word," unpublished paper, 2. Used by kind permission of the author. He puts forward Martin Luther as the prime example of a reformer whose work reveals this unresolved tension. One could also cite Luther's contemporary, Philip Melanchthon,

to suggest may provide a way to participate in Christian theological discourse without succumbing to a truncated, fundamentalist lust for power, a dissipation of faith into amorphous relativism, some version of hyper-pluralism, or, as I want to highlight, the instrumentalization of the theological task as taking on the primary role of identity formation. Instead of attempting to solve questions of certainty and ambiguity prior to theological inquiry, we should pursue the theological task in a way that is shaped by the nature of theology itself, which in my view includes dimensions of (a) reticence that pursues a "learned ignorance"; (b) reverence that celebrates the wonder of theology; (c) repentance that realizes the brokenness of theology; and (d) restlessness that recognizes the mobility of theology.[14]

Four Dimensions of Theological Method

Reticence: The "Educated Ignorance" of Theology

The nature of theology calls for an element of reticence within theological work, the willingness to say less than we are tempted to say, to resist saying more than should be said.[15] The tone of

---

for support of the same point. In his introduction to *Loci Communes Theologici*, Melanchthon makes the following claim regarding the usual main headings in theology: "Just as some of these are altogether incomprehensible, so there are others which Christ has willed the universal body of Christians to know with greatest certainty. We do better to adore the mysteries of Deity than to investigate them." Melanchthon, *Loci Communes Theologici*, in *Melanchthon and Bucer*, edited by William Pauck (Philadelphia: Westminster, 1969), 21.

[14] The fourfold list of dimensions of the theological task is obviously not comprehensive. To provide just one more example of a dimension of the theological task that challenges misplaced (especially triumphalist) certitude and security, see Chris Huebner's work on the role of martyrdom in the formation of identity in Huebner, *Precarious Peace*, esp. 189–212. Further, I do not intend to assert some kind of causal sequence to the order of these dimensions. At most, I want to suggest that reticence, reverence, and repentance are constituent parts of the restlessness for which I am arguing, which explains why that dimension appears last in the order.

[15] As Stanley Hauerwas puts it, we are "tempted to use the simulacra of Christian speech in an effort to say more than can be said." Hauerwas, *Working with Words*,

theological discourse loses its authenticity when any note of triumphalism is allowed to carry the day. This is not to say that theological truth cannot be shared but to assert that it cannot be considered a possession or commodity that can be fully grasped or owned.[16]

Further, just as faulty attempts at coherence serve only to create multiple possibilities of crises, so too assuming complete or even nearly complete understanding multiplies the possibilities of misapprehension. Therefore, it is crucial to the theological task that we recognize that "the closer we are drawn to God, the more that we begin to gain some understanding of the holy mystery of God, the more that what we are and what we say and what we do refracts the character of God's Word, the more conscious we become of the depths of our unknowing. God becomes *more* unknown, not less, the more we understand Him. That is why the tradition speaks of '*docta ignorantia*,' of '*educated ignorance*.'"[17]

To embrace educated ignorance is to engage rigorous pursuit of understanding in a spirit or stance of humility that recognizes the possibility of deception, including self-deception, deception by those who teach us, and the misleading of those whom we teach. Teresa of Avila's writings provide a historical example of the importance of humility in the discernment of evil and good. According to Susan Schreiner, Teresa recognized the dangers of reliance on experience as the basis of accurate discernment since experience of the supernatural itself is subject to ambiguity. For Teresa, humility

---

88. Johannes Harder, in an essay included in a collection of reflections on Mennonite identity, asserts, "Perhaps we have testified too much in our history and thought too little." Johannes Harder, "To Be or To Become a Mennonite," in *Why I Am a Mennonite: Essays on Mennonite Identity*, edited by Harry Loewen (Scottdale, PA: Herald, 1988), 117. I am grateful to Professor Grace Kehler of McMaster University for alerting me to this passage in Harder's essay. Further, while I use the term "reticence" here, it seems to me that "restraint" might also serve a similar function (although I am not encouraging reluctance to engage in the theological task). See Nicholas Lash, "'An Immense Darkness' and the Tasks of Theology," in *God, Truth, and Witness: Engaging Stanley Hauerwas*, edited by L. Gregory Jones, Reinhard Hütter, and C. Rosalee Velloso Ewell (Grand Rapids: Brazos, 2005), 276–78.

[16]Nicholas Lash, *Holiness, Speech, and Silence: Reflections on the Question of God* (Burlington, VT: Ashgate, 2004), 31.

[17]Lash, *Holiness, Speech, and Silence*, 76. Lash refers here specifically to the work of Nicolas of Cusa.

acted as the most important safeguard against deception by evil forces, including the work of Satan. Humility kept the soul aware that it did not deserve, and was incapable of receiving, favors and delights of God based on its own merits. Only in humility could the soul receive as gift any of God's "effects,"[18] including the truths of theology.

So, although we acknowledge that the theological task in some sense defies us and is dangerous, we ought not to let these factors deter us from that faithful pursuit. After all, theology is not the exercise of a technique, some "vaguely spiritual response to free-floating, ill-defined omnivorous human desire."[19] Rather, the nature of the task calls for the stance of humility, which engenders reticence. In Harry Huebner's words, "Although Christians may see Jesus, as the writer of Hebrews reminds us (Heb 2:8-9), the task of knowing how to embody Jesus in our settings requires an ongoing corrective challenge of simplification and complexification, construction and subversion. Perhaps most important is learning the art of knowing when to pick up which challenge. That requires insight and humility."[20]

It is important to note that the Scriptures offer encouragement along these lines. For example, passages such as Isaiah 55 and Psalm 84 highlight the fact that the God of whom we haltingly try to speak is our sun and shield, that here is a God who bestows honor and favor and does not withhold good things from those who walk uprightly. Here we have a God who invites us to abundant life, who cheerfully sends rain and sets in motion the process wherein we are fed with all manner of good things. Theological work embraces danger and possible failure; it also embraces a gift, which is not to be received in isolation. Rather, workers in the theological enterprise join with other workers as recipients of the gift—to participate in something that is already going on, and on a scale that is truly global, seeing how it is given to the whole earth, which in turn responds in an attempt to articulate praise to the one from whom every good and perfect gift proceeds: mountains, hills shall burst into song; trees

---

[18]Schreiner, Schreiner, *Are You Alone Wise?*, 312ff.
[19]William Willimon, "Making Ministry Difficult: The Goal of Seminary," *Christian Century* 130, no. 4 (February 4, 2013): 11.
[20]Harry Huebner, "Learning Made Strange," in Jones, Hütter, and Ewell, *God, Truth, and Witness*, 306.

will clap their hands. Joining with others in participating in the joyful receiving of God's gifts is a giving over of oneself to the hope that the words with which we work, and which we offer together to all creation, will not return empty.

Reverence: The Wonder of Theology

The same impulses that encourage reticence ought also to lead to reverence and wonder, dimensions of Christian theology for which rational certitude are not required. Such reverence and wonder are not just a matter of perpetual surprise; rather, theological wonder is connected to the object of study, or so Karl Barth would have it. For Barth, astonishment is indispensable if theology is to be perpetually renewed as a modest, free, critical, and happy science.[21]

Insofar as theology requires the embrace of some level of uncertainty, then, it does so in a particular way. Here uncertainty is not so much relativism, pluralism, or the pursuit of doubt as if it were a fully Christian stance or virtue; what is required by the nature of Christian theology itself is a kind of uncertainty that is reverent. To follow Marilynne Robinson's moving discussion of these matters, while there is "something about certainty that makes Christianity un-Christian," it is possible to cultivate uncertainty, itself "a form of reverence," which in turn is connected inextricably to the practice of humility.[22]

The only certainty Robinson allows herself is confidence that she remains in error in significant ways that are as yet unknown to her. Rejecting the notion that such a recognition generates a paralyzing effect, or that assertion of faith that exists without certainty somehow creates a stultifying impact on the life and work of the Christian believer, Robinson argues instead that "faith in God is a liberation of thought, because thought is an ongoing instruction in things that pertain to God," resulting in the (perhaps counterintuitive) reality of "a religious belief in intellectual openness."[23] Robinson's notion of intellectual openness is not some amorphous version of

---

[21]Barth, *Evangelical Theology: An Introduction* (Grand Rapids: Eerdmans, 1963). See his chapter titled "Wonder."
[22]Marilynne Robinson, "Credo," *Harvard Divinity Bulletin* 36, no. 2 (Spring 2008): 23.
[23]Robinson, "Credo," 27.

"all opinions are equally valid." Rather, she is seeking a robust investigation and expression of what we encounter in this world, which she believes to be God's world. The embrace of truth, history, humility, and uncertainty as reverence moves Robinson to assert,

> By my lights an appropriate reverence for God, for this shining garment of reality in which he is revealed and concealed, for the unique and deeply sacred mystery of his dealings with any person—an appropriate reverence for these things is not consistent with the idea that we can judge those other souls it has pleased God to make partakers of this great mystery, the great sacrament, Being itself.[24]

Thus the pursuit of theology, of God, of truth, of relationship, and so much more is given its shape neither by certainty nor by uncertainty but by reverence. For the Christian, that reverence is not pursued for its own sake or directed toward just any object but is rather directed at God, who is not one object among other objects. To assert that the reverence of Christian theology ought to be directed to God may appear at first glance to state the perfectly obvious. However, it remains a struggle, theologically speaking, to retain reverence directed to God as a shaping power in our theological work. To have the first word of the theological task to be "God," as Karl Barth liked to say, is difficult to sustain in the face of the temptation to have our theology do "work." To state this more pointedly in an Anabaptist/Mennonite key, it has often (always?) been tempting to forget or omit reverence in our haste to pursue ethics or politics or some such basis of social action. The concern regarding the superfluity of reverent theology by Mennonites is raised explicitly by Paul Martens, who brings to view what he sees as an anthropocentric focus in the work of Harold Bender, John Howard Yoder, and J. Denny Weaver. This anthropocentric emphasis, when pursued in combination with a distillation trajectory that is primarily interested in politics and ethics, renders Mennonite theology superfluous, according to Martens.[25] Put another way, the

---

[24]Ibid., 26.
[25]Paul Martens, "How Mennonite Theology Became Superfluous in Three Easy Steps: Bender, Yoder, Weaver," *Journal of Mennonite Studies* 33 (2015): 149–66.

temptation brought to view here is that the pursuit of Mennonite theology may ironically render that exact work superfluous.

Facing the present danger of rendering reverent theology superfluous through an anthropocentric focus and distillation trajectory toward politics and ethics need not—indeed *ought not*—to lead to the ignoring of politics and ethics. Rather, the embrace and practice of reverence for *God* opens up possibilities of seeking political and ethical practices that would be unavailable to our imaginations on any other grounds—practices rooted in the *kingdom of God*.

Repentance: The Brokenness of Theology

The theological task pursued with appropriate reticence and humility also requires repentance, given humanity's perpetual need for correction—a need that goes beyond technicalities or factual content of theological discourse. Put another way, theology has to articulate and confront not only the falsehoods external to it but also its internal temptations. Such self-awareness, attentiveness to theology's inner workings, calls not for narcissism but for penitence. As Rowan Williams states, "The repentance of theological discourse can be shown in the readiness of any particular version of it to put in question not only this or that specific conclusion within its own workings, but the adequacy or appropriateness of its whole idiom."[26]

Such impetus for theology's self-study and correction can come from sources outside of Christian theology, given that theology may well become blind to its own shortcomings. Not all criticisms of Christian theology and practice are equally insightful or capable of providing corrective discernment to Christian theology. Christian philosopher Merold Westphal argues that the reading of substantive critics such as Friedrich Nietzsche, Karl Marx, and Sigmund Freud

---

[26]Rowan Williams, *On Christian Theology* (Malden, MA: Blackwell, 1999), 9. The importance of penitence is recognized in discourses other than theological as well. For example, philosopher Aaron James attempts to define, with considerable philosophical rigor, what constitutes being an asshole. Interestingly, according to James, "Penitence is usually a sign of not being an asshole." Aaron James, *Assholes: A Theory* (New York: Doubleday, 2012), 85.

may serve just such purposes for Christian thought. These so-called masters of suspicion might be read profitably, claims Westphal, not for immediate resistance or attempts to defeat their respective criticisms but rather to embrace whatever truth and insight regarding the state of Christian thought and practice needs to be acknowledged as being all too true—all with a view to repentance. Thus, according to Westphal, modern atheism serves a "religious use," that of generating penitence.[27]

Rather than seeking rational certainty as a way to approach a fully orbed understanding of God, the mourning of repentance may be thought to constitute a medium by which God makes himself present to the soul.[28] It is impossible to suggest of what theology must repent at any given time, since it may fall prey to various temptations within particular contexts.[29] Within the context of contemporary Mennonite theology, occasion for repentance seems obvious, as we struggle to cope with the theological, institutional, and personal legacy of the work and life of John Howard Yoder, for example. Many kinds of attention need to continue to be paid in this context (i.e., including and in addition to theological attention), especially to the role of repentance—not only for what has and has not been done but also increasingly importantly to what kinds of temptations Mennonite theology has succumbed to within this larger context, whether that be an unwillingness to be appropriately critical of powerful and compelling theological work, especially

---

[27]Merold Westphal, *Suspicion and Faith: The Religious Uses of Modern Atheism* (New York: Fordham, 1998). See also his essay "Taking Suspicion Seriously: The Religious Uses of Modern Atheism," *Faith and Philosophy* 4, no. 1 (January 1987): 26–42. David Bentley Hart's book *Atheist Delusions* (New Haven: Yale University Press, 2009) provides an example of both the resistance to atheism that does not provide constructive challenge to Christianity and the serious engagement with atheism that deserves to be taken seriously.

[28]Gary Kuchar, *The Poetry of Religious Sorrow in Early Modern England* (Cambridge: Cambridge University Press, 2008), 1.

[29]Historically, it seems that theology has a tendency to be tempted by idolatry, an observation Susan Schreiner makes repeatedly in *Are You Alone Wise?* (see, for example, 122, 327ff). Nicholas Lash's articulation bears repeating here: "Insofar as what we worship is some fact or feature of the world, some object or ideal, commodity or dream or theory, nation, place or thing (and most of us include ourselves among the things we worship), then we are idolaters. To learn to worship only God, only the holy and unmasterable mystery that is not the world nor any part of it, is an unending task." Lash, "'Immense Darkness,'" 261.

when that work has afforded Mennonites the seductive result of becoming more widely known and even admired.

It is precisely in this dimension of theological work, that of repentance, that we might draw on a long-standing emphasis in our Mennonite theological heritage, reaching back to Menno Simons—not only on acts of repentance but also on a sustained penitent existence, a "pattern displayed in the liturgical life that transforms the sacraments into daily practice," as P. Travis Kroeker, drawing on Menno, asserts in an argument that nicely draws together reverence and repentance.[30]

Restlessness: The Mobility of Theology

To understand theological inquiry as something other than a search for rational certainty or ecclesial stability is an important dimension of the pursuit itself. Watching our language and working with words in the light of faith are construals that resist the notion that the task of theology requires a definitive beginning and an identifiable conclusion. Nicolas Lash uses the term "understanding" as opposed to "explanation" to signal the relevant pursuit. For Lash, explanation, unlike understanding, if successful, comes to an end,[31] but it is not the task of theology to come to the kind of end explanation offers. Rather, theology is constantly on the move. In a closely related observation, the nature of faith itself is also "mobile"—or perhaps better put, dynamic. For example, Flannery O'Connor, in a series of letters addressed to a friend whose faith seems to be faltering, describes faith in "mobile" terms. In the letters, she assures her searching friend that, although faith does not include absolute certitude, it offers enough certainty to be able to make our way; faith comes and goes, rises and falls. For O'Connor,

---

[30]P. Travis Kroeker, *Empire Erotics and Messianic Economies of Desire*; J. J. Thiessen Lectures (Winnipeg: CMU Press, 2016), 79–81. Kroeker's work in messianic political theology returns to and explores the importance of penitent existence at length, among many other theological dimensions. See P. Travis Kroeker, *Messianic Political Theology and Diaspora Ethics: Essays in Exile* (Eugene, OR: Cascade, 2017).
[31]Lash, *Holiness, Speech, and Silence*, 9. Karl Barth's massive *Church Dogmatics* project is perhaps the best and best-known example of pursuing theology in a way that (literally) never ends.

the cry "I believe; Help my unbelief" is the foundational prayer of faith.[32]

The theological task, then, includes an essential restlessness, which should be embraced by Mennonites if we are to resist the grasping and controlling impulses along with the temptation to idolatry that accompanies the work of theology, especially if it is being instrumentalized primarily in the service of identity formation. A resistance or refusal to force a closing-off of possibilities is intrinsic to the nature of theology itself. Williams argues that a push for complete coherence does not produce any such thing (as coherence); instead, the possibility of crisis is multiplied in the same way that tidying up an unsystematized speech often results in great loss.[33] This is not to say that theology or religious talk of all kinds is satisfied only with provisional statements in perpetuity. If such talk purports to be about the moral universe, it declares itself to be "under judgment" and to be dealing with what supremely *resists* the urge to finish and close what is being said. Put another way, theology is not an attempt to say a last word but a *prohibition* against a would-be final account.[34]

Embrace of this restlessness, this mobility, carries with it the temptation to assert the necessity of rejection of anything that resembles or approaches authoritative creedal or even confessional statements. However, restlessness and mobility are not synonymous with some version of agnosticism, with cynicism regarding truth, or more radically with nihilism. Rather, if Williams is right about the essentially restless nature of Christian theology, then it becomes possible to avoid the dangers of certainty and the frustration of

---

[32] See Flannery O'Connor, *The Habit of Being* (New York: Farrar, Straus and Giroux, 1988), 92, 476–77.
[33] Williams, *On Christian Theology*, xii, xvi.
[34] "To the extent that the relation of the Spirit to Logos is still being realized in our history, we cannot ever, while history lasts, say precisely all there is to say about Logos. What we know, if we claim to be Christians, is as much as anything a set of negations. We know that the divine is not simply a pervasive ground and source, incapable of being imaged, but we know that the historical form of Jesus, in which we see creation turning on its pivot, does not exhaust the divine. We know that the unification of all things through Christ is not a matter of a single explanatory scheme being manifested to us, but the variousness of human lives being drawn into creative and saving relation to the divine and to each other." Williams, *On Christian Theology*, 178.

relativism while nonetheless pursuing real meaning. Kuchar expresses this insight in this way: "Mystery that is intelligible but not ultimately comprehensible, interpretable but not, as it were, containable . . . allows for the possibility of spiritual meaning without excessive, exaggerated certitude."[35]

Conclusion

Restlessness as theological method resists an idolatrous grasping for control. It is central to struggling against self-delusions and unintelligibility to ourselves of the kind that Hauerwas and others have warned against.[36] Rather than control—the pursuit of certitude and stability—theological work calls for a turn to God, a turn that engenders the kind of reticence congruent with such a turn, a reticence enabled in part by reverence that is "due" to God, and a perpetual stance of repentance that continually seeks to root out delusions, many of which are idolatrous. Theological method understood in this way is not a pursuit of the possession of a body of knowledge; rather, it can be understood, embraced, and pursued as, in Rowan Williams's words, the

> dispossession in respect of what is easily available for religious language . . . a dispossession of the entire identity that exists prior to the paschal drama, the identity that has not seen and named its self-deception and self-destructiveness . . . a *strategy* of dispossession, suspicion of our accustomed ways of mastering

---

[35]Kuchar, *Poetry of Religious Sorrow*, 1, 14. In his specific treatment of George Herbert's work, Kuchar observes that Richard Sibbes and Herbert's *The Temple* share the same exigency: "to ensure that scripture be experienced as a mystery into which one is repeatedly initiated as though it were an ever-renewing circle of possibility rather than a problem to be resolved for the sake of one's interpretive certainty" (12). Such an understanding of Scripture complements Williams's take on the task of theology. See also my colleague Chris Huebner's fine discussion of related matters in the introduction to *Precarious Peace*.

[36]Brian Brock, in a recent book-length interview of Hauerwas, describes Hauerwas as "challenging settled habits and narratives" (within the academic guild of ethicists and theologians) and doing so "without offering any alternative habits or any alternative at all really." Brian Brock and Stanley Hauerwas, *Beginnings: Interrogating Hauerwas*, edited by Kevin Hargaden (New York: T&T Clark, 2017), 73.

our environment. If theology is itself a critical, even suspicious discipline... it seeks to make sense of the practice of dispossessed language "before God." It thus lives with the constant possibility of its own relativizing, interruption, silencing; it will not regard its conclusions as having authority independently of their relation to the critical, penitent community it seeks to help be itself.[37]

Such an embrace of restlessness as theological method in the Mennonite context implies that our theological work be pursued by a community of penitents that resists doing its work through grasping modes of domination. This suggests that the work of theology cannot be isolated within our educational institutions alone; the cultivation of strong collaborative and interconnected relationships between the academy and the church is critical to the pursuit of the theological task in a restless posture. To conclude with just one brief example, the pursuit of the revision of confessional statements of faith calls not only for an emphasis on specific content or the articulations of moral or ethical "positions" but also for the ongoing pursuit of understanding embedded within liturgical practices (of reverence), a continued penitential stance, and the refusal to think or act as if this will be the final word. Thus, the pursuit of understanding would ask not only what content to embrace but also how to embrace that content, and it would also seek to discern as part of such work the nature of confessions themselves. To pursue theology restlessly opens the possibility of remaining open to God and resists the temptation to intrumentalize theology, to press it into the service of ends that we think are valuable on some other ground; put another way, theology serves the God whom we worship.

---

[37]Williams, "Theological Integrity," in *On Christian Theology*, 10–13. I acknowledge helpful discussions of earlier versions of this chapter with Professor Grace Kehler, Professor P. Travis Kroeker, Dr. Denny Smith, and members of the Mennonite Seminary community in Amsterdam (December 7, 2017), especially Professor Fernando Enns.

CONTRIBUTORS

Jeremy M. Bergen is Associate Professor of Religious Studies and Theological Studies and Director of Theological Studies at Conrad Grebel University College, University of Waterloo, Waterloo, Ontario.

Stephanie Chandler Burns is a bisexual, queer Mennonite who recently received her MTS at Conrad Grebel University College, Waterloo, Ontario.

Paul Doerksen is Associate Professor of Theology and Anabaptist Studies at Canadian Mennonite University, Winnipeg, Manitoba.

Melanie Kampen is an independent scholar whose research is at the intersection of sexual violence, settler colonialism, and theological ethics.

Karl Koop is Professor of History and Theology at Canadian Mennonite University, Winnipeg, Manitoba.

Paul Martens is Associate Professor of Ethics and Director of Interdisciplinary Programs in the College of Arts and Sciences at Baylor University in Waco, Texas.

Carol Penner is Assistant Professor of Theological Studies and Coordinator of Applied Studies at Conrad Grebel University College, University of Waterloo, Waterloo, Ontario.

Myron A. Penner is Professor of Philosophy and Director of the Humanitas Anabaptist-Mennonite Centre at Trinity Western University in Langley, British Columbia.

Laura Schmidt Roberts is Professor of Biblical and Theological Studies at Fresno Pacific University in Fresno, California.

R. Bruce Yoder is an independent scholar of church history and world Christianity in Ontario, Canada.

BIBLIOGRAPHY

Akam, E. J. *Fasting or the School of God*. Ibesikpo, Nigeria: The International Supreme Temple of Prayer Fellowship, [n.d.].
Akam, E. J. *The Voice of Warning*. Uyo, Nigeria: Voice of Warning, 1970.
Amamkpa, Edet William. *A Short History of Ibesikpo*. [N.p.]: [Amamkpa], 1979.
Barth, Karl. *Church Dogmatics* 1/1. Edinburgh: T&T Clark, 1956/1963.
Barth, Karl. *Church Dogmatics*, 1/2. Edinburgh: T&T Clark, 1956/1963.
Barth, Karl. *Evangelical Theology: An Introduction*. Grand Rapids: Eerdmans, 1963.
Becker, Palmer. *Anabaptist Essentials: Ten Signs of a Unique Christian Faith*. Harrisonburg, VA: Herald, 2017.
Becker, Palmer. *What Is an Anabaptist Christian?*, rev. ed. Elkhart, IN: Mennonite Mission Network, 2010 (2008).
Bender, Harold S. "The Anabaptist Vision." *Church History* 13, no. 1 (March 1944): 3–24.
Bender, Harold S. *The Anabaptist Vision*. Goshen, IN: Mennonite Historical Society, 1944.
Bender, Harold S., Robert Friedmann, and Walter Klaassen. "Anabaptism." *Global Anabaptist Mennonite Encyclopedia Online*, 1990 (1955), http://gameo.org/index.php?title=Anabaptism&oldid=143474.
Bergen, Jeremy M. "The Holy Spirit and Lived Communion from the Perspective of International Bilateral Dialogues." *Journal of Ecumenical Studies* 49 (2014): 193–217.
Bergen, Jeremy M. "Lutheran Repentance at Stuttgart and Mennonite Ecclesial Identity." *Mennonite Quarterly Review* 86 (2012): 315–38.
Bergen, Jeremy M. "Problem or Promise? Confessional Martyrs and Mennonite–Roman Catholic Relations." *Journal of Ecumenical Studies* 41 (2004): 367–88.
Berkman, John and Michael Cartwright, eds. *The Hauerwas Reader*. Durham, NC: Duke University Press, 2001.
Blough, Neal. "The Anabaptist Vision and Its Impact among French Mennonites." *Mennonite Quarterly Review* 69, no. 3 (July 1995): 369–88.

Bonhoeffer, Dietrich. *The Collected Sermons of Dietrich Bonhoeffer.* Edited by Isabel Best; translated by Douglas W. Stott. Minneapolis: Fortress, 2012.

Brock, Brian, and Stanley Hauerwas. *Beginnings: Interrogating Hauerwas.* Edited by Kevin Hargaden. New York: T&T Clark, 2017.

Burkholder, J. Lawrence. *The Problem of Social Responsibility from the Perspective of the Mennonite Church.* Elkhart, IN: Institute of Mennonite Studies, 1989.

Buschart, W. David, and Kent D. Eilers. *Theology as Retrieval: Receiving the Past, Renewing the Church.* Downers Grove, IL: IVP Academic, 2015.

Cartledge, Mark J., and David Cheetham, "Introduction." In *Intercultural Theology* edited by Mark J. Cartledge and David Cheetham, London: SCM, 2011, 1–10.

Chandler Burns, Steph. "Non-binary Identity in Ruth and the Restructuring of Power." Presentation at the Women Doing Theology Conference, Leesburg, VA, November 4–6, 2016.

Cheng, Patrick S. *Radical Love: An Introduction to Queer Theology.* New York: Seabury, 2011.

Confession of Faith in a Mennonite Perspective. Scottdale, PA: Herald, 1995.

Congar, Yves. *True and False Reform in the Church.* Translated by Paul Philibert. Collegeville, MN: Liturgical Press, 2011.

Conlan, Maureen. "Women Crossing Worlds: Women-Church Fuels Worldwide Movement." *Sojourners* 16, no. 11 (December 1987): 7.

Cramer, David C. "Mennonites Systematic Theology in Retrospect and Prospect." *Conrad Grebel Review* 31, no. 3 (Fall 2013): 255–73.

Driedger, David. "Just Let Him Finish; Or, You Cannot Serve Both Process and Advocacy." David CL Driedger (blog). January 16, 2017, https://davidcldriedger.wordpress.com/2017/01/16/just-let-him-finish-or-you-cannot-serve-both-process-and-advocacy.

Driedger, Leo, and J. Harold Kauffman, "Urbanization of Mennonites: Canadian and American Comparisons." *Mennonite Quarterly Review* 56 (1982): 269–90.

Dueck, J. Alicia. *Negotiating Sexual Identities: Lesbian, Gay, and Queer Perspectives on Being Mennonite.* Zurich: Lit Verlag, 2012.

Dueck-Read, Alicia. "Breaking the Binary: Queering Mennonite Identity." *Journal of Mennonite Studies* 33 (2017): 115–33.

Durnbaugh, Donald F. "Believers Church." *Global Anabaptist Mennonite Encyclopedia Online*, 1987, http://gameo.org/index.php?title=Believers_Church&oldid=128086.

Dyck, Cornelius J. "Hermeneutics and Discipleship." In *Essays on Biblical Interpretation: Anabaptist–Mennonite Perspectives*, edited Willard M. Swartley. Elkhart, IN: Institute of Mennonite Studies, 1984, 29–44.

Edwards, James R. "Earthquake in the Mainline." *Christian Century* 110, no. 1 (May 12, 1993): 38–43.
Eiler, Kent. "Rowan Williams and Christian Language: Mystery, Disruption, and Rebirth." *Christianity and Literature* 61, no. 1 (Autumn 2011): 19–32.
Enns, Fernando. "Introduction." In *Mennonites in Dialogue: Official Reports from International and National Ecumenical Encounters, 1975–2012*, edited by Fernando Enns and Jonathan Seiling. Eugene, OR: Wipf &Stock, 2015, 1–17.
Enns, Fernando. *The Peace Church and the Ecumenical Community: Ecclesiology and the Ethics of Nonviolence*. Translated by Helmut Harder. Kitchener: Pandora, 2007.
Ensign-George, Barry. *Between Congregation and Church: Denomination and Christian Life Together*. London: T&T Clark, 2018.
Epp, Kathleen, and Aiden Schlichting Enns. "Women's Theology Conference Provides 'Hospitable Space.'" *Mennonite Reporter* 26, no. 11 (May 27, 1996): 1, 5.
Epp-Tiessen, Esther. *Mennonite Central Committee in Canada: A History*. Winnipeg: CMU Press, 2013.
Estep, William R. *The Anabaptist Story: An Introduction to Sixteenth-Century Anabaptism*. 3rd ed. Grand Rapids: Eerdmans, 1996.
Falola, Toyin, and Matthew Heaton. *A History of Nigeria*. New York: Cambridge University Press, 2008.
Finger, Thomas. "Appropriating Other Traditions While Remaining Anabaptist." *Conrad Grebel Review* 17, no. 2 (Spring 1999): 52–68.
Flores, Gilberto. "Church as an Instrument of Hope." In *Anabaptist Visions for the New Millennium*, edited by Dale Schrag and James Juhnke. Kitchener: Pandora, 2000, 43–47.
Friesen, Duane K. *Artists, Citizens, Philosophers: Seeking the Peace of the City; An Anabaptist Theology of Culture*. Scottdale, PA: Herald, 2000.
Friesen, Duane K. "A Critical Analysis of Narrative Ethics." In *The Church as Theological Community: Essays in Honor of David Schroeder*, edited by Harry Huebner. Winnipeg: Canadian Mennonite Bible College Publications, 1990.
From Conflict to Communion: Lutheran–Catholic Common Commemoration of the Reformation in 2017. Report of the Lutheran–Roman Catholic Commission on Unity. Leipzig: Evangelische Verlagsanstalt; Paderborn: Bonifatius, 2013.
Fuchs, Lorelei F. *Koinonia and the Quest for Ecumenical Ecclesiology*. Grand Rapids: Eerdmans, 2008.
Goossen, Rachel Walter. "'Defanging the Beast': Mennonite Responses to John Howard Yoder's Sexual Abuse." *Mennonite Quarterly Review* 89 (2015): 7–80.

Gregory, Brad. *The Unintended Reformation: How a Religious Revolution Secularized Society.* Cambridge, MA: Harvard University Press, 2012.

Grenz, Stanely J., and John R. Franke. "Scripture: Theology's 'Norming Norm.'" In *Beyond Foundationalism: Shaping Theology in a Postmodern Context,* 57–92. Louisville: Westminster John Knox, 2001.

Grimsrud, Ted. *Embodying the Way of Jesus: Anabaptist Convictions for the Twenty-First Century.* Eugene, Oregon: Wipf & Stock, 2007.

Groff, Anna. "Women Are To Be 'Apostles to the Apostles,'" *The Mennonite* 17, no. 4, April 2014, 32–33.

Guest, Deryn. *When Deborah Met Jael: Lesbian Biblical Hermeneutics.* London: SCM, 2005.

Hall, Douglas John. *Thinking the Faith: Christian Theology in a North American Context.* Minneapolis: Fortress, 1991.

Hamilton, Brian. "The Ground of Perfection: Michael Sattler on 'The Body of Christ.'" In *New Perspectives in Believers Church Ecclesiology,* edited by Abe Dueck, Helmut Harder, Karl Koop, 143–160. Winnipeg: CMU Press, 2010.

Harder, Johannes. "To Be or To Become a Mennonite." In *Why I Am a Mennonite: Essays on Mennonite Identity,* edited by Harry Loewen. Scottdale, PA: Herald, 1988.

Harder, Lydia Neufeld. *The Challenge Is in the Naming: A Theological Journey.* Winnipeg: CMU Press, 2018.

Harder, Lydia Neufeld. "Guest Editorial." *Conrad Grebel Review* 14, no. 2 (1996): [iv–vi].

Harder, Lydia Neufeld. *Obedience, Suspicion and the Gospel of Mark: A Mennonite–Feminist Exploration of Biblical Authority.* Waterloo, ON: Wilfred Laurier University Press for the Canadian Corporation for the Studies in Religion, 1998.

Hart, David Bentley. *Atheist Delusions.* New Haven, CT: Yale University Press, 2009.

Hart, Drew. *Trouble I've Seen: Changing the Way the Church Views Racism.* Scottdale, PA: Herald, 2016.

Hauerwas, Stanley. "In Defense of Cultural Christianity: Reflections on Going to Church." In *Sanctify Them in the Truth: Holiness Exemplified.* Nashville: Abingdon, 1998.

Hauerwas, Stanley. "Whose Church? Which Future? Whither the Anabaptist Vision?" in *In Good Company: The Church as Polis.* Notre Dame, IN: University of Notre Dame Press, 1995.

Hauerwas, Stanley. *Working With Words: On Learning to Speak Christian.* Eugene, OR: Cascade, 2011.

Hauser, Gordon. "The Dignity of Doing Theology," *The Mennonite* 1, no. 19, July 7, 1998, 7.

Healy, Nicholas M. *Church, World, and the Christian Life: Practical–Prophetic Ecclesiology*. Cambridge: Cambridge University Press, 2000.

Healy, Nicholas M. "What Is Systematic Theology?" *International Journal of Systematic Theology* 11, no. 1 (2009): 24–39.

Heelas, Paul, Scott Lash, and Paul Morris, eds. *Detraditionalization: Critical Reflections on Authority and Identity*. Cambridge, MA: Blackwell, 1996.

Heinrichs, Steve, ed. *Buffalo Shout, Salmon Cry: Conversations on Creation, Land Justice, and Life Together*. Scottdale, PA: Herald, 2013.

Hiebert, Paul G. "Contextualization's Challenge to Theological Education." *Occasional Papers of the Council of Mennonite Seminaries and Institute of Mennonite Studies* 2 (1981): 32–44.

Hockman, Cathleen. "Women Challenged to Explore New Visions for Anabaptist Feminism at Theology Event." *Gospel Herald* 87, no. 28, July 12, 1994, 9.

Hockman, Cathleen. "Women Do Theology without the Stereotypes." *Mennonite Weekly Review* 72, no. 27, July 7, 1994, 1.

Hockman-Wert, Cathleen. "Women Envision Theology of Service." *Canadian Mennonite* 5, no. 11, June 4, 2001, 18.

Hollander, August den, Alex Noord, Mirjam van Veen, and Anna Voolstra, eds. *Religious Minorities and Cultural Diversity in the Dutch Republic: Studies Presented to Piet Visser on the Occasion of his 65th Birthday*. Leiden: Brill, 2014.

Hostetler, S. J. "Report of Visit of S. J. and Ida Hostetler to the Church in the Calabar Province." Accra, Ghana: November 28, 1958.

Huebner, Chris. *A Precarious Peace: Yoderian Explorations on Theology, Knowledge, and Identity*. Scottdale, PA: Herald, 2006.

Huebner, Harry. "Imagination/Tradition: Conjunction or Disjunction?" In *Mennonite Theology in Face of Modernity: Essays in Honor of Gordon D. Kaufman*. North Newton, KS: Bethel College, 1996.

Huebner, Harry. "Learning Made Strange." In *God, Truth, and Witness: Engaging Stanley Hauerwas*, edited by L. Gregory Jones, Reinhard Hütter, and C. Rosalee Velloso Ewell. Grand Rapids: Brazos, 2005.

Huebner, Harry. "Participation, Peace, and Forgiveness: Milbank and Yoder in Dialogue." In *The Gift of Difference: Radical Orthodoxy, Radical Reformation*, edited by Chris K. Huebner and Tripp York. Winnipeg: CMU Press, 2010.

Hunt, Mary E. "Women-Church." *Encyclopedia of Women and Religion in North America*, vol. 3, edited by Rosemary Skinner Keller and Rosemary Radford Ruether. Bloomington, IN: Indiana University Press, 2006.

Inglis, Nathanael. "The Importance of Gordon Kaufman's Constructive Theological Method for Contemporary Anabaptist–Mennonite Theology." *Conrad Grebel Review* 34, no. 2 (Spring 2016): 131–54.

International Methodist–Catholic Dialogue Commission, "Encountering Christ the Saviour: Church and Sacraments" (2011), no. 24, www.vatican.va/roman_curia/pontifical_councils/chrstuni/meth-council-docs/rc_pc_chrstuni_doc_20110612_durban-document_en.html.

International Methodist–Catholic Dialogue Commission, "The Grace Given You in Christ: Catholics and Methodists Reflect Further on the Church" (2006), no. 14, www.vatican.va/roman_curia/pontifical_councils/ chrstuni/meth-council-docs/ rc_pc_chrstuni_doc_20060604_seoul-report_en.html.

James, Aaron. *Assholes: A Theory*. New York: Doubleday, 2012.

Janzen, Mark. *Mennonite German Soldiers: Nation, Religion, and Family in the Prussian East, 1772–1880*. Notre Dame, IN: University of Notre Dame, 2010.

Kanagy, Conrad, Elizabeth Miller, and John D. Roth, *Global Anabaptist Profile: Belief and Practice in 24 Mennonite World Conference Churches*. Goshen, IN: Institute for the Study of Global Anabaptism, 2017.

Kauffman, Daniel, ed. *Bible Doctrine: A Treatise on the Great Doctrines of the Bible, Pertaining to God, Angels, Satan, the Church, and the Salvation, Duties and Destiny of Man*. Scottdale, PA: Mennonite Pub. House, 1914.

Kauffman, Daniel. *Doctrines of the Bible: A Brief Discussion of the Teachings of God's Word*. Scottdale, PA: Mennonite Pub. House, 1928.

Kauffman, Daniel. "How Far Should the Home Church Project Its Policies into the Church on the Field?" In *Twenty-Seventh Annual Report of the MBMC*. Elkhart, IN: Mennonite Board of Missions and Charities, 1933.

Kauffman, Daniel. *Manual of Bible Doctrines: Setting Forth the General Principles of the Plan of Salvation, Explaining the Symbolical Meaning and Practical Use of the Ordinances Instituted by Christ and His Apostles, and Pointing out Specifically Some of the Restrictions Which the New Testament Scriptures Enjoin upon Believers*. Elkhart, IN: Mennonite Pub. Co., 1898.

Kaufman, Gordon D. "Doing Theology from a Liberal Point of View." In Doing *Theology in Today's World: Essays in Honor of Kenneth S. Kantzer*, edited by John D. Woodbridge and Thomas Edward McComisky. Grand Rapids: Zondervan, 1991.

Kaufman, Gordon D. *An Essay on Theological Method*. 3rd ed. Atlanta: Scholars, 1995.

Kaufman, Gordon D. *Nonresistance, Responsibility, and Other Mennonite Essays*. Newton, KS: Faith and Life, 1979.

Klaassen, Walter, ed. *Anabaptism in Outline*. Scottdale, PA: Herald, 1981.

Klaassen, Walter. *Anabaptism: Neither Catholic nor Protestant*. Kitchener, ON: Pandora, 2001.

Koontz, Gayle Gerber, and Willard Swartley, eds., *Perspectives on Feminist Hermeneutics*. Elkhart, IN: Institute of Mennonite Studies, 1987.

Koop, Karl. "Anabaptist and Mennonite Identity: Permeable Boundaries and Expanding Definitions." *Religion Compass* 8, no. 6 (2014): 199–207.

Koop, Karl. "A Complication for the Mennonite Peace Tradition: Wilhelm Mannhardt's Defense of Military Service." *Conrad Grebel Review* 34, no. 1 (Winter 2016): 28–48.

Koop, Karl, ed. *Confessions of Faith in the Anabaptist Tradition 1527–1660*. Kitchener, ON: Pandora, 2006.

Koop, Karl. "Worldly Preachers and True Shepherds: Anabaptist Anticlericalism in the Lower Rhine." In *The Heart of the Matter: Pastoral Ministry in Anabaptist Perspective*, edited by Erik Sawatzky, 24–38. Scottdale, PA: Herald, 2004.

Kraus, C. Norman. "American Mennonites and the Bible, 1750–1950." *Mennonite Quarterly Review* 41, no. 4 (October 1967): 309–29.

Kraybill, Becca. "Second Women Doing Theology Conference Focuses on Power. Daily News/Updates. *The Mennonite*, Nov. 7, 2016, https://themennonite.org/daily-news/second-women-theology-conference-focuses-power/.

Kroeker, P. Travis. *Empire Erotics and Messianic Economies of Desire*. Winnipeg: CMU Press, 2016.

Kroeker, P. Travis. "Making Strange: Harry Huebner's Church–World Distinction." In *The Church Made Strange For the Nations: Essays in Ecclesiology and Political Theology*, edited by Paul Doerksen and Karl Koop. Eugene, OR: Wipf & Stock, 2011.

Kroeker, P. Travis. *Messianic Political Theology and Diaspora Ethics: Essays in Exile*. Eugene, OR: Cascade, 2017.

Kuchar, Gary. *The Poetry of Religious Sorrow in Early Modern England*. Cambridge: Cambridge University Press, 2008.

Kuchar, Gary. "Sounding the Temple: George Herbert and the Mystery of the Word." Unpublished paper.

Küster, Volker. "Intercultural Theology Is a Must." *International Bulletin of Missionary Research* 38, no. 4 (October 2014): 171–76.

Lapp, George Jay. *The Christian Church and Rural India: A Report on Christian Rural Reconstruction and Welfare Service*. Calcutta: YMCA Publishing House, 1938.

Lapp, George Jay. [*Menno Simons and the Mennonite Church*]. Jabalpur, India: 1929.

Lapp, John A. "The Global Mennonite History Project: The Vision and Process." *Mission Focus Annual Review* 19 (2011): 41–45.

Lapp, John A. *The Mennonite Church in India, 1897–1962*. Scottdale, PA: Herald, 1972.

Lapp, John A., and C. Arnold Snyder, eds. *Global Mennonite History Series*. 5 vols. Intercourse, PA: Good Books, 2006.

Lash, Nicholas. "'An Immense Darkness' and the Tasks of Theology." In *God, Truth, and Witness: Engaging Stanley Hauerwas*, edited by L. Gregory Jones, Reinhard Hütter, and C. Rosalee Velloso Ewell. Grand Rapids: Brazos, 2005.

Lash, Nicholas. *Holiness, Speech, and Silence*: Reflections on the Question of God. Burlington, VT: Ashgate, 2004.

Lehman, M. C. *Our Mission Work in India*. Elkhart, IN: Mennonite Board of Missions and Charities, 1939.

Leith, John H., ed. *Creeds of the Churches: A Reader in Christian Doctrine from the Bible to the Present*. 3rd ed. Atlanta: John Knox, 1982.

Leithart, Peter J. *The End of Protestantism: Pursuing Unity in a Fragmented Church*. Grand Rapids: Brazos, 2016.

Linden, Ian. *Global Catholicism: Diversity and Change Since Vatican II*. London: Hurst, 2009.

Loewen, Howard John. *One Lord, One Church, One Hope, and One God: Mennonite Confessions of Faith*. Elkhart, IN: Institute of Mennonite Studies, 1985.

Loewen, Royden. "The Poetics of Peoplehood: Religion and Ethnicity among Canada's Mennonites." In *Christianity and Ethnicity in Canada*, edited by Paul Bramadat and David Seljak, 330–64. Toronto: University of Toronto Press, 2008.

Luther, Martin. "The Freedom of a Christian (1520)." In *A Reformation Reader: Primary Texts with Introductions*, edited by Denis R. Janz. Minneapolis: Fortress, 1999.

Lutheran–Roman Catholic Dialogue. "Facing Unity" (1984), nos. 9–12. In *Growth in Agreement II*, edited by Jeffrey Gros, Harding Meyer, and William G. Rusch. Grand Rapids: Eerdmans, 2000.

Lutheran World Federation and Mennonite World Conference. "Healing of Memories, Reconciling in Christ" (2010). In *Mennonites in Dialogue: Official Reports from International and National Ecumenical Encounters, 1975–2012*, edited by Fernando Enns and Jonathan Seiling, 187–307. Eugene, OR: Wipf &Stock, 2015

Lutheran World Federation and Mennonite World Conference. "Healing of Memories, Reconciling in Christ." In *Mennonites in Dialogue: Official Reports from International and National Ecumenical Encounters, 1975–2012*, edited by Fernando Enns and Jonathan Seiling. Eugene, OR: Wipf &Stock, 2015

Martens, Paul. "How Mennonite Theology Became Superfluous in Three Easy Steps: Bender, Yoder, Weaver." *Journal of Mennonite Studies* 33 (2015): 149–66

Martin, Dennis D. "Nothing New Under the Sun? Mennonites in History." *Conrad Grebel Review* 5 (1987): 1–27.

Melanchthon, Philipp. *Loci Communes Theologici, in Melanchthon and Bucer*, edited by William Pauck. Philadelphia: Westminster, 1969.

Mennonite Central Committee, Gifts of the Red Tent, web.archive.org/web/20030313130735/http:/www.mcc.org/womendoingtheology/.

Mennonite Church Canada. "Being a Faithful Church 7: Summary and Recommendation on Sexuality 2009–2015." PowerPoint Presentation at Mennonite Church Canada Assembly, Saskatoon, July 7–9, 2016, www.home.mennonitechurch.ca/BFC.

Mennonite Church USA Archives, Elkhart, IN.

Mennonite Church USA staff, "Daily News Posts." *The Mennonite*, August 23, 2016, www.themennonite.org/daily-news/women-theology-conference-speakers-announced/.

Messenger, John Cowan. "Anang Acculturation: A Study of Shifting Cultural Focus." PhD diss., Northwestern University, 1957.

Migliore, Daniel. *Faith Seeking Understanding: An Introduction to Christian Theology*. 3rd ed. Grand Rapids: Eerdmans, 2014.

Miller, Keith Graber. "Anabaptist Ethics." In *The Dictionary of Scripture and Ethics*, edited by Joel Green. Grand Rapids: Baker Academic, 2011.

Miller, Paul. "Worship among the Early Anabaptists." *Mennonite Quarterly Review* 30, no. 4 (October 1956): 235–46.

Murray, Stuart. *Biblical Interpretation in the Anabaptist Tradition*. Kitchener: Pandora, 2000.

Murray, Stuart. *The Naked Anabaptist: The Bare Essentials of a Radical Faith*. Scottdale, PA: Herald, 2010.

Neustaedter Barg, Darryl, and Irma Fast Dueck (producers). Listening Church Project. www.listeningchurchproject.ca.

Nigeria and Department of Statistics. Population Census of the Eastern Region of Nigeria, 1953. Lagos: Census Superintendent (the Govt. statistician), 1955.

O'Connor, Flannery. *The Habit of Being*. New York: Farrar, Straus and Giroux, 1988.

Ollenburger, Ben C. "The Hermeneutics of Obedience." In *Essays on Biblical Interpretation: Anabaptist–Mennonite Perspectives*, edited Willard M. Swartley, 45–61. Elkhart, IN: Institute of Mennonite Studies, 1984.

Ollenburger, Ben C., ed. *So Wide a Sea: Essays on Biblical and Systematic Theology*. Elkhart, IN: Institute of Mennonite Studies, 1991.

Orobator, Agbonkhianmeghe E. *Theology Brewed in an African Pot: An Introduction to Christian Doctrine from an African Perspective*. Nairobi: Paulines Publications Africa, 2008.

Osbourne, Troy. "TS 640: The Mennonite Tradition in the Historical Context." Course at Conrad Grebel University College, Waterloo, ON, January–April 2017.
Penner, Carol. "Women Doing Theology: A Conference Report." *Women's Concerns Report* 105 (November–December 1992): 1–2.
Phan, Peter C. *In Our Own Tongues: Perspectives from Asia on Mission and Inculturation.* Maryknoll, NY: Orbis, 2003.
Pinches, Charles. "Considering Stanley Hauerwas." *Journal of Religious Ethics* 40, no. 2 (2012): 193–201.
Pinches, Charles, Kelly Johnson, and Charles Collier, eds. *Unsettling Arguments: A Festschrift on the Occasion of Stanley Hauerwas's 70th Birthday.* Eugene, OR: Wipf & Stock, 2010.
Pratten, David. "Mystics and Missionaries: Narratives of the Spirit Movement in Eastern Nigeria." *Social Anthropology* 15, no. 1 (2007): 47–70.
Price, Tom. "Yoder's Actions Framed in Writings." *Elkhart Truth*, July 15, 1992.
Radner, Ephraim. *The End of the Church: A Pneumatology of Christian Division in the West.* Grand Rapids: Eerdmans, 1998.
Rambo, Shelly. *Spirit and Trauma: A Theology of Remaining.* Louisville: Westminster John Knox, 2010.
Razack, Sherene. *Looking White People in the Eye: Gender, Race, and Culture in Courtrooms and Classrooms.* Toronto: University of Toronto Press, 1998.
Reimer, A. James. *Mennonites and Classical Theology: Dogmatic Foundations for Christian Ethics.* Kitchener, ON: Pandora, 2001.
Reimer, A. James. "Mennonites and the Church Universal." In *Without Spot or Wrinkle: Reflecting Theologically on the Nature of the Church*, edited by Karl Koop and Mary Schertz. Elkhart, IN: Institute of Mennonite Studies, 2000, 93–111.
Reimer, Margaret Loewen. "Women Explore 'Doing Theology' in Their Own Voices." *Mennonite Reporter* 22, no.10 (May 18, 1992): 1.
Reno, R. R. "The Debilitation of the Churches." In *The Ecumenical Future: Background Papers for "In One Body Through the Cross: The Princeton Proposal for Christian Unity,"* edited by Carl E. Braaten and Robert W. Jenson, 46–72. Grand Rapids: Eerdmans, 2004.
"Report on the Re-Imagining Conference." *Journal of Feminist Studies in Religion* 11, no. 1 (Spring 1995): 137–38.
Ricoeur, Paul. *The Conflict of Interpretations: Essays in Hermeneutics.* Edited by Don Ihde. Evanston: Northwestern University Press, 1974.
Ricoeur, Paul. "The Hermeneutical Function of Distanciation." In *Hermeneutics and the Human Sciences*, edited and translated by John B. Thompson, 131–44. Cambridge: Cambridge University Press, 1981.

Ricoeur, Paul. "Hermeneutics and the Critique of Ideology." In *Hermeneutics and the Human Sciences*, edited and translated by John B. Thompson, 63–100. Cambridge: Cambridge University Press, 1981.

Ricoeur, Paul. *Interpretation Theory: Discourse and the Surplus of Meaning*. Fort Worth: Texas Christian University, 1976.

Ricoeur, Paul. *Oneself as Another*. Translated by Kathleen Blamey. Chicago: University of Chicago Press, 1990.

Ricoeur, Paul. *Time and Narrative*. 3 vols. Translated by Kathleen McLaughlin and David Pellauer. Chicago: University of Chicago Press, 1984–1988.

Robert, Dana L. "Shifting Southward: Global Christianity Since 1945." *International Bulletin of Missionary Research* 24, no. 2 (2000): 50–58.

Roberts, Laura Schmidt. "The Church in the World: Shifting Notions of Ecclesial Identity among North American Mennonites." *Dialog: A Journal of Theology* 51, no. 1 (March 2012): 53–61.

Roberts, Laura Schmidt. "(Re)Figuring Tradition." *Conrad Grebel Review* 21, no. 2 (Spring 2003): 71–81.

Robinson, Marilynne. "Credo." *Harvard Divinity Bulletin* 36, no. 2 (Spring 2008): 22–32.

"Role of Catholic Women Debated." *Sojourners* 13, no. 1 (January 1984): 6–7.

Roman Catholic Church and World Evangelical Alliance, "Church, Evangelization, and the Bonds of Koinonia [2002]." No. 18, in *Growth in Agreement III*, edited by Jeffrey Gros, Thomas F. Best, and Lorelei F. Fuchs. Geneva: WCC Publications; Grand Rapids: Eerdmans, 2007.

Roman Catholic–Mennonite International Dialogue, "Called Together to be Peacemakers" (2003). In *Mennonites in Dialogue*, edited by Fernando Enns and Jonathan R. Seiling, 19–114. Eugene, OR: Pickwick, 2015.

Roth, John D. "The Challenge of Church Unity in the Anabaptist Tradition." Lecture at Conrad Grebel University College, Waterloo ON, 2012.

Roth, John D. "Community as Conversation: A New Model of Anabaptist Hermeneutics." In *Anabaptist Currents: History in Conversation with the Present*, edited by Carl F. Bowman and Stephen L. Longenecker. Bridgewater, VA: Penobscot, 1995, 51–64.

Roth, John D. ed. *Engaging Anabaptism: Conversations with a Radical Tradition*. Scottdale, PA: Herald, 2001.

Roth, John D. "Living Between the Times: 'Anabaptist Vision and Mennonite Reality' Revisited." In *Refocusing a Vision*, edited by John D. Roth. Goshen: Mennonite Historical Society, 1995.

Roth, John D. "Pietism and the Anabaptist Soul." In *The Dilemma of Anabaptist Piety*, edited by Stephen L. Longnecker, 17–33. Bridgewater: Forum for Religious Studies, 1997.

Roth, John D., and James M. Stayer, eds. *A Companion to Anabaptism and Spiritualism, 1521–1700*. Leiden: Brill, 2007.

Sawatsky, Rodney J. "Domesticating Sectarianism: Mennonites in the U.S. and Canada in Comparative Perspective." *Canadian Journal of Sociology* 3 no. 2 (1978): 233–44.

Sawatsky, Walter. "20th Century Anabaptist–Mennonites Re-shaped by Context: First, Second, and Third Worlds." In *Prophetic and Renewal Movements: The Prague Consultations*, edited by Walter Sawatsky. Geneva: World Alliance of Reformed Churches: 2009, 177–87.

Sawatsky, Walter. "Teaching Christian History in Seminary: A Declension Story." *Conrad Grebel Review* 30, no. 3 (Fall 2012): 265–85.

Schlabach, Gerald. "Just Policing: How War Could Cease To Be a Church-Dividing Issue." *Journal of Ecumenical Studies* 41 (2004): 409–30.

Schlabach, Gerald, ed., *Just Policing, Not War: An Alternative Response to World Violence*. Collegeville, MN: Liturgical Press, 2007.

Schlabach, Gerald. *Unlearning Protestantism: Sustaining Christian Community in an Unstable Age*. Grand Rapids: Brazos, 2010.

Schlabach, Gerald. "You Converted to What? One Mennonite's Journey." *Commonweal* 134, no. 10 (June 1, 2007): 14–17.

Schlabach, Theron F. *Gospel versus Gospel: Mission and the Mennonite Church, 1863–1944*. Scottdale, PA: Herald, 1980.

The Schleitheim Confession. Edited and translated by John Howard Yoder. Scottdale, PA: Herald, 1977.

"The Schleitheim Confession of Faith (1527)." In *The Protestant Reformation*, edited by Hans Hillerbrand, 129–36. London: MacMillan, 1968.

Schreiner, Susan E. *Are You Alone Wise? The Search for Certainty in the Early Modern Era*. New York: Oxford University Press, 2011.

Schreiter, Robert J. *Constructing Local Theologies*. Maryknoll, NY: Orbis, 1985.

Schreiter, Robert J., ed. *Faces of Jesus in Africa*. Maryknoll, NY: Orbis, 1998.

Second Vatican Council, *Unitatis Redintegration: Decree on Ecumenism* (1964).

Séguy, Jean. *Les Assemblées Anabaptistes–Mennonites de France*. Paris: Mouton, 1977.

Sensenig, Kristine. "Women gather to share under 'Red Tent,'" *The Mennonite* 6, no. 12 (June 17, 2003): 21.

Sensenig, Kristine. "Women Share Talents, Theological Insights under a 'Red Tent.'" *Mennonite Weekly Review* 81, no. 24 (June 16, 2003): 3.

Shenk, Wilbert R. *By Faith They Went Out: Mennonite Missions 1850–1999*. Elkhart, IN: Institute of Mennonite Studies, 2000.

Shenk, Wilbert R., ed., *Enlarging the Story: Perspectives on Writing World Christian History*. Maryknoll, NY: Orbis, 2002.

Shenk, Wilbert R. "A Global Church Requires a Global History." *Conrad Grebel Review* 15, no. 1 (1997): 3–18.

Shenk, Wilbert R. "'Go Slow through Uyo': A Case Study of Dialogue as Missionary Method." In *Fullness of Life for All: Challenges for Mission in Early 21st Century*, edited by Inus Daneel, Charles Van Engen, and Hendrik Vroom, 329–40. New York: Rodopi, 2005.

Shenk, Wilbert R. *Henry Venn: Missionary Statesman*. Maryknoll: Orbis, 1983.

Shenk, Wilbert R. *Mennonite Board of Missions: A Theology of Mission in Outline*. Elkhart, IN: Mennonite Board of Missions, 1978.

Shenk, Wilbert R. "Theological Education in Historical and Global Perspective." In *Theology in Missionary Perspective: Lesslie Newbigin's Legacy*, edited by Mark T. B. Laing and Paul Weston. Eugene, OR: Pickwick, 2012, 221–43.

Shenk, Wilbert R. "Toward a Global Church History." *International Bulletin of Missionary Research* 20, no. 2 (April 1996): 50–57.

Shenk, Wilbert R. ed., *The Transfiguration of Mission: Biblical, Theological, and Historical Foundations*. Scottdale, PA: Herald, 1993.

Sider, J. Alexander. "Self and/as Victim: A Reflection on 'Mennonite' Ethics." *Conrad Grebel Review* 34, no. 3 (Fall 2016): 27–39.

Simons, Menno. *The Complete Writings of Menno Simons, c. 1496–1561*. Edited by J. C. Wenger; translated by Leonard Verduin. Scottdale, PA: Herald, 1984 (1956).

Snyder, C. Arnold. *Following in the Footsteps of Christ: The Anabaptist Tradition*. Maryknoll, NY: Orbis, 2004.

Stayer, James M., Werner O. Packull, and Klaus Deppermann, "From Monogenesis to Polygenesis: The Historical Discussion of Anabaptist Origins." *Mennonite Quarterly Review* 49 (1975): 83–121.

Stendahl, Krister. "To Speak about God." *Harvard Divinity Bulletin* 36, no. 2 (Spring 2008): 8–9.

Toews, Paul. *Mennonites in American Society, 1930–1970: Modernity and the Persistence of Religious Community*, vol. 4, *Mennonite Experience in America*. Scottdale, PA: Herald, 1996.

Tracy, David. *Plurality and Ambiguity: Hermeneutics, Religion, Hope*. San Francisco: HarperCollins, 1989.

Tuhus, Melinda. "Conference Celebrates Women–Church Movement." *Sojourners* 18, no. 1 (January 1989): 11–12.

van Braght, Thieleman J. *The Bloody Theater or Martyrs Mirror*. Translated by Joseph F. Sohn. Scottdale, PA: Herald, 1950.

van den Toren, Benno. "Intercultural Theology as a Three-Way Conversation: Beyond the Western Dominance of Intercultural Theology." *Exchange* 44 (2015): 123–43.

Veen, Mirjam van, Piet Visser, and Gary Waite. *Sisters: Myth and Reality of Anabaptist, Mennonite and Doopsgezind Women, ca. 1525–1900.* Leiden: Brill, 2014.

Verduin, Leonard. *The Reformers and Their Stepchildren.* Grand Rapids: Eerdmans, 1964.

Vischer, Lukas. "The Reformation Heritage and the Ecumenical Movement." In *Towards a Renewed Dialogue: The First and Second Reformations*, edited by Milan Opočenský. Geneva: World Alliance of Reformed Churches, 1996, 161–69.

Vischer, Lukas, Ulrich Luz, and Christian Link. *Unity of the Church in the New Testament and Today.* Grand Rapids: Eerdmans, 2010.

Visser, Piet. *Broeders in de geest: De doopsgezinde bijdragen van Dierick en Jan Philipsz. Schabaelje tot de Nederlandse stichtelijke literatuur*, 2 vols. Deventer: Sub Rosa, 1988.

Weaver, Edwin I. "This Year in the Church." In *Report of the Forty-Third Annual Meeting of the MBMC*, 104–8. Elkhart, IN: Mennonite Board of Missions and Charities, 1949.

Weaver, J. Denny. "A Believers' Church Christology." *Mennonite Quarterly Review* 58, no. 2 (April 1983): 112–31.

Weaver, J. Denny. "The General versus the Particular: Exploring Assumptions in 20th-Century Mennonite Theologizing." *Conrad Grebel Review* 17, no. 2 (Spring 1999): 17–51.

Weaver, J. Denny. "Mennonite Theological Self-Understanding: A Response to A. James Reimer." In *Mennonite Identity: Historical and Contemporary Understandings.* Edited by Calvin Wall Redekop. Lanham, MD: Institute for Anabaptist and Mennonite Studies, 1988, 39–61.

Weaver, J. Denny. "Mennonites: Theology, Peace, and Identity." *Conrad Grebel Review* 6 (Spring 1988): 119–45.

Weaver, J. Denny. "Reading Sixteenth-Century Anabaptism Theologically: Implications for Modern Mennonites as a Peace Church." *Conrad Grebel Review* 16 (Winter 1998): 37–51.

Weaver-Zercher, David. *Martyrs Mirror: A Social History.* Baltimore: Johns Hopkins University Press, 2016.

Wenger, J. C. *Introduction to Theology: A Brief Introduction to the Doctrinal Content of Scripture Written in the Anabaptist–Mennonite Tradition.* Scottdale, PA: Herald, 1966.

West, Traci C. *Wounds of the Spirit: Black Women, Violence, and Resistance Ethics.* New York: New York University Press, 1999.

Westphal, Merold. *Suspicion and Faith: The Religious Uses of Modern Atheism.* New York: Fordham Press, 1998.

Westphal, Merold. "Taking Suspicion Seriously: The Religious Uses of Modern Atheism." *Faith and Philosophy* 4, no. 1 (January 1987): 26–42.

Wiebe, Katie Funk. "Responses." *Conrad Grebel Review* 10, no. 2 (Spring 1992): 209–14.

Williams, Peter. "'Not Transplanting' Henry Venn's Strategic Vision." In *The Church Mission Society and World Christianity, 1799–1999*, edited by Kevin Ward and Brian Stanley, 147–72. Grand Rapids: Eerdmans, 2000.

Williams, Rowan. *On Christian Theology*. Malden, MA: Blackwell, 1999.

Willimon, William. "Making Ministry Difficult: The Goal of Seminary." *Christian Century* 130, no. 4 (February 4, 2013): 11–12.

"Women–Church and Diversity." *Christian Century* 110, no. 16 (May 12, 1993): 512–13.

Working Group of the World Council of Churches and the Roman Catholic Church, "The Nature and Purpose of Ecumenical Dialogue" (2004). In *Growth in Agreement III*, edited by Jeffrey Gros, Thomas F. Best, and Lorelei F. Fuchs. Grand Rapids: Eerdmans, 2007.

World Council of Churches. "Canberra Statement"; www.oikoumene.org.

World Council of Churches. "Called To Be the One Church: The Porto Alegre Statement" (1996), www.oikoumene.org.

World Council of Churches, "The Church: Towards a Common Vision" (2013), www.oikoumene.org.

World Council of Churches. "New Delhi Statement on Unity" (1961); www.oikoumene.org.

World Council of Churches. *A Treasure in Earthen Vessels: An Instrument for an Ecumenical Reflection on Hermeneutics, Faith and Order*. Geneva: WCC, 1998.

World Council of Churches. "The Unity of the Church—Gift and Calling: The Canberra Statement" (1991); www.oikoumene.org

Wright, Jeff. *Urban and Anabaptist: The Remarkable Story of Rapid Growth Among Mennonites in Southern California*. Elkhart, IN: Mennonite Board of Missions, 2001.

Yamasaki, April. "In Search of Wholeness." *MCC Women's Concerns Report* 105 (November–December 1992): 4.

Yoder, Elizabeth, ed. *Peace Theology and Violence Against Women*. Elkhart, IN: Institute of Mennonite Studies, 1992.

Yoder, John Howard. "Anabaptist Vision and Mennonite Reality." In *Consultation on Anabaptist–Mennonite Theology*, edited by A. J. Klassen. Fresno, CA: Council of Mennonite Seminaries, 1970, 1–46.

Yoder, John Howard. "The Hermeneutics of the Anabaptists." In *Essays on Biblical Interpretation: Anabaptist–Mennonite Perspectives*, edited Willard M. Swartley, 11–28. Elkhart, IN: Institute of Mennonite Studies, 1984.

Yoder, John Howard. *The Original Revolution: Essays on Christian Pacifism*. Scottdale, PA: Herald, 2003.

Yoder, John Howard. *The Politics of Jesus: Vicit Agnus Noster*. 2nd ed. Grand Rapids: Eerdmans, 1994 (1972).
Yoder, John Howard. *The Priestly Kingdom: Social Ethics as Gospel*. Notre Dame, IN: University of Notre Dame Press, 1984.
Yoder, John Howard. "The Recovery of the Anabaptist Vision." *Concern* 18 (July 1971): 5–23.
Yoder, Kelli. "Women's conference asks 'Is love enough?'" *Mennonite World Review* 92, no. 5, March 3, 2014, http://www.mennoworld.org/archived/2014/3/3/love-enough
Zacharias, Robert, ed., *After Identity: Mennonite Writing in North America*. Winnipeg: University of Manitoba Press; University Park, PA: Pennsylvania State University Press, 2015.
Zacharias, Robert. "Ceremonies of Belief: Unsettling Mennonite Stories." *Canadian Mennonite*, April 19, 2017, http://www.canadianmennonite.org/stories/ceremonies-belief.

INDEX

acculturation 5, 7, 139, 140
Anabaptist Vision 4, 7, 12, 16, 33, 42, 96, 107, 111, 146, 153, 154. *See also* Harold S. Bender
authority 12, 24, 27, 37, 42–5, 68, 89, 101, 112, 134, 143, 149, 156, 167

baptism 82–3, 104
  adult 106
  believer's 4, 23, 112, 120
Barth, Karl 26–7, 160, 161, 164 n.31
Becker, Palmer 74, 107 n.10
Bender, Harold S. 3–8, 10, 12–15, 26 n.16, 33, 42, 70, 96, 107, 111, 118, 137–8, 146–7, 154, 161. *See also Anabaptist Vision*
Bible 8, 28, 35, 40–4, 47, 54, 66, 71, 72, 75, 90, 124, 131, 139, 141, 143. *See also* scripture
  colleges 139, 140
  interpretation 29–30, 75, 87
  New Testament 6, 9, 111
  Old Testament 60
  scholarship 8, 30
  study 5, 74, 146
  theology 8, 81

Cheng, Patrick 78, 86
Christendom 47, 88, 112, 154
classism 67
clergy 58, 65, 68, 85
coercion 11, 48
colonialism 5, 98–9, 134. *See also* post-colonialism
communion 23, 105, 106, 115
confessional tradition 19, 113, 115
confessions of faith 5, 19, 20, 22, 25, 139, 152, 165, 167
  Augsburg 112
  Schleitheim 4
conscientious objector 93, 94, 101
Constantinianism 9, 12, 14
conversion 115, 124
Cramer, David C. 17 n.1, 18 n.3
creed 101, 165

dance 59, 63, 69
deconstruction 46, 47
denominationalism 14, 20, 34, 40, 60, 64, 71, 75, 103, 107, 115, 118–21, 139, 140, 148
discipleship 7, 23, 26, 29, 68, 94, 95, 97, 115, 143, 140, 147
distinctives 22, 23, 50–2, 104, 112–14, 130–7
diversity 51, 53, 56, 59, 60, 64, 67, 71, 75, 115, 118, 129, 149
  Anabaptist 21, 145, 147, 148
  Christian 38, 106, 110
  racial 58

INDEX

"right" 114, 119, 122
  theological 128, 129
drama 59, 69, 166
dress 131, 137
Dueck-Read, Alicia J. 80–3, 90

ecclesiology 28, 94, 110, 111, 125
Eilers, Kent D. 22 n.10
Enns, Fernando 28, 117
ethnicity 10, 13, 14, 47, 118, 120

faithfulness 14, 26, 29, 93, 103, 104, 109, 111, 114, 117, 119, 124, 131, 137, 143, 149
fellowship 23, 105, 106, 112, 140
feminism 66–70, 72, 74, 75
  methodology 64, 68, 69
  theology 9, 53, 54
Finger, Thomas 115–16
Fiorenza, Elisabeth Schüssler 65, 68
fundamentalism 107, 131, 157

Gadamer, Hans-Georg 36–7, 46 n.28
gender 14, 47, 74, 77–80, 82, 85, 86, 90, 126
  cis- 87, 95, 97
  trans- 97–9
genocide 93 n.1, 97
globalization 144
Global South 21, 59, 148
Goossen, Rachel Waltner 11
gospel 4, 9, 15, 26, 109, 110, 114, 125, 139, 143, 145, 147, 153
Graber, Joseph D. 135–8
Gregory, Brad 152
Grimsrud, Ted 70, 74

Hamilton, Brian 26 n.16
Harder, Lydia Neufeld 59, 62–3, 72, 97–8
Hauerwas, Stanley 10, 152–5, 157 n.15, 166
Healy, Nicholas M. 85, 110–11
historiography 2, 3, 19, 33, 34, 118
  monogenesis 3
  polygenesis 3, 19, 34, 42, 118
homophobia 97
Huebner, Chris K. 155 n.11, 157 n.14, 166 n.35
Huebner, Harry 24, 30, 159
humility 32, 114, 125, 158
Hunt, Mary E. 67

idealism 20, 34, 94, 111, 112, 114, 116, 119
ideology 46–8, 52, 118

justice 44, 81, 90, 91, 97, 117, 120

Kauffman, Daniel 25 n.15, 131–2, 137
Kaufman, Gordon D. 10, 44
Klaassen, Walter 71
Kroeker, P. Travis 155 n.11, 164
Kuchar, Gary 156, 166

land 20, 93 n.1, 97, 120
Lapp, George Jay 132
Lapp, John A. 16
Lash, Nicolas 164
LGBTQ 59, 78–84, 86–91, 95
liberation theology 77, 125, 145
love 32, 56, 82, 83, 146
  God's 79, 83
  nonviolent 44
Luther, Martin 3, 87–8, 109, 156 n.13

marginalization 47, 60, 62, 89
Martin, Dennis D. 88, 107–8
martyrs 22, 120, 121, 124
Martyr's Mirror 4, 72
Mennonite Central Committee (MCC) 54–6, 61, 81, 82
militarism 20, 67, 138
military service 6, 137, 146
misogyny 97
Murray, Stuart 34, 73, 111, 118. See also *The Naked Anabaptist*
music 63, 66, 69
    hymns 22
    song 23, 25, 69, 86, 159
mutual aid 20, 23
mystery 15, 24, 156, 158, 161, 166

The Naked Anabaptist 34, 118. See also Stuart Murray
neo-Anabaptism 10, 34
nonconformity 6, 7, 10, 82, 112, 130–2, 135, 136
nonresistance 6, 20, 23, 96, 112, 137, 138, 146
nonviolence 7, 94, 96, 101, 112

O'Connor, Flannery 164–5
orthodoxy 17, 23, 115, 132
orthopraxy 23

patience 124
patriarchy 69, 96–9, 114
peace 44, 81, 91, 96, 98, 99, 101, 104, 135, 136, 138, 147
    building 23
    making 112
    theology 90, 94–7, 116
    witness 115, 117
penitence 162, 163
persecution 47
pilgrimage 24, 30, 32

poetry 22, 63
The Politics of Jesus 9, 96, 116. See also John Howard Yoder
post-colonialism 140, 141, 145. See also colonialism
prayer 30, 79, 122, 146, 165
    books 22, 25
    veil 131
Protestantism 28, 31, 87, 89, 116
purity 94, 99

race 47, 67, 90
racism 54, 67, 97
Rambo, Shelly 100–2
reconciliation 44, 105, 109, 120, 122
reconstruction 2, 3, 6
reformation 3, 8, 19, 156
    Protestant 2, 28, 88
    radical 3, 10
Reimer, A. James 17, 18 n.5, 115–17
repentance 108, 109, 115, 121, 124, 157, 162–4, 166
Ricoeur, Paul 34–46, 48–52
Robinson, Marilynne 160–1
Roth, John D. 4, 70, 89
Ruether, Rosemary Radford 66, 68, 72

sacrament 105, 115, 161, 164
Sattler, Michael 26 n.16, 72
Sawatsky, Walter 109, 118
Schlabach, Gerald 113, 117
Schreiner, Susan E. 156, 158, 163 n.29
scripture 19, 23, 25–31, 59, 70–4, 80–6, 99, 105, 112, 124, 147, 149, 156, 159. See also Bible
Second World War 4, 129, 133, 137, 138

INDEX

sectarianism 8, 17, 107, 113, 123
Sensenig, Kristine 57–8
sexism 67, 97
sexual
  abuse 11, 12, 96
  bi- 83, 87, 102
  hetero- 81, 87, 95
  orientation 47, 67, 78, 85, 86, 90
  violence 1, 11, 15, 97–9, 101
sexuality 77–9, 82
Shenk, Wilbert R. 127–8, 141–3, 147–9
Sider, J. Alexander 113–14
Simons, Menno 5, 8, 25–6, 94, 133, 164
Stendahl, Krister 151
suspicion 23, 35, 163, 166
  hermeneutics of 35, 46–50, 87, 88

van Braght, Thieleman J. 5, 8. *See also Martyr's Mirror*
victimization 80, 121
victim-survivor 98–101
Vischer, Lukas 113, 123
voluntary church membership 7, 9, 146, 147

war 6, 96, 117, 147. *See also* Second World War
Weaver, Edwin I. 133–6, 138–40
Weaver, Irene 133–6, 138–40
Weaver, J. Denny 43, 116, 161
Wenger, J. C. 5, 7–8
Wesleyan quadrilateral 31, 86, 90
Wiebe, Katie Funk 61, 73
Williams, Rowan 162, 165–7
witness 89, 100, 101, 105, 109, 144
  eye- 27, 31
  of Jesus 47
  peace 115, 117
  of scripture 25–7, 31
Woman-Church 65
World Council of Churches (WCC) 65, 109, 110, 124, 144

Yoder, John Howard. *See also The Politics of Jesus*
  mission work 136–8
  sexual violence 11–13, 47 n.31
  theology 8–11, 13–15, 29, 96–7, 116–17, 161

Zacharias, Robert 120

www.ingramcontent.com/pod-product-compliance
Ingram Content Group UK Ltd.
Pitfield, Milton Keynes, MK11 3LW, UK
UKHW021901220326
469204UK00008B/118